D0334960

The Real Stanley Baxter

The Real Stanley Baxter

BRIAN BEACOM

Luath Press Limited

EDINBURGH

www.luath.co.uk

This book is dedicated to the force of nature that is Florence Beacom and the quite brilliant Brenda Paterson.

First published 2020

ISBN: 978-1-910022-05-4

The paper used in this book is recyclable.
It is made from low chlorine pulps
produced in a low energy, low emission manner
from renewable forests.

Printed and bound by
CPI Books, Chatham

Typeset in 12 point Sabon by Main Point Books, Edinburgh

Contents

	Foreword STANLEY BAXTER	7
	Introduction BILLY CONNOLLY	8
	Preface	9
	Prologue	13
1	A Star is Born	15
2	The Infirm and the English	20
3	Little Ethel Merman	27
4	The Norman Bates Experience	32
5	3,000 Volt Love	39
6	The Red Coal Minor	45
7	De-bollocking	51
8	Carry on Sergeant	58
9	Buggery, Bestiality and Necrophilia	65
10	To Be Had	71
11	Poofter Hell	80
12	Ménage à Deux	88
13	Life Gets Glamourouser	97
14	The Get Out of Jail Free Card	105
15	Bob Hope or Bill Holden?	111
16	Stage Frights	118
17	Fruit-flavoured Mother-love	125
18	Five-buck Blow Jobs	131
19	The Scots Cain and Abel	137
20	Padding, Tits and Wigs	142

21 Kommandant Baxter 150
22 There's Nothing Funny About Stanley 158
23 Spanked Bottoms 173
24 Dick Swap 177
25 Loving Sydney 184
26 Arse Banditry 189
27 The Wee Culver City Collapse 197
28 Nymphromania 207
29 The Suicidal Zapata 217
30 Love in Leeds 226
31 The Morally Inhibited 231
32 Death by Porridge 241
33 Santa's Sack 251
34 Benny from *Crossroads* 258
35 The Languid Moon Vanishes 267
36 Ugly Flowers 274
37 David Niven's Blow Job 280
38 Shadows Becoming Darker 285
39 The Wasp Sting 295
40 Cancelling the Newspapers 300
Endnotes 309
Timelines 313
Acknowledgements 318
Picture Credits 319

Foreword

Not all my relations with the press in Scotland have been highly satisfying but one relationship has and that's with the man whom I've chosen to write my biography. He not only has my good wishes but my gratitude. The process of working on the book over almost 20 years has been enjoyable, except in the difficult areas, but the writer was kind and patient, and in the end, all was revealed.

Stanley Baxter
September 2020

Introduction

Stanley Baxter was a radio star when I was a little boy in Scotland. He was also a star of dramatic theatre and vaudeville. When television got its act together, he became a star of that too. His talent is so huge that it is quite difficult to nail down and state exactly what it is. He has also oozed a certain classiness whether he was doing *Parliamo Glasgow* as an English language professor or impersonating some leggy starlet with the most extraordinary attractive legs you have ever set eyes on!

I found some video tapes of his performances on television recently and found myself laughing out loud at stuff he had recorded 30 or 40 years ago.

Stanley Baxter is a hero of mine and a legend in his own lifetime.

Billy Connolly
Spring 2020

Preface

CHRISTMAS, 1999. The dull calm of a very slow Friday afternoon newsroom was crashed by the harsh trill of the office phone. But the startle was nothing compared to what the caller on the other end of the line had to say.

'How would you like to write Stanley Baxter's biography,' asked the actor's agent, Tony Nunn, clearly in Santa mode.

Would I? The elusive, enigmatic Stanley Baxter, a man I'd watched on television since I was ten years old, a performer whose TV specials could clear streets, a man of a thousand on-screen personalities who'd managed to reveal very little about his own...

'We think you're exactly the right person to handle it,' said the agent.

Wow. How flattering. I'd interviewed Stanley a few times over the years and we had gotten on well. Yet, this offer was unexpected. Stanley Baxter opening up entirely to a journalist? Clearly, the comedy legend must have thought it time to tell all – and I deemed worthy to become Boswell to his Dr Johnson.

Not quite. 'Stanley wants his official biography written because he thinks someone will write an unofficial one,' said the agent, as the sound of a giant balloon burst in my head.

'This is a way of stopping that happening. But he wants it to come out posthumously. Are you still interested?'

'Well, yes, Tony. But if it's coming out posthumously, there's time for someone else to write it in the meantime? And why choose me in particular?'

'Stanley reckons the journalist most likely to write the unauthorised version would be the writer who knows him most, the person who's had most access to him over the years. And that's you.'

'Come on, Tony. I've never thought of going behind his back. And in any case, there's so much I don't know.'

'Well, anyway, Stanley would prefer to work with you on it. At least, when word gets out you're writing it that could spike others' guns. From your point of view however it may not be published for some time. Stanley's in great health. Are you still interested?'

'Of course. Yes, great, let's get it going.'

Arrangements were made to meet Stanley at his home in Highgate Village in London at lunchtime, as stipulated. But as he showed me upstairs into his sitting room, he didn't look like a man set to enjoy a nice Italian lunch around the corner. He was brooding and anxious as he reached into his pocket, pulled out a wad of notes and thrust them into my hands. My face immediately took on the miserable countenance of the three BAFTA masks on his sideboard. I sensed what was coming.

'That's £100, which should cover your air fare,' he said in sheepish voice. 'I'm sorry to have brought you all the way down from Glasgow and wasted your time but I can't go ahead with this. It's embarrassing, but I'm too afraid.'

I pushed his money back at him. He insisted. I made a desperate suggestion.

'Look, Stanley, I don't know what your concerns are but let's go to lunch at least. I'm here anyway. And during lunch if you tell me your darkest secret, off the record, we'll both weigh up the consequences and decide where to go from there. If we can't agree, I'll be back on the plane to Glasgow, we'll stay chums and our conversation will never have happened.'

He thought for what seemed the longest moment imaginable. I smiled, but in reality my heart was thumping. The chance to write Stanley's story was dependent upon his decision at this exact second. Eventually, he shrugged. But it was a warm, wonderful shrug. The lunch was on. And during that lunch he slowly revealed the darkest secret that defined his personal and professional life. And I chewed on the information and smiled and said, 'Is that it? No robbery, murder or incest? It's going to be a dull book.' Thankfully, he laughed.

'I thought you would think very badly of me,' he said of his revelation, in soft, thankful voice, sipping on his cappuccino. 'I couldn't bear that.'

So the book was on. But Stanley's story didn't gush out of the mouth of the man who'd always seemed so confident on television and on stage. Indeed, it emerged in a cautious trickle.

Yes, he would be delightfully indiscreet where others could be concerned, but Stanley was always conscious of how he would be perceived. It didn't matter if the book was not to be published in his lifetime, he could still be judged by his audience, which, for the moment, happened to be me.

The interview process was lengthy. Over 17 years in fact. As our relationship developed, he offered little insights into his life, layering on detail, correcting himself and developing new, often painful, levels of introspection.

We saw each other more; we holidayed together at his villa in Cyprus. And at one point, the book, now written and approved, was set to be published. Stanley had changed his mind about the posthumous agreement. But on the day of signing contracts he changed it back again.

'I'm too afraid of what people will think of me,' he said in soft, appealing voice. 'I got into this business to be loved. I don't wish that to stop.'

'That won't happen, Stanley. Not when they read the whole story.'

This year he changed his mind again. Now, he's willing to allow the world to make up its own mind.

Prologue

LONDON, 16 JANUARY 1962. It's early morning and a young actor is driving his black Ford Zephyr along the streets of London's West End as the city begins to go about its business. And as he checks his mirror, he realises he has just driven past the two major West End theatres in which his name had been up in lights only a short time ago. The Empire Leicester Square had screened his first film hit, *Very Important Person* the previous year. A couple of streets away, the Phoenix Theatre played home to the clever satirical comedy, *On the Brighter Side*.

Today, the driver is set to head west, to Beaconsfield, to recommence filming on *Crooks Anonymous*, a movie in which he is playing an incredible eight roles and starring alongside screen darling Julie Christie and the very clever Wilfred Hyde-White.

But as he drove around Piccadilly Circus, the actor knew his career was heading in anything but the right direction. And for once, the constant anxiety which so often blighted his life was entirely justified.

As he sidled onto Shaftesbury Avenue, the actor's worst fears were realised when a newspaper billboard screamed out at him:

'FILM STAR STANLEY ON MORALS CHARGE'.

His heart was now racing, and he felt sick to the pit of his stomach. His mind began to throw out all sorts of questions; Would he go to jail? Would his career survive this? Could he carry on living?

But another terrifying thought occurred: what would Bessie Baxter say when she heard the news?

I

A Star is Grown

ON A FREEZING late spring night of 1933 and well past most kids' bedtime, in a tiny hall in the Partick area of Glasgow, a 6-year-old boy in a sailor suit is on stage belting out 'I'm One Of The Lads Of Valencia' to a hundred adults squashed up on wobbly wooden seats. Incongruous? Inappropriate? You bet. The song had helped make heartthrob Al Bowlly the biggest singing star of the 1930s, but it was laced with saucy adult lyrics:

> You can't beat a Spaniard for kissing!
> Oh, ladies do you know what you're missing?

The 6-year-old seducer then continues with:

> I've got such a fine Spanish torso.
> It's just like a bulls only morso!

The little boy will go on to sing hundreds of risqué songs during his career, mostly pastiches of popular hits. But back in Partick, he looks a sight. His hair has been tortured into unnatural waves and his scalp is still burning from scorching tongs, his mother having carelessly touched skin. And if that weren't enough to involve social services, he's wearing more make-up than a Parisian streetwalker.

As the boy goes for the big finish, movement at the side of the stage catches his eye. An angry figure in a green velvet frock is half rising from the piano stool and winking wildly at him. The boy panics but picks up his cue from the pianist (who happens to be his mother) and directs a cheeky wink at the fat lady in the front row, as he has been trained to do. The applause instantly doubles.

But the act's not over as the little lad very far from Valencia produces a stream of celebrity impersonations, from local legend Tommy Morgan to superstar Mae West, to Laurel and Hardy.[1]

The audience loves it and the pint-sized prodigy leaves the hall with a 10s note and a little certificate, his first prize for Top Entertainer picked up for beating the competition, mostly adults, in these X Factor-like variety shows, before falling exhausted into bed.

Not a normal childhood?

'I guess not,' says Stanley, that same little boy 80-odd years on, offering a wry smile. 'I appeared in a series of those talent shows all over the West of Scotland, in tiny village halls and community centres in the likes of Milton of Campsie or Clydebank, going up against singers, jugglers and ventriloquists. These talent shows were massively popular, but they were tough. Yet, I learned so much about how to please an audience.'

Overall, Stanley enjoyed his stage appearances over the two years, performing to Depression audiences desperate to be entertained.

'At this time, I felt mostly excitement rather than fear. And when the other mums gazed up at me and shouted "Oh, look at that wee boy! Listen to him do Mae West." I loved that.'

But paradoxically, as Stanley's success on the circuit grew, so did his anxiety. This need to be loved by an audience was always accompanied by an acute fear of failure. And the twin emotions were to define the performer for rest of his life.

Stanley's director-mother Bessie Baxter had no idea of the adverse psychological imprint she was making on her tiny son with his huge smile and pixie ears. Yet, while she would take the reviews from the likes of the *Milton of Campsie Gazette* in 1933 and delight in showing them to her friends – 'Young Master Stanley Baxter and his clever impersonations of popular comedians brought the house down' – she seldom praised her son.

'It was bewildering for me,' says Stanley. 'I'd go on stage and get rapturous applause from a hundred people shouting Bravo! and beating the adults to the prizes. And I'd start to think I must be awfully good.'

'I sensed my mother was pleased when I'd get the standing

ovations, but the problem was she could rarely show it. As my manager and director, she demanded more and more, and probably felt if she praised me I'd try less hard. And over the time, I began to become more fearful. I began to be scared someone else *would* do better than me on stage and my mother would clatter me.'

What kind of woman would burn her wee boy's head ('Ach, you've got to suffer for your art, Stanley!'), dress him up like Little Lord Fauntleroy and use fear as an encourager?

Bessie Baxter may have been a Glasgow blacksmith's daughter, but she was a showbiz mother right out of the 1962 film musical *Gypsy*, in which Rosalind Russell's Rose Hovick will stop at nothing to make sure her beautiful daughter June, played by Natalie Wood, becomes a star. But it's not surprising that Bessie, born in December 1889, lived vicariously and played the Rosalind Russell role with consummate ease. Five feet and two inches of blonde dynamite, the lady was a born entertainer and a talented pianist. Alongside her sisters Molly, Alice (Stanley's favourite aunt) and Jeannie, the McCorkindale sisters had been sent to *Kinderspiels* (infant schools that taught performance skills) as little girls.

Stanley's sister Alice recalls seeing an old family photograph that tells as much about her mum and her aunts than a collection of diaries ever could.

'Aunt Alice was dressed as Napoleon, Aunt Molly was dressed as a gypsy, my mother was dressed as a man with a suit and a trilby hat and Jeannie was a Scottish soldier. This dressing up, performance-thing was very much a fundamental in the McCorkindale side of the family. I suppose it all helped make the McCorkindales seem more immune to the harsh realities of life around them.'

The McCorkindale girls – think of a Victorian von Trapp Family living in fog, with grey skies and dirty, oily shipyard cranes as a backdrop rather than snow-peaked mountains – would perform to anyone who would listen. Dressing up at home they would excitedly re-enact dramatic tales of exotic heroes and heroines and their fantasy lives. Their living room was peopled by everyone from Romeo and Juliet to Marie Lloyd, the turn-of-the-century music hall star who sang 'My Old Man Said Follow the Van'.

'I can remember as a child that the McCorkindales were always running to pianos, singing and dancing,' says Stanley.

The sisters appeared as vestal virgins or Vesta Tilley, the music hall performer who dressed up as male characters such as 'Burlington Bertie'. The McCorkindales could shift their programme from Will Shakespeare to Will Fyffe, the Dundonian-born music hall star who satirised drunkenness with his song 'I Belong to Glasgow'. This incredible homespun drama saw the precocious young ladies develop an imagination way beyond the limits of their experience. On one level they were all fairly poor, ordinary Glasgow lassies, but they loved to think they were rather bohemian and cultured. Even a little eccentric.

Bessie McCorkindale grew up with showbiz airs. As a young lady her cigarette holder contained only Russian cigarettes and she even sounded like the archetypal drama queen, constantly gushing out words such as 'Wonderful!' or 'Marvellous!' It didn't matter she'd grown up with her three sisters and two brothers in a small flat in the city's Argyle Street. Yet, while the sisters could dream of becoming actresses, it could never be a reality. This was industrial, smog-filled, grimy turn-of-the-century Glasgow after all. Not sunny Tinseltown. Actresses were seen as a short step up from streetwalkers.

What was Bessie to do? She desperately needed a little sparkle in her life. Working as a clerk on at Mr Neergaard's shipping company on Clydeside was a means to an end but her daily existence was entirely starved of the glamour and sophistication she'd see in some of Glasgow's 100 cinemas or 30 theatres. (Part of the city's shipbuilding wealth had filtered downward to a populace that craved entertainment.)

'She decided if she couldn't become an actress, my mother would create a new role for herself,' says Stanley, grinning. 'She'd become a society hostess, with a lovely home where she would entertain her friends.'

How? Like a character from a Jane Austen novel, Bessie reckoned she simply had to marry the right young man. Yet, that wouldn't be easy. Although an attractive woman with a huge personality, suitors were few. 'All the good ones have been killed in the war,' she would often tell friends (there was talk she had been in love with a young Glasgow airman who had lost his life in the Great War). More worryingly, at 35, time was not on her side.

However, fate took her by the hand one night at a local dance when Fred Baxter waltzed into her life. The young insurance actuary didn't actually send shivers of excitement down her spine (although he was handsome enough) but he added up to possibility. And when he told her he thought her beautiful, she told him she was 29. The couple married soon after but, as in Jane Austen novels, hopes are dashed as often as gentlemen doff their caps.

In her wedding year Bessie opened her arms to embrace the promises of the new post-war Labour Government: better housing, cheaper living costs – it was all so exciting. But she had to close them again fairly quickly after the couple moved into their first home. Glasgow's gentrified, leafy West End may have been a couple of miles away from the grime and noise of Govan's many shipyards, but Bessie and Fred move into a tiny, one-bedroomed flat in a tenement building.

Two years after their wedding the couple were still living in that little flat in Fergus Drive. Fred's salary at the Commercial Union wasn't enough to buy Bessie the grand Glasgow residence she had hoped for. The family didn't even have a car, and, heaven forfend, her brother Archie had one. The dream of a more glamourous life seemed to be slipping away.

However, in the autumn of 1925, Bessie found herself pregnant. And with that news a gleam of possibility sparked in the lady's powder-blue eyes. What if this child became an entertainer? What if she taught Baby Baxter all the McCorkindale skills? Could she grow her own little star?

2

The Infirm and the English

STANLEY LIVINGSTONE BAXTER arrived into the world at 2.15am on 24 May 1926, just 12 days after the end of the General Strike and almost at the same time as the Hollywood release of *The Son of the Sheik*, the silent adventure film based on Edith Maud Hull's romance novel in which Rudolph Valentino plays both the father and the eponymous role.

Baby Baxter created his own little melodrama when he revealed a hugely swollen head. An indicator he would one day take himself as seriously as Rudolph Valentino had in his film swansong?

'It may have been an early sign of megalomania, or perhaps it was because the doctor had to pull me out by the side of the head using forceps.

'Anyway, my mother blamed the doctor for the swelling and told me later she was so angry she pushed him right across the room.'

Bessie was immediately besotted with her little star-to-be. By day, she would push Stanley proudly around the nearby Botanic Gardens in his swanky Silver Cross pram. At night, the baby boy slept in the only bedroom while husband and wife occupied the bed-recess in the kitchen. And as Stanley grew, any warmth Bessie once had for her husband was saved for her son.

'I grew up realising my mother was always criticising my father and indeed the whole Baxter clan, exclaiming, "They're awfy dull."'

To defend Bessie Baxter a little, compared to the McCorkindales they were. While Bessie and her sisters loved to leap into a four-part harmony of the hits of the period such as 'Baby Face' and 'Bye

Bye, Blackbird', the Baxters were Highland-bred Presbyterians, hell-bent on singing nothing more than hymns on a Sunday.

How did Fred Baxter cope with his wife's growing coldness? Well, it was made a little easier because he adored her. And so what if she sucked most of the oxygen from any room she walked into, that she was pretentious or her conversation almost inevitably became a performance? He could put up with it. And how could he complain about a mother loving her son? Fred loved his boy too and was determined to spend every moment away from the Commercial Union with him. However, it was a connection Bessie was keen to keep as loose as possible.

'She wanted it to be about me and her alone. She didn't go to the theatre with my father to see Tommy Lorne at the Pavilion, Dave Willis singing "My Wee Gas Mask" at the King's or a vaudeville show at the Empress. She'd take four-year-old me.'[2, 3]

Bessie focused on her toddler's performance skills. She played piano for him and taught him to sing and to mime the stars of the day. Stanley learned to become Mae West via Bessie's interpretation. Meanwhile, Fred Baxter could only watch on from the wings.

Bessie's overall masterplan began to play out. On 22 May 1930, she produced a baby sister for Stanley. Alice was named after Stanley's favourite aunt and Bessie Baxter was delighted, if for no other reason than a family of four could no longer be confined to a one-bedroomed flat. Thankfully, Fred could now afford a move, not to the des res Bessie had dreamed of but a rented four-bedroomed, fourth-storey, top floor flat on a hill at 150 Wilton Street.

It wasn't a swish townhouse but the red sandstone building with its polished green tiles at the entranceway was certainly one of the classier Glasgow closes. What augmented the delight for Bessie however was the discovery that part of the street had once been known by the much grander title of Wilton Mansions. Within hours of picking up the keys she was off to the printers to have her own headed notepaper made up heralding '5 Wilton Mansions'.

Stanley says, grinning, '5 Wilton Mansions became her own Versailles. We had a big wooden shower – very unusual at the time – and quickly had a phone installed. And when it would ring my mother's voice would go all Celia Johnson-posh and she'd trill "Maryhill 2680!" She loved all that show.'

Bessie now had the home – and the son – to show off. The front room with its large bay window became the parlour – and the stage – where the first lady had a grand piano installed. And although Fred's income was limited – he earned less than £1,000 a year – Bessie, ignoring the absurdity of it all, insisted they have a permanent live-in servant. She hired a succession of Catholic maids (Catholics at this time in Glasgow tended to be poorer, from Irish immigrant families), who were actually made to wear coffee-coloured uniforms in the afternoon and black at night. Later, during the Second World War, when there was only a fire for the kitchen, the family sat at the kitchen table and the poor wee maid sat alone at a card table near the stove.

'It was *Upstairs, Downstairs* in a Glasgow tenement. You see how she would have loved to have lived the Bellamy life.'

While Glasgow battled the impact of the Depression (the city's defiant attitude saw it continue to pack its 11 ballrooms and 70 dance halls), Bessie still pursued her dream of glamour and sophistication. Afternoons at 5 Wilton Mansions would see her friends arrive for tea – served up by the maid – and the ladies would play whist or the Chinese board game mahjong, or Bessie would play the piano until it was time for Fred to arrive home from work. (One of her West End friends was Mrs Jackson who had a son, Gordon. As fate would have it, Gordon Jackson would go on to become a British television star, best known for his role as Hudson the butler in the ITV drama *Upstairs, Downstairs*. Years later Stanley would impersonate Gordon when he parodied the classic series.)

Bessie also began to showcase her little boy. He remembers stepping out from behind the parlour room curtains to impersonate Harry Lauder singing 'Roamin' in the Gloamin', and Marlene Dietrich.[4] But with the applause from the mahjong ladies still ringing in his ears, Bessie would give Stanley notes, telling him where he'd gone wrong.

'She was terrified that I would be a failure. My mother had sort of come to terms with her own situation, but she thought the sky was the limit as far as I was concerned – so long as I didn't fuck up.

'But when you are continually told "Don't fail", regardless of how much natural talent you have to begin with, inevitably, the real worry sets in.'

Stanley was already a top-class worrier in August 1931, when he attended Hillhead High School, a (Corporation-subsidised) private school in Glasgow's Cecil Street in the West End.

'I was completely terrified on that first morning, so my mother came into the classroom and sat beside me. I was given a crayon and a bit of paper and the lovely Miss McNeely said encouragingly, "Just draw whatever you feel like, Stanley." But I was paralysed. My mum said, "What's wrong?" and I blurted out "I'm sure to get it wrong!"'

Don't most kids suffer nerves on the first day? Stanley reckons he was more worried than most, thanks to a heightened sense of being judged. But he says there was another problem to contend with; his counting skills were limited. Stanley clearly hadn't inherited his father's arithmetic gene.

Yet, although fearful about schoolwork, Stanley wasn't shy when it came to entertaining. During playtimes, the impish little boy would regale the other kids with stories and impersonations. He was great fun to have around says former schoolmate Eddie Hart. (Bessie wasn't there to give Stanley notes.)

Stanley recalls the days when his classmates became his audience.

'On a Friday afternoon Miss Pattison would say, "Stanley, I'm bored, come out and entertain us before the bell goes." I can't even remember exactly what I did, probably tell the class about a show my mother had taken me to see at the Empress Theatre, and I'd just talk nonsense and the class would laugh.'

Bessie's coaching and Stanley's raw talent was paying off. But the Hillhead High teachers weren't always pleased with Master Baxter. Thanks to his church hall competition appearances he struggled to stay awake in class. Fred Baxter wasn't happy either.

Fred hadn't seen his son perform at this point – the thought of it filled him with dread. But one night, after a show, Bessie told her husband about Stanley's standing ovations and thunderous applause, and she insisted he see for himself. Fred had to be dragged along 'to see what all the fuss was about'.

On the bus on the way home Bessie said, 'Well?'

'Well what?'

'What did you think of your son?'

'I'll tell you what I think! If I ever go to see that boy on the stage again, have me certified insane!'

The sight of the sailor suit and the Mae West dresses was clearly too much for the subdued Highlander. (Fred however came to eat his words, or rather, Bessie forced them down his throat at regular intervals and he would see Stanley perform many times later in life.)

'I guess that night must have been horrendous for him, to sit and listen to a big fat soprano singing sharp and then watch a conjurer drop his balls, all before it was Sonny Boy's turn. No wonder he didn't want to see it again.'

Bessie Baxter wasn't entirely unhappy to see her husband unhappy; it meant she had almost total control of Stanley's development as an entertainer. Yet, if Stanley were now the leading man in Bessie's life, little Alice was way down the bottom of the bill.

You might assume Bessie would have tried to double her chances of creating a star, as Natalie Wood's mother had, pushing younger daughter Lana into the slipstream. But Bessie was content with one star to hothouse. Alice recalls she had only three dance lessons. And just as few piano lessons.

'No matter what I did it was never good enough. And my mum was already caught up with Stanley.' (Alice would go on to make it as an actress and comedy feed, working the variety theatres of the West of Scotland, but this was more due to raw talent – and perhaps a little osmosis – than encouragement from her mum.)

Meanwhile, Fred Baxter tried to push his son in the direction of ordinary little boy interests. He had him join the Cub Scouts, but Stanley says he hated the very idea of washing out his little dixie can in the mud.

'I couldn't be doing with the pack thing. I didn't mind the little units of kids but not when it became too big. It seemed pointless.'

Former First Glasgow cub pal Bob Reid however recalls Stanley was a little more in tune with cubbing than the actor remembers.

'He would come alive when he led the singing sessions and he really seemed to enjoy it, keeping the campfires going. He loved to ging gang goolie. We all thought he was good fun to have around.'

Fred also tried push Stanley towards the sports field, but his son believed the very idea of kicking a ball around to be pointless. Stanley reckons this made him less popular with the other boys in his class.

'I found myself to be not quite part of it all. And I was bullied. As a result, my isolation caused me to befriend others who were outsiders.' He adds with a wry smile, 'I was left to play with the infirm and the English.'

His schoolmates who were neither infirm nor English don't remember it that way. But there's no denying Stanley was out of synch with many of the boys. And the happy times he remembers came about when performing.

He was popular with some of the girls however, and indeed he had a couple of little girlfriends. But they weren't selected for the role because his tiny heart was beating fit to burst.

'I used to flirt with Dorothy Miller and I'd shock the rest of the boys by kissing her,' he recalls of his mini-performances. 'This wasn't the sort of things wee boys did.'

What wee boys – and girls – did was delight in the Saturday morning ABC Minors shows at the local cinema. Stanley lived for the weekend when he would skip a mile down the road to the Hillhead Salon. From the moment he stepped inside the dark theatre the schoolboy realised this was a very special place.

That's not to say he would whoop and holler every time Gene Autry rode across the range on Champion, or giggle when Laurel and Hardy got themselves into yet another fine mess. Nor did he salivate over space films which used so obviously fake ray-guns or wallow in the westerns where the actors wore phoney cowboy moustaches. (He did like the camp theatre of *Flash Gordon* however.)

'For the most part, the children's films bored me, but the world of the cinema was absolutely captivating. I remember looking up at the screen and seeing the child actors and thinking I could do that just as well.'

What he also loved was the grown-up world of theatre, his mother taking him to see the likes of Henry Hall (the BBC dance band leader) and during the summer months, the Howard & Wyndham (H&W) variety shows. (Stanley would later headline these *Half Past Eight* shows, which became *Five Past Eight Shows*, the title relating to the time the curtain went up, running at the King's Theatre).[5] The precocious little boy was enthralled by Harry Gordon, the Aberdeen-born comedian and impressionist, actress Beryl Reid, who would later win a Tony Award for her role as a lesbian soap opera star in *The Killing of Sister George,* and high-kicking, arms-linking international dance troupe, The Tiller Girls. Even *Flash Gordon* couldn't compare.

But if Stanley enjoyed variety theatre, his little eyes were on stalks the first time his parents took him across the River Clyde to the Princess's Theatre. It was there the schoolboy watched his first-ever panto, *Aladdin*, from a box (Fred landed the treat thanks to the Commercial Union's connection with the theatre) and gaped at George Lacy, the London-born panto star who delivered working-class gags in a posh accent as the principal comic (with whom Stanley would later co-star with). What this seating meant was that little Stanley could see into the wings. He could see stagehands scurrying around with bits of scenery. He could see wonderful new worlds being created. He could enjoy fabulous, energetic performances and he could see how the audience was lapping it up. It was all frenetic, exciting and daring. This was a world he sorely wanted to become part of. Bessie Baxter noted her son's envious blue eyes – and smiled.

3
Little Ethel Merman

LITTLE STANLEY NEVER took a holiday from performing. Even on summer holiday. Bessie would never allow it. When Stanley and his aunts, uncles and cousins took off to the little island of Cumbrae off the coast of Largs, during the half hour ferry trip the Baxter clan would be entertained by an on-board accordion trio. No sooner had the families arrived at the boarding house, with the suitcases still in the hall, Bessie would be banging on the lounge piano, offering up her Winifred Atwell's to the watching world.

'My father, as you can imagine, would be black affronted,' says Stanley, shaking his head.

During daytime at the beach Stanley would create little short act plays for his cousins to perform, and the little director would use the rocks, a cocktail cabinet, a lampstand or a sofa as stage pieces.

But at nights he had to step down as director when his mother produced the show.

'One night, my mother and my cousin Alma and I had to perform for the other guests. Incredibly, Bessie had us recreate a show she had seen on the vaudeville stage, one of the 'dirty quickies' based around a ménage à trois, with the plot involving two men talking about their marital problems.

'Just imagine a nine-year-old boy pretending to be a grown man.'

It's easier to imagine when you factor in that the schoolboy was incredibly precocious. Meantime, other holidays offered Stanley the chance to reveal his talent for mimicry. When the family went to Portrush one summer, Stanley captured the Ulster accent and refused to surrender it for days afterwards. After holidaying in Blackpool, Stanley sounded remarkably like George Formby (whom he later impersonated on television). Fred Baxter thought this performance-thing nonsense of course but Bessie would hear no criticism of her Sonny Boy. Not even from a teacher. Not even when the teacher realised Stanley was playing with his penis in class.

One day at school, the seeds of sexual awakening seemed to bloom in Stanley before most of his classmates. And he discovered if he played with his little organ with a pencil, via a hole in his trouser pocket, it could be quite pleasurable. But eagle-eyed Miss Morton spotted the secret fiddling, called Stanley out to the front of the class, took out a huge needle and some big green wool and sewed up the gateway to pleasure.

'That night I went home, and my mother immediately demanded to know why the pocket was sewn up. I muttered, "I've no idea." And my mother cut away the green wool. This panicked me and I cried, "Oh, Miss Morton will kill me if I go back in with the wool gone." But my mother said emphatically, "Don't you worry, I'm going to write a stiff note to her."

'So I walked into school next day, and as expected Miss Morton yelled at me, demanding to know where the green wool was, and I gave her the stiff note. She sat down to read it and I could see the colour building up in her face. I don't know what it contained – I didn't dare read it – but it did the trick.

'But this was a case of Sonny Boy being backed against someone who had good reason to reprimand me. At the time I was left with a feeling of smug triumph, but it backfired because a little later I was left with a sense of even greater alienation from the rest of the class.'

And Fred Baxter's input into the pencil and the penis trick? None, because he was clueless.

'I guess it was because my mother wore the breeks in the family.'

Bessie's unconditional support for Sonny Boy crossed the boundaries of sensible parenting. When kids at school would tease Stanley for being too self-important (on the days they weren't laughing at his performances) Bessie would yell, 'Good! Good! That means they're jealous – and you're on the way up!'

Stanley breaks into 'Everything's Coming Up Roses' at this recollection, complete with Ethel Merman voice.

There's no doubt Bessie's mothering imbued Stanley with a sense of being special, a necessary character trait in a future showbiz star. But other kids came to see Stanley as an entertainer rather than their pal.

The little Ethel Merman's sense of displacement at school was soothed however by even more visits to the cinema. Most days on hearing the final school bell, Stanley raced to the movies to get there before 4.30pm – at which time the prices went up from the 5d he paid. Bessie's prepared banana and marmalade sandwiches (Stanley had decided he would become vegetarian for reasons he can't recall) were the fuel to take Sonny Boy on his journey into fantasy.

Not children's films. The world he escaped to was one of eternal triangles, bitter-sweet romances and melodramas featuring screen divas such as Bette Davis in *Of Human Bondage* or Greta Garbo in *The Painted Veil*. There are lots of actors who sought comfort in cinema as an escape from the harsh realities of their world as a child. But few aged nine who wallowed in adult relationship tales.

And it's not as if Stanley was hiding from Glasgow's searing religious bigotry. Nor was he suffering the endemic poverty of the families crammed ten to a room-and-kitchen in slum areas such as the Gorbals. The schoolboy wasn't escaping from the city's human misery, he was escaping *into* Hollywood's human misery, in the form of melodramas such as *Mutiny on the Bounty*.

'I loved all that angst, but I did quite like *Tarzan* movies too, although I wasn't sure why I seemed to like him more than I liked Jane.'

Stanley's world however wasn't without real trauma. One mid-October day in 1935, as he made his way home from a school chum's birthday party, the nine-year-old was approached by a threatening stranger.

'I had been wearing a kilt and he came up to me and he said, "What have you got on under your kilt then?"

'Of course, I'd always been taught by mother to be nice to adults, but then she'd never included the coda, "Unless they happen to be paedophiles," so I mumbled something like, "Well, it's just my trews." And at that he lifted up my kilt, exposed himself – and ran off.'

Stanley had no idea who the man was, but although shocked by the experience he told no one. It was a mistake. Three weeks later on Hallowe'en night as he returned home from buying a new false face, Stanley realised the same man was following.

'It was one of those brown, foggy nights and I was a few streets from my house when I heard the footsteps in the same rhythm as my own. My heart sank.

'I began to move quicker, and he moved quicker – and quicker – and by the time I reached my close I had broken into a run. I was breathing hard and sweating buckets. But he caught up with me as I flew up the second flight of stairs and he grabbed me.

'Again, I had been wearing a kilt and he put his hand between my legs and pulled and clawed at me for the longest time. I was grief-stricken. Stunned and frightened out of my wits. I shouted out, "Please, please, I don't want to! Let me go!"

'And after a while he did finally let me go. It was my screaming, I guess. And I was left shaking and absolutely terrified.'

No one heard the screams. And again Stanley told no one.

'But a few weeks later I broke down crying in my bedroom one night and told my father about it. Like a lot of children who are abused you wonder if you are to blame in some way. And I suppose to absolve some of that guilt you confess.'

Fred Baxter, unusually, took control of the domestic crisis.

'He explained to me that there were quite a lot of men around who do this sort of thing and said, reassuringly, "You are not to worry about it, Stanley." He added that it had happened to boys in his class. He then said, "You must point out this man to me because it's against the law, you know."'

Stanley never did see the child molester again. And Fred's patient counselling had helpedallay the worst fears. Interestingly, the experience brought about a father and son closeness which had never manifested itself before. Nor was it to ever reappear. Bessie Baxter would make sure of that.

Another story of sexual discovery suggests Stanley wasn't entirely alienated from his school chums. Now ten, he and his little friends would get together for group masturbation sessions in each other's bedrooms in pursuit of the collective erection. And perhaps, on a good day, the individual Etnas would erupt.

'The wanking parties were not uncommon. Not at all,' says

Stanley. 'And it wasn't all little poofs-to-be, getting together. It was just something someone did.' (Indeed. Willy Russell writes extensively and coloufully about the same group sex adventures of little boys in his novel, *The Wrong Boy*, as does Roddy Doyle in *Angela's Ashes*.)

Bessie *did* believe however that Stanley's little chums were corrupting him. There were signs that Stanley's polite West End tones were being infected by his little school pals, many of whom adopted the Glasgow vernacular in order to avoid being tagged public school pansies.

This is not to suggest that Stanley's diction had degenerated into Gorbals working-class, later used to wonderful comic effect in his classic *Parliamo Glasgow* TV sketches; but he certainly didn't speak like a tiny Trevor Howard. The new Glesga accent had to go. Received pronunciation was vital.

'I was rushed down to the College of Music and Drama to see a man called Percival Steed,' Stanley recalls with real drama in his voice, as if he'd been discovered to have had head lice and sent to the nit nurse.

'His character perfectly suited his name. He was an eccentric Englishmen who was bald but with frizzy hair at the side and he looked like he'd been created by Dickens.

'To develop our speech, he would encourage us to use our diaphragm, and he'd point out the geography of this organ. But curiously, we learned later that with the little girls he taught, the diaphragm was a little higher up.'

Stanley's speech hardly improved during the Steed period, but meanwhile his acting skills did, thanks to Aunt Alice who'd dress him and his cousins up as actors and rehearse them in the likes of scenes from *Hamlet*. Stanley once played Hamlet to cousin Sheila's Queen of Denmark and he managed to find laughs in the performance. (If future directors of serious theatre had seen this, they'd have realised it was pointless trying to contain Stanley's obvious predilection for comedy.) Here was yet another example of Stanley being stage-managed by adults who lived to perform. And he was being applauded by them. The words of encouragement by Ethel Merman rang out in his head. He had begun to believe them.

4
The Norman Bates Experience

ACT TWO OF Stanley's school life saw him move up to the Seniors where, he says, he felt even more out of sorts than he had at primary. It didn't help he was under male tutelage for the first time. And not only was Form Head Mr Fletcher a man, he was also 'a man's man', a games master. Stanley says Flecky was totally confused by this rather effete young boy with the Peter Pan ears who didn't know which end of a ball to kick.

'He was really quite a decent bloke, but I think he was actually embarrassed for me. I can remember the class being asked to bring in some work they did at home, a lamp they'd made or whatever, and I brought in poetry I had written.'

Mr Fletcher worried about Stanley. The boy seemed bright enough but this wasn't reflected in his exam marks. Stanley was also worried; it was bad enough being consigned to the infirm and the English without being trapped in the lower-stream classes with the hard of thinking. But he just couldn't focus in class.

'My parents were so worried about my poor performance that they threatened to send me off to boarding school, thinking this would improve me. Luckily, I knew they could hardly pay the fees at Hillhead.'

The glorious summer of 1938 and the arrival of the Empire Exhibition which came to Glasgow's Bellahouston Park distracted Stanley's mind a little from the dreaded exam results wait. But, when the circus left town, Stanley was left with the rubbish in the form of low exam marks. And he suffered the indignity of being shoved into the lower of the two First Year classes. The part of Dunce was definitely not the role he would have chosen.

But not all aspects of the schoolboy's life was so depressing. Just before he turned 13, a leading lady entered his world and together they performed wonderfully together. The theatre was Stanley's bedroom. Bessie was still employing a succession of young ladies as maids – she had her standards to keep up – with names such a Gracie Glancey, Sadie Thomson and Cathy Scott. But Cathy considered her role in looking after the Baxter family to have the widest remit.

'She was 14 at the time, and one night in the kitchen, while the family were in the living room, she just set upon me. Cathy was a very sexy girl and I was completely randy. And there we were getting up to all kinds of fun, everything I suppose but full sex. So then I took her to my bedroom where I tried my very best to fuck her. But she drew the line at that. However, these little bedroom encounters went on for a while – until my mother began to suspect.'

Bessie, still desperate to stage manage her Sonny Boy, was to play the Fear Card, the psychological weaponry she carried in the way other women carried a compact. In a scene with resonances of the Norman Bates *Psycho* experience, Bessie worried her son so gravely about the consequences of fooling around with the fairer sex he froze with fear.

'She started telling me about these two boys who once took a wee girl into a haunted house up the road and did terrible things to her. And they were birched! Beaten with sticks! Well, that was it. I wouldn't dare touch Cathy from then on. And Cathy got so frustrated that I wouldn't keep on playing. My mother had put the kybosh on any openings for me.'

Stanley and Cathy were reduced to playing Lexicon, a Scrabble-like game of the period. Which could still be rather dangerous.

'Cathy would try and come up with rude words whenever possible. I remember once playing with her, Alice and Alma, and Cathy placed the letters 'UCK' on the table. Then she looked up at me with big, simpering eyes and said, "I can't think of a letter to put down to make a real word, can you, Stanley?" At this point I covered her attempts, to stop Alice seeing what was going on.'

He could have suggested an 'S' but that would have compounded Cathy's frustration. As it was, the rejected maid announced her departure from 5 Wilton Mansions. And when the day came, Lana

Turner couldn't have played the scene any better.

'Cathy said a polite goodbye to everybody then when it came to my turn she mouthed a soft and alluring, "Bye, Stanley," and ran up and kissed me hard right on the lips, for the longest time.'

Bessie almost choked on her own tongue.

'My mother then played it down, of course. She said later, "That was awful nice. She was very fond of you right enough."'

It wasn't *just* that Bessie had a suspicion that Stanley and Cathy were soon-to-be lovers and was terrified her Sonny Boy would father the maid's child.

'She didn't want me going with anyone else,' he says, softly. 'She had to be the only woman in my life.'

With Cathy gone home, and a new replacement installed (who had neither the looks nor the sense of adventure), life looked grim for the volcanic schoolboy. Yet world events were to intervene and ensure Stanley had more than his libido to think about. In 1939, it seemed only a matter of time before Glasgow became a prime target for the Luftwaffe; the city's shipyards, munitions and naval vessels were essential to the war effort.

As a result, fearful parents decanted their kids to relatives around the safer areas of country. Rather than pack Stanley and little nine-year-old Alice off to live with distant relatives or even well-meaning strangers, Bessie decanted Stanley and Alice off to the safety of Lennoxtown, a village 20 miles outside Glasgow. There they lived with a schoolmistress friend of Aunt Alice, Kate Taylor. Bessie hated the six months living with Ms Taylor because the teacher was every bit as bossy as she was. And Kate Taylor reckoned The Performing Baxters were too much to bear. What was especially poignant about the six months in exile was, as far as Stanley can recall, his dad never came to visit.

'He had to work during the week of course and perhaps he didn't get on with Kate Taylor. But I really think my mother told him not to come. I only appreciated later how lonely it must have been for him to be back in Glasgow alone without his family.'

When it looked as though the Germans had decided not to wipe Glasgow from the face of the earth, Bessie and her brood returned home. Stanley was delighted to see his dad and at the same time meet a new chum who'd arrived at Hillhead High. Norman Connolly wore thick glasses, was as thin as a ration coupon and had an obvious speech impediment.

'I guess Norman came into the category of the lame, infirm and the English, all of whom were bullied mercilessly at school. I guess he liked me because I was aware of that.'

Norman's dad was a clergyman and his mother taught Classics at a school in the south side, but 'could have been mistaken for a bag lady'.

'His shoes were always held together by bits of string just like those of his brother, the brilliant James Logie Baird. Norman lived on Colebrooke Street, just along from Glasgow Academy, in a home that looked like the House of Usher, with cats climbing all over the kitchen table.

Stanley and his new oddball chum would hang out in Norman's wee bedroom and listen to records by Stéphane Grappelli, the French jazz violinist and his guitarist partner Django Reinhardt.

Their music appreciation sessions were halted when Stanley was enlisted by the BBC. Kathleen Garscadden, a producer of the hugely successful *Children's Hour* radio programmes, had been talent spotting, searching out the drama stars of the future, when she came across Stanley singing at a Band of Hope concert in his church in Belmont Street, Glasgow.[6] Dressed in his tailcoat, he performed a Fred Astaire and a Harry Lauder turn. Garscadden had discovered exactly what she was looking for.

'Up until this time Auntie Kathleen, as she was called by the kids in her series, had been using a very small and very nice lady called Elsie Payne, who specialised in playing small boys. I guess Auntie Kathleen figured it was time to replace Elsie with a real boy.'

Stanley Baxter was to become that real boy, and a professional actor.

'The drama was called *The Unicorn Stamp*, I remember they had to put me on a box to be at the same height as the rest of the actors. I can't recall what the show was about although I think it was pretty daft. Regardless, it worked, and I was offered a whole series of roles – at a guinea for each one.'

Children's Hour, recorded on Queen Margaret Drive, just

a few hundred yards from his home, was the start of Stanley's professional career and he managed to complete more than a hundred performances before being called up for National Service, loving every moment of his time on air.

Almost.

'I remember one show called *Trader Horn*, which I think ended with two children being swept out to sea – it was a real cliffhanger – and I thought it was wonderful. But to my horror, to stop the listening kids having nightmares, Auntie Kathleen stepped in and announced that Archie and June would be alright in the week ahead and "Not to worry, children!"'

'I thought, "Fuck it. That's spoiled it!" But regardless of the spoiler I fell in love with radio broadcasting.'

Bessie's delight at Sonny Boy becoming a radio star was uncontainable, except in front of Sonny Boy himself. Fred Baxter was initially uncomfortable with Stanley's new radio work; even the hint of an entertainment career worried the actuary. But gradually, Stanley's radio performances drew his respect. Still 14, Stanley also found his way into theatre and performed with an amateur company the Nessie Night Club. During rehearsals he became friendly with amateur actor Alan MacKill, a man in his 40s. It was a chance meeting which would later have a major impact on Stanley.

But while radio provided the real excitement in his life, sadly there was crackly interference from school. His tall and imposing headmaster at Hillhead High was a man with a rather Dickensian – and ironic – name. Dr Merry liked to single out Master Baxter for special treatment. But it was never positive. During assemblies he referenced Stanley's radio success but pointed out it was all rather pointless if academic results didn't match.

'It's called sadism, isn't it?' says Stanley, the anger still rising when he thinks about the one-dimensional outlook of his educator.

Stanley's schoolmates such as Tom Forrester however were 'in awe' of the radio star. 'But of course Glaswegian boys would never acknowledge they had a talent in their class,' says Tom. 'It wasn't the thing to do.' Stanley's separation from the mainstream saw him spend much of his free time at the House of Usher or at the movies, very often now with his mother. On the night of 15

March 1941, Stanley and Bessie sat in the stalls of the Grosvenor cinema watching *The Lady in Question.*[7] But the real drama was taking place outside the cinema.

The Luftwaffe had finally chosen to unleash its fury upon Glasgow. After raining down their death loads onto the shipbuilding town of Clydebank on the Clyde estuary, the returning Germans unloaded their remaining bombs onto the leafy, genteel West End of the city. While Rita Hayworth and Glenn Ford played out their emotional turmoil on screen, outside, people were running for their lives as homes were being demolished and streets destroyed. Stanley and his mother were unaware of Hitler's flying hoards until they, and the rest of the audience, tried to leave the cinema and were barred at the door.

'We were told Glasgow was being bombed, and to sit tight.'

All the captive audience could do was await the all-clear and try to sleep in their seats throughout the night.

'I was terrified. My dad was at home looking after Alice and we had no idea if they'd been bombed. We just had to sit there all night while the cinema played music, the same four songs on a loop. I remembered all the words to all of them for years, but they've slipped away now.'

Stanley had no idea of the devastation which was being rained down on Glasgow. The Luftwaffe, aiming to destroy the shipyards, had dropped more than 1,000 bombs, most landing in nearby Clydebank, just a few miles away. (It was later discovered that 1,200 people had died and 1,000 seriously injured.)

The West End of Glasgow wasn't spared being showered by terror. The next morning, Byres Road looked like a post-apocalyptic nightmare. The street was entirely covered in swirling white plaster dust and there was powdered glass everywhere. Standing on the pavement surveying the scene, Stanley felt he was in the inside of a snow ornament.

'I looked across the road and McKean's Pork Butchers had been totally destroyed. Then we heard that a parachute-mine had hit Wilton Street, some of the streets around my house had been blitzed, and my mother expressed the only declaration of concern for my father I can ever remember. She said, "Oh my God, I hope he's alright." We got home eventually – and he was.'

The following day the bombing continued, and the Baxter family spent the night in a doctor neighbour's safer ground-floor flat at 151 Wilton Street, or rather they spent it under the doctor's big dining table.

Fred and Bessie agreed that this was all too dangerous. The kids couldn't stay in Glasgow. They had to leave – again. This time the answer was to move to Millport, on the island of Great Cumbrae in the Firth of Clyde, their little holiday haven. In recent months Bessie had bought a little upstairs flat.

'I think perhaps my uncle Archie, who inherited the smithy when his dad died, had slipped her the money to buy it. The flat would have cost a few hundred at most.'

Fred was left home alone again with the Home Guard as his family decanted to the island, although he did make it to Millport at weekends. All of this again meant huge upheaval to the Baxter kids. But it turned out to be the most wondrous upheaval imaginable.

5
3,000 Volt Love

FROM THE AGE of ten or so Stanley decided organised religion would play no part in his life. The precocious boy had seen how Glasgow's sectarian battles had been waged in the name of religion. But if he had to project a view of Paradise onto a screen it would have looked like Millport in the summer of 1941. Even the prospect of having to share a room with his little sister couldn't dampen his spirits; anyway, the pair were quite close and would giggle at nights and tell each other stories.

The key to the Millport success was its school. There were only three or four kids to a teacher, as opposed to 40 at Hillhead. Stanley loved the attention and wallowed in the opportunity to ask questions.

And there was still the chance to act. During his stint on the island of dreams, the 15-year-old would travel to Glasgow to take part in *Children's Hour* and several other BBC series. For a time he was 'The Boy' in a series called *Nature Watch*, who would exclaim inane lines such as, 'Uncle Bob, what's that flower up there?'

'All the time behaving like an excited idiot,' he reflects.

Stanley would travel alone to Glasgow, first by ferry to the mainland and then by train from the small village of Wemyss Bay to Glasgow Central. But one freezing night in early December 1941, days before the Japanese mounted a surprise attack on the US Navy base at Pearl Harbor, a heavy snowfall saw Stanley's train held up for several hours just outside Glasgow. There was no heating on the train and the teenager, still in short trousers, was freezing. As a result, he suffered a middle-ear condition. Later, Stanley would have thanked the Lord for this hearing problem, if he believed in Him.

Back in Millport, Stanley spent the following year studying hard and growing up. (He even graduated to long trousers, a Scottish rites of passage in those days.) And the year over, it was an emboldened teenager who (accompanied by his dad) returned to Hillhead High and declared he simply *had* to study Higher French and Lower Latin.

Meanwhile, Stanley's education into the ways of the world continued via the many cinemas he frequented, but one night in 1943, the 16-year-old felt a little flummoxed. *Stormy Weather* was showing at the Ascot Cinema in Anniesland featuring Lena Horne. Horne was the first African American woman to sign a long-term contract with a major studio (MGM) as a 'speciality performer', meaning that she was initially cast in parts and subplots (usually separate singing scenes) that could be edited out for showings in Southern theatres. But now she was playing the female lead.

And for some inexplicable reason, Stanley became aware of a little high pressure developing around his southern regions. This had nothing to do with the almost non-existent plot of this flimsy excuse to feature a collection of America's finest black performers. No, Stanley stared at the screen transfixed as the beautiful star sang 'There's No Two Ways About Love'.

'I was certainly sexually attracted to her,' he recalls. 'I really felt the stirrings.'

What was going on? Had he become beguiled by older women? By black women? What about the girls at Hillhead? Bessie certainly never asked her son if he had a wee girlfriend.

'She would have been horrified if I had!' says Stanley in loud, serious voice. 'After all, she wanted me all to herself.'

Stanley had no idea about his sexuality. All he knew was he had been intrigued by Tarzan, had tried to penetrate the maid Cathy and Lena Horne made him feel rather, well, horny.

The new school term however brought about a test to the schoolboy's predilections. English teacher, Miss Caldwell, had more on her mind than teaching Fifth Year boys the machinations of *Macbeth*.

'She wouldn't sit down at her own desk to talk to the class. No, she'd sit high on top of one of our desks. And the skirt would be at our eye level. Then she would go on talking of the love poems of Keats and Shelley and when she'd tell us to *open* at page 22 it would be in the most suggestive manner possible.'

Most of the boys loved every minute of Miss C's *Summer of '42*-like performance, so redolent of the 1971 film in which a young war widow seduces a 15-year-old boy. This Hillhead showcase was the stuff of adolescent dreams. Well, some adolescent's dreams.

'I just thought, conniving cow! She's trying to bring us all on. And it may be working with them but it's no' working with me.'

Stanley wasn't sure why, but no matter. He had other things on his mind. His future career, for example.

Back in the cinema, this time with his mother, the pair went along to see new British war movie, *The Foreman Went to France*. The film was an engaging flag-waver, but it wasn't the content which raised Stanley and Bessie's interest – it was the cast list. Alongside Robert Morley and Tommy Trinder was a young Scot making his film debut – Gordon Jackson. Mrs Jackson's boy from up the road. Bessie Baxter looked up at the screen, turned to Sonny Boy and unleashed weaponry the Luftwaffe would have been proud of.

'It should be you up there!' she yelled, pointing to the screen and stunning those in the stalls. Stanley was struck dumb by the assault. He faced a dilemma. What could he do to progress his acting hopes – and manage to keep his dad happy by passing his exams? He certainly didn't give up on radio.

But Stanley didn't stop studying either, not just school subjects but politics and philosophy. By 1943, the war had heightened his political awareness and he hoovered up works by socialist writers such as Hegel and Engels, he studied Plato and existentialists such as Sartre. The schoolboy began to appreciate that while he lived in a relatively cosy lower middle-class world, life in most of Glasgow's tenement closes was close to Dickensian. He knew of the cramped living conditions whereby 44 per cent of the population lived in seriously overcrowded conditions, and parents slept in kitchen recesses in fold-down beds. Glasgow's engineering works were working to capacity during wartime, but Stanley knew from reading socialist worker pamphlets he'd picked up on the streets, that its mortality rates were the highest in Britain, and that the number of tuberculosis cases was higher than in any other Scottish city.

Stanley had another reason for devouring Marx's *Das Kapital* and Hegel's *The Phenomenology of Spirit* and the history books which told of why the Government had sent tanks to the city's George Square in 1919 to quell uprising. He had found a new friend. And this friendship was to impact upon him in a way he could never have imagined.

Bill Henry was a blond teenager who lived a couple of miles along the road in Jordanhill and looked like thin-lipped French film star Jean Gabin, who found international fame with the 1937 release of *Pépé le Moko* and would build a huge career playing anti-heroes. Bill, like Stanley, had strong sympathies with the Scots' working-class struggle (despite also being lower middle-class) and had left Hillhead High School the year before to study art. But that departure hadn't stopped the pair keeping in touch. The relationship grew and somehow, Bill's regular girlfriend never managed to get in the way. Over the months, Stanley and Bill became inseparable. Indeed, they were so pally they practically lived in each other's homes.

'We were so close to the extent that my mother would say, "That boy's never out of this house!" And we'd talk, talk, talk and read together. We'd read Plato and Marx and Freud, and he would teach me about artists such as Modigliani and Dufy. I was a very serious person then. Not at all like today, where I'm so frivolous and read mostly showbiz biographies. But Bill and I would read Tolstoy and talk into the night, and if we ended up at his place and it was too late, he'd put me up for the night. And we'd share a bed.

'Sometimes we'd even end up at Jordanhill and say, "Och, it's early yet, it's only midnight." So we'd walk back to my place and then get talking again until we fell asleep, exhausted.'

So close were the pair, Stanley didn't even take umbrage when Bill declared Stanley's future dream of becoming an actor to be 'terribly downmarket'. 'He said I shouldn't even think about acting.' Despite Bill's snooty sense of artistic purity, Stanley's fondness for Bill Henry grew, an affection which transcends the years.

'He was my soulmate,' he says, with a soft voice. 'We'd swap ideas and notions constantly, we'd go down to the art school where

I'd meet his girlfriend Betty Low – who went on to become Bet Low, a very famous artist (one of the acclaimed group umbrellaed under the name The Glasgow Girls) – and then we'd talk into the night. There was no limit to what the imagination could come up with in conversation.'

The relationship wasn't a perfectly balanced one. Stanley came to realise his feelings for his pal involved much more than mateyness. (Betty Low, before she passed away in 2007, wouldn't discuss her or Bill Henry's relationship with Stanley, a silence which speaks volumes.)

'Looking back, I was in love with Bill,' Stanley says, softly. 'But he certainly wasn't in love with me. He probably knew the way I felt about him but he didn't give any indication. It was all a bit upsetting. And although we'd spent lots of times in each other's beds nothing happened.'

Each time they met, Stanley found himself placed in an impossible situation. He had these massive uncontainable, yet unexplained feelings. He was uncomfortable, yet happy. He was excited, yet disappointed.

What was going on? He had tried to have sex with Cathy Scott, he had been stirred into life by Lena Horne. Now, he had feelings for his best pal. However, they had to be contained. Stanley was acutely aware of the huge danger that one wrong move could destroy the real friendship the pair had together – and he would lose the light of his life.

Then Stanley began to understand homosexuality. The pair read Havelock Ellis's *Sexual Inversion*, the first book in English to treat homosexuality as neither a disease nor crime and maintained that it was inborn and unmodifiable. Interestingly, Stanley didn't instantly conclude he was himself a homosexual (although the signposts were pointing in that direction). What he did know however was he was becoming an emotional wreck where Bill was concerned. Yet what to do? His great love had a girlfriend. Bill preferred women.

The terminally frustrating status quo between Stanley and Bill looked certain to remain. Until one night the impossible dream came true.

'We were back at my house in my bed, which was now in the

maid's bedroom where I'd had the wee arousal with Cathy Scott, and I confessed to Bill, all very dramatically, that I was so randy I was going to have to get up and think of going to see a prostitute.'

It was as much an emotional cry for help as it was a physical need.

'Anyway, Bill, referring to the prostitute idea said, "Oh, you don't have to do that. And look at the time. It's too late." And I said, oh so dramatically, "Oh, I have to. I can't tell you what I'm feeling!" And I turned my back to him.'

Stanley's angst was noted. 'As I turned my back, he drew his finger lightly down my spine – and it was like a 3,000-volt electric current going through me. Then I turned in the other direction and we made love. Not in any penetrative sense – gay sex is far less penetrative than people would imagine – but in that moment I thought the world had changed for me.

'Afterwards I gasped, "Have you ever done this before?" And he said, dismissively, "Oh yes, I've had all my friends." I thought "You bastard!" Here was me holding everything back. And so much for the girlfriend!'

In the weeks that followed, Fred and Bessie sensed something going on.

'One time my mother yelled to my dad, "It's ridiculous! It's every second night that boy's living here, or Stanley's over there. What's his mother and father going to think?"'

Fred Baxter simply shrugged. And Stanley carried on adoring Bill Henry. But even though they had become lovers, Stanley didn't for a second assume they were in a relationship. Bill, it seemed to Stanley, was simply having a bit of fun. But Stanley wasn't. This was complete infatuation. His heart was entirely engaged. And he sensed it would soon be broken.

6

The Red Coal Minor

STANLEY WORKED HARD to pass his upcoming final exams in June 1943, although not just to please his dad. The 17-year-old simply hated the idea of failure. And the showbiz dream was still very much alive.

'Stanley would practise signing his signature for autographs,' Alice recalls. 'He would even toy with different stage names believing that "Stanley Baxter" sounded awfully dreary. But he never came up with an alternative.'

During the last few weeks of the term, Stanley convinced his teachers he was Glasgow's answer to Orson Welles, and he should stage a revue, with himself as impresario, producer, director and star turn of *Paper Doll.*

'There was a song out at the time called 'Paper Doll', and I borrowed the name from that. Part of this show included a burlesque of Hamlet's meeting with his mother which I rewrote into Americanese. Instead of "How now Hamlet, thou hast thy father much offended", it became "Say, Junior, you shuah got your old man seeing red..."'

It was the sort of pastiche Stanley would perform so many times later on television. And already he was revealing his love for the risqué.

'I picked a very talented girl from one of the junior classes for my Gertrude, 14-year-old Josephine.'

The young Welles had star-spotted well. Josephine Martin Crombie would become a well-known actress and marry acting legend Donald Pleasence (his second of four wives).

However, Dr Merry wasn't excited by Stanley's production.

'The Doctor was ill with worry,' says Stanley, with a wicked smile of understatement. 'It was the usual complaints about me, being too raunchy ["the usual" referring to the complaints that would come much later in his television life]. But he did have a point. I had a girl of 14 lying on stage in a split skirt smoking a cigarette seductively.'

Start as you mean to go on, Stanley.

'With great reluctance, Dr Merry did let it go on.'

Stanley's risqué revue made the *Scottish Daily Express*. Glasgow's very own Orson was ecstatic, and in August was happier still when he achieved the full set of Highers passes. Yet he soon realised he had passed his way into misery. Fred Baxter demanded his son become 'a teacher of English'.

'I thought, "Oh, fuck! The mind-numbing weariness of it all."'

Stanley had hated being a kid and now here he was expected to spend his working life teaching them. To compound the gloom, he couldn't share his angst with Bill Henry – who still reckoned acting to be pointless, and in any case Betty Low was becoming fed up with sharing her boyfriend. All Stanley could do was try hard to find acting work and then worry about his father.

The Citizens' Theatre Company had opened the previous year, based in the Athenaeum Theatre in Glasgow's Buchanan Street. Its directive was to establish a Scottish national theatre company, and it all sounded so exciting. Stanley lined up a meeting with famous playwright and Citizens' director, James Bridie. But the teenager's hopes, however thin, were ripped apart.

'Bridie was a nice old boy. Like a big bear. But he said, "I'm sorry, Stanley, we'd love to take you on but you are due to be called up. We really can't start someone who is certain to be whipped away."'

Bridie was right. Rome had been liberated in June, but the Normandy beach landings of the same month proved the Germans were still prepared to fight on. Stanley faced being conscripted. But if he knew this, he put it to the back of his mind. A few days later reality whacked him hard on the head when he was called to attend Forces assessment. Recruitment officers told Stanley he was short-sighted, but it didn't mean the schoolboy was unfit for service. He was informed, to his horror, the Navy would take him on.

Yes, he could have sought refuge in university but that would only have delayed the process – and given his father hope of a teaching career. The teenager resigned himself to the fact he'd have to do his three-year stint, probably serving on some mid-Atlantic troop ship that could be bombed at any moment.

'I was shit scared of the whole idea,' he says, shuddering in recall.

At least in these winter months he began seeing more of Bill; Betty Low had loosened the rope a little, and Bill made sure his horny chum didn't need to think about professional sex services. Stanley was also thankful to learn Bill wouldn't be called up as his army medical had revealed some little heart abnormality; 'Nothing to worry about.'

But in the New Year, Stanley discovered life on the ocean wave wasn't for him after all. The buff envelope containing his call-up papers arrived and the teenager discovered he would be appearing in a movie so much darker and grimmer than he could ever have imagined.

'IT'S THE MINES! IT'S THE MINES!' yelled Bessie, piercing Stanley's slumber that Saturday morning in the spring of 1944, Bill Henry dozing beside him.

The words not only shattered Stanley's serenity, they announced the world had in fact come to an end. Stanley was to become a Bevin Boy, joining the cast of thousands in what was one of the war effort's more questionable productions.

A shortage of miners and coal saw Minister of Labour Ernest Bevin introduce a ballot to determine whether conscripts should go into the armed services, or work in the mines. Stanley was to work down the pits, or rather *at* the pits because youngsters weren't actually sent underground.

'I thought going away on ships that might be bombed was bad enough but to go and work in the mines… and asking a late adolescent at 17 to suddenly learn to work coal? It was madness.

'And how could I tell my new workmates I was a radio actor, still appearing on *Children's Hour* and other shows? They'd punch me in the face.'

The black-faced coal commandos would most likely have struggled to embrace Stanley's latest creative project.

'I had seen this ballet recently at the Theatre Royal in Glasgow with Betty Low [they'd become closer pals] and thought it was wonderful, so we decided to write the book of the ballet based on the life of *Arthadekowtama the Buddha*.'

Of course, you did, Stanley. It's an obvious choice.

'Looking back, it's all so pretentious I can't fucking believe it. Nothing ever came of it of course, but it shows where my head was at the time.'

Slightly lost perhaps, somewhere between *Swan Lake* and *Shit Creek*.

Bessie meantime was relieved her Sonny Boy wasn't going off to war. At least he 'wouldn't be murdered'. Regardless, Stanley knew grim times lay ahead.

In the waiting months, he made the most of his time at home, still hanging around with Bill and, at times, Betty. But in October 1944, the black day finally arrived when the heavy-hearted 18-year-old packed a hefty suitcase and set off for a training mine near Dunfermline in the North East of Scotland.

The Bevin Boys were billeted in a 'horrid and claustrophobic' hostel but fortunately, Stanley discovered a kindred spirit in future Scottish Office Minister J Dickson Mabon (the 'J' was for Jesse, which, had the other members of Camp Coalface known, would have caused a few smirks).

Dick Mabon, who had won a scholarship to a private school in Glasgow, had similar traits to Stanley: a good sense of humour, sympathies with the socialist movement, a driving ambition and an understanding that they were two young men cast in the wrong roles.

'I liked him straight away,' said Dick, who passed away in 2008. 'He seemed a confident type, not shy or introverted at all. And I was pleased that like me he was furious to be posted to the mines.'

Together the two new chums learned of the dangers of poisoning, to keep their food in tins so the rats wouldn't get at it. And they learned about fire damp, the sudden release of methane gas which can cause coal to explode in the face of those mining it.

And it was all awful.

'The ex-miners seconded to train us were salt of the earth people, but they faced a real task with the improbables and the ludicrous like me,' says Stanley.

After training, Stanley and Dick were posted to Kingshill, a mining pit in Shotts, a village about six miles outside of Glasgow, and consigned to another hostel with the rest of the Bevins. But if those nasty mines people thought Sonny Boy was to endure this horrid existence Bessie Baxter had other ideas.

'Her little boy living in a Bevin Boys hostel and pouring beer down his throat every night? Goodness! And God knows what hoors he would be taken to by these rough boys.'

And so Ma and Pa Baxter took preventative measures.

'My father had a friend named Carmichael, who lived locally in Wishaw, and my dad asked if I could be taken in as a lodger.'

During the day, Stanley would go to the pit head and work in an open shed with the rest of the black-faced teenage boys as they suffered the pain of cut hands from lifting razor-sharp rocks. And to add to the horror of it all, Scotland's winter in 1944 was close to Siberian. At night, the Carmichaels would come to regret saying to filthy young Stanley that he should not bother to use the pit baths.

'You couldn't get the dirt off the rim of their lovely lilac bath with a chisel.'

The pit work involved a conveyor belt delivering a constant line of coal mixed up with stones and Stanley and Co. had to remove the stones, break them up with an 18-pound hammer into smaller pieces and then push them through a grille on the ground. However, as the bars on the grille were fixed close together, it made for far more stone breaking. Naturally, Stanley found this situation to be intolerable.

'By the time I got the bloody stones broken up other stones had gone into the truck with the coal'

Infuriated, Stanley left his post and went back to the canteen to find the foreman.

'[With Kelvinside silver spoon in mouth.] I simply must speak with you!'

'[With pipe in mouth.] Oh, aye. Whit dae ye want, son?'

'Do you realise what's going on down there?'

'No, what?'

'No? Well, I'll tell you…' He does, and concludes: 'And if there's any more of this nonsense well, we're going to WALK OUT.'

Stanley's interpretation of Marx and Engels was unleashed. However, he could have been quoting Groucho Marx for all the foreman cared.

'Walk out? Walk out? You're working for His Majesty's Service here, son. Do you realise you could be shot for what you're saying to me?'

'Shot? Shot? Well, em. Shot, you say? Em, well, regardless, something ought to be done. [Softened, conciliatory tone appears.] It's really not good enough.'

'Aye, well. We'll see what can be done about taking away a couple of the bars.'

Threat of dawn execution passed and the young revolutionary at the vanguard of coal mining improvement schemes had his way. (In a few years' time Stanley's union work with Equity would see him described in a *Glasgow Evening Times* headline as 'RED BAXTER'.)

But before Red could really make his name as a political activist, fate kicked in. When a very bad cold and his old earache flared up, so did Bessie. Her little Bevin Boy, she felt, *had* to come out of the mines. Bessie insisted Sonny Boy be given a new National Service medical, but it was only after protracted discussion the board reluctantly agreed to free Master Baxter from the chains of coal mining oppression.

'They looked at me rather aggressively and said, "We're dropping you down to B1 status. But don't think you won't be called up for one of the services!" And I said, "Look, I'm not asking *not* to be called up at all."

'All they said in dismissing me was, "Well, be on your way." But I didn't know where my "way" was at all.'

While Stanley was being derided by Her Majesty's recruiters, young Gordon Jackson had been recruited by the Citizens' Theatre Company, a fact which Bessie rubbed into Sonny Boy deeper than Shotts' coal dust. The Citizens' had moved to a new home in The Princess's Theatre in the Gorbals, which would become, according to the *Daily Record*, 'Glasgow's Old Vic'. And while Gordon faced a welcoming and delighted audience in this wonderful new world of Scottish theatre, all Stanley could do was wait to be decided upon.

7

De-bollocking

RELEASED IN THE spring of 1945 from the pit of misery, Stanley had some unexpected time on his scratched and torn hands. And for a while he managed to delude himself that Her Majesty's Forces may well have forgotten he ever existed. After all, what use could he be to the war effort now that it looked to be over? Dresden had been bombed flat, the Red Army was about to enter Berlin and the British and Canadians were set to liberate Belsen.

But just in case he *were* called up, Stanley determined to make at least a little hay while Freedom's sun shone. Time was again spent at the movies, catching a tram out to the Boulevard in Knightswood to see the likes of Judy Garland's *Meet Me in St. Louis*.

Stanley smiles as he agrees this particular days' delights offered a clue to his sexuality. Yet, his sexual predilection wasn't *entirely* clear. Lena Horne made him feel light on his feet, but the mere thought of Bill Henry caused the teenager to defy gravity.

Stanley, now almost 19, certainly didn't think to explore the Glasgow world of teen heterosexuality. He didn't like bars and the city's vast array of glittering dancehalls/pick-up palaces such as the Locarno and the Dennistoun Palais – Glasgow now had more than 150 – held no real appeal.

'I did go dancing with cousin Alma a few times to Green's Playhouse in the city centre because she didn't have a boyfriend, and I was there to be dragged around.'

But if Stanley was gay and in love with Bill what could he do about it? Bill wasn't gay. He much preferred tea but would have the occasional coffee – when it was presented on a tray.

When Stanley wasn't thinking of Bill Henry he was dreaming of a life in acting. In May 1945, just before his birthday, Betty Low (a keen actor as well as an artist) suggested Stanley audition for the radical Unity Theatre Group, based at Glasgow's Athenaeum Theatre. To his utter relief he was successful. Here was a chance to prove to his dad he could make a career as a performer.

'The only problem was this was I found myself in a workers' theatre milieu, so I thought I'd better play up the mines and play down Hillhead – both school and district. But I didn't fool anyone with my baggy brown corduroys and turtle-necked navy blue jersey and wise nods to Marx and Engels.

'I was uncomfortably aware that the real thing, a young actor called Roddy McMillan, (who would become an iconic TV and film star) was controlling his mirth with difficulty.'[8]

Stanley appeared in one play at Unity (he can't recall the title – 'I think it was a George Munro play.') playing an old man and he loved it, but regrets he had to learn to smoke for the role and was hooked for life.

'But the next part coming up, I figured, would be truly immense for me. The play was called *Remembered For Ever* and it was the story of a young soldier who was blinded. A real womb trembler. I thought, "There won't be a dry eye in the house."'

The female lead went to Josephine Crombie, his school siren.

However, Stanley didn't get to play alongside his Paper Doll. Days before the opening, a manila envelope plopped onto the landing with the letters OHMS on the back. It was the worst of news. Stanley had been called up.

He could of course have followed in the footsteps of Alfie Hill, later to change his name to Benny, who had decided to become a moving target and worked (hid) in the theatres of England for six months (Benny was caught and punished before being sent to a unit).

Then again, he could have become a conscientious objector and refused to enlist, as playwright Harold Pinter did – and was fined £30. But Stanley had never skipped school, far less a civil ruling you could be jailed for. And that would certainly have created scandal amongst Bessie's mahjong ladies.

In June 1945, a month after VE day, Stanley set off for Pinefields camp in Elgin to join the Seaforth and Camerons. He was sad to leave behind his dad, Alice and erstwhile lover Bill, whom he'd said a brief goodbye to over the phone. Leaving his mother behind however was far less of an ordeal.

'It was too close,' he says of the relationship. 'I badly wanted to get out of the house. I didn't want to join the army, but one consolation was Bessie wasn't coming with me.'

Stanley was sad however to leave the BBC behind and a developing career in acting on radio in series such as *Kidnapped*. But his saddened heart sank even lower than his battered seat covering when he looked out of the train window.

'As the train made to move off, I saw this shambolic figure of Mrs Connolly rushing along holding the hand of Norman. And I nearly died at this realisation he was coming to Pinefields with me.'

Norman was all too much of a reminder of the outsider Stanley had been before he found his own set. And Stanley had more than enough adjustments to make on his own, what with moving into a wooden hut in the camp with '11 other hairy-arsed soldiers'.

'When I walked in I thought a rat had died. The place stank of sweaty feet.'

There was another personal issue to contend with.

'I was terrified to find that you had terrible trouble having a wank, down to the bromide they put in the tea. The army said they didn't ever do such a thing but believe you me I am living proof that they carried out pharmaceutical de-bollocking. The number of nights I sat in that loo working up to a sweat that would pour down my face – with nothing to show for it but a wee feeling – convinced me we had all been tampered with.

'I hoped that this wouldn't go on for my entire army career, and fortunately it didn't.'

But despite the stinking socks and sexual emasculation, being cut from Bessie's umbilical cord was just what he needed. Stanley began to breathe on his own.

'I got on awfully well with the corporal in charge of our hut because I started doing impressions of the Regimental Sergeant Major. In fact, he said to a personnel officer, "Take a look at Private Baxter, sir. He has his Higher Leaving Certificate. Could he be officer material?"

'And this chinless wonder of an officer looked me up and down and with a derisory sneer, produced an Oxford accent and declared, "I don't think so."

'I laughed at the time, thinking, "You are so fucking right!" I never did make officer.' (Technically, he did – much, much later Stanley would be awarded the awesomely grand title of Brigadier.)

Meantime, he settled in nicely. Learning to march at Pinefields came easy, thanks to Alma's dancing lessons. Yet poor Norman may have been brilliant academically but couldn't march, or even fold a blanket.

'He went AWOL. He ran back to mummy and the House of Usher. And after a few days she brought him back to the camp, by the hand. The commanding officer looked at Norman's baffies, still held together by string, and his mum holding his hand and clearly felt sorry for the pair of them. He was sent to the Pioneer Corps to do some manual labour and I never heard of him again.'

Stanley was sent to Byefield Camp in Woking, Surrey to be trained as a touch typist clerk (Class 3). Then came the announcement that he was on the road to Bombay, to be sent to a holding camp while the army determined his future.

Bessie, who wrote every week, was horrified to learn her Sonny Boy was to be sent to this strange and exotic world. If she worried about the 'hoors' of Scotland's mining villages, what would he get up to when faced with the torrid temptations of the East? Stanley also wondered what he would get up to. And grinned.

Sailing into Bombay – Stanley's first time abroad – he was immediately heady with excitement. This was World Theatre.

'I was stunned at the sight of this huge archway, the Gateway to India, which was like a stage on which the curtain had gone up. All around there were the bright blue porters' uniforms and saffron turbans and carts and donkeys and men wearing dhotis. It was all so colourful.

'The theatricality of it all just thrilled me. It was like a massive Drury Lane pantomime or the opening of 'Arabian Nights' come to life. And at the same time you could see dead bodies covered in flowers and wee boys of eight offering their sisters to you for fuckie-fuckie, "Very white inside, just like Queen Victoria!" And I would be shouting, "No, no!" It was all a massive culture shock.'

Yet, not at all a frightening one. Arriving at the Kalyan holding camp, it was an effervescent Stanley who offered himself up for the position of Head of Camp Entertainment – which he had just invented – and announced plans to produce a little show with the acting troupe he'd formed.

'I had met up with a guy from Yorkshire called Reggie Short, a very likeable, slim bloke with splayed feet and we decided we would put on shows for the entire transit camp.'

Why not? Yet, instead of putting on a concert party, which the troops would have appreciated, Stanley and Reggie decided to stage a sort of outrageous Elizabethan fantasy called *Ducks and Drakes*, in which Reggie played Queen Elizabeth and Stanley became Francis Drake. It was heavy with political satire and laced with contemporary army gags and had huge songs written by Reggie. This outrageous idea also involved having period costume made up, but Stanley somehow managed it.

'And for this Rodgers and Hammerstein-like epic of course we hired a very big theatre. It was all so ludicrously ambitious.'

It hinted at the scale of production Stanley would later demand on television and in panto. But back then, in the late autumn of 1945, more was certainly less.

The soldiers weren't remotely interested in an Elizabethan extravaganza full of British topical references and the show didn't run to a second night. Stanley was seriously embarrassed but at least he had learned quickly what services audiences *didn't* want. What he also learned – just as importantly – was that the army had been prepared to indulge entertainers on an ad hoc basis.

Thanks to Japan having surrendered in September, the top brass realised the real battle on their hands was to maintain troop morale. That was why Stanley and Reggie had been allowed to work on *Ducks and Drakes* for several months. The young performers made another discovery during those months.

After one very late night of rehearsals, Stanley and Reggie crashed out together on Queen Elizabeth's prop bed. Curious fumbles turned into free-flowing passion and by the time the Indian sun rose in the morning Stanley had his moment of clarity.

'I knew then I was probably gay. I'd half thought Bill Henry just may have been some sort of an infatuation but this night with Reggie gave me a fair idea where my preference lay.'

'Reggie,' says Stanley, 'wasn't gay.'

'It was just one of those nights. Sometimes people do the unexpected, and being away from home… It may sound odd but lots of heterosexual men have gay affairs. Perhaps it's curiosity. Who knows?'

Reggie was to be sent to another part of India and it would be many years later before they would meet again, in very different circumstances.

In the meantime, Stanley was transferred to Rangoon, the Burmese capital, a far less exotic placement than Bombay. Bomb craters lined the streets where beautiful shops had once stood; it was a world beginning to rebuild itself, resonating with both sadness and hope.

Stanley was based at the army station at Rangoon Racecourse, where all the spectators' stands had been filled with gunny sacks and where all sorts of supplies were stored. His clerical job was to supervise a hundred Japanese POWs on the road up from their camp to the supply depot, where they would load up these bags, to be sent to army camps in the likes of Mandalay. (In reality, much of the foodstuffs such as dried eggs were being sent back to Britain by officers on the fiddle.) Stanley was promoted to corporal after meeting the HQ's Major Savage – who liked the fact Stanley was 'posher' than the other two supply clerks, who were in fact a couple of tearaways. Percival Steed's elocution lessons had not been in vain.

Army life became very relaxed. The very polite soft-spoken major was due to be de-mobbed soon but far too lazy to type up his job applications to prospective employers. That became Stanley's job. The major wasn't overly ambitious and Stanley typed up just two letters in six months, the rest of the time he spent reading.

The easy army life however surrendered to stupefying boredom. Touchy typist Stanley felt he was going out of his mind with nothing to do all day but look out of the window at the unceasing rain. This wasn't glorious theatre at all. This was torturous tedium, punctuated with tiny intermissions when the parcels arrived from home. Bessie wrote each week of course, and Fred would send his son tins of Senior Service cigarettes.

However, one morning the rain stopped – and a little rainbow formed in his head. Corporal Baxter spied a sign that suggested a whole new way of army life. And he began to feel giddy with excitement.

8

Carry on Sergeant

IN 1974, THE BBC broadcast a new sitcom series, *It Ain't Half Hot Mum* written by Jimmy Perry and David Croft, featuring the tales of a collection of misfits who made up the Royal Artillery Concert Party in wartime India. Led by bulldog Battery Sergeant Major Tudor Bryn 'Shut Up' William played by the wonderful Windsor Davies, the 'physically challenged and the pooftahs' teamed up to entertain the troops.

Twenty-eight years earlier, thoroughly frustrated typist (Class 3) Stanley Baxter hoped the real thing could be his saviour. The sign on the regimental notice board read:

> ENSA [Entertainments National Services Organisation] is being disbanded. A new organisation called Combined Services Entertainment [CSE] will be formed, combining for some time civilian and service artists, eventually phasing out civilian artists altogether.

Without a war raging there was nothing to kill but boredom. CSE offered an outlet for the frustrated performers and chance to keep the servicemen smiling. Win-win!

> If you can sing, dance, play a musical instrument, or whatever, please apply.

Corporal Baxter's eyes lit up like neon. This was it, the chance to pick up where he had left off at the BBC and Unity Theatre, to act, to entertain, to wallow in applause once again, to prevent him going out of his Brylcreemed head. He simply HAD to be accepted.

Stanley applied, as a straight actor, along with hundreds of other Forces hopefuls from all over India, Burma and the HQ in Singapore. Young officers who had run amateur dramatic societies in Civvy Street were chosen to filter out the absolute rubbish from the talented.

'I had to go before one of these "chinless wonders" and audition. On the day, I was given a part to read from the Patrick Hamilton play, *Rope*.'

Rope was a tale of homicide and homoeroticism, a meaty play in which Stanley would later appear in Scotland – and fail to win over an audience. But his performance in Rangoon hit the mark.

'Mmm, yes, that's pretty good,' recalls Stanley, imitating the slightly sibilant officer. 'And that's the best we've heard this week. You'll be sent down to Singapore (CSE HQ) for a second audition. Of course, we can't guarantee you'll get in. And if they don't accept you you'll be sent back to your unit.'

What? If he heard, 'Next!' he would be RTU'd. Returned To Unit. 'Goodbye and thank you. Life-fucking-over.'

Stanley could hardly contain his fear – and excitement – when, on the appointed day on 31 December 1946, he flew to Singapore on the Sunderland Flying Boat, his first time on a plane. On arrival, he was surprised to see that Singapore looked relatively untouched, in spite of merciless Japanese bombing during the time of British occupation.

'It was all lit up and there was a hugely colourful feel about the place. I thought, "This is a bit more glamourous than Rangoon."'

The frisson heightened when Stanley learned the meeting place was the famous Raffles Hotel, which served as an information centre. When he arrived at Raffles in the mid-afternoon, the soldier-typist was told the next lorry to take him to the transit camp at Nee Soon, where he'd be interviewed, didn't leave until one o'clock in the morning.

'I headed for The Cheery Cafe to pass the time and have steak, eggs and chips but at the time I didn't feel all that cheery. I felt alone and anxious.

'Then I got talking to some soldiers in the cafe, who didn't seem to mind hanging around at all. "Dekko the tarts in the rickshaws," said one corporal. His head gave a jerk window-wards and my eye followed. Chinese girls (in the obligatory split satin skirts) were seated on small couches which were being propelled along by very scraggy, barefoot cyclists wearing straw hats.

'If I had been a bit older, I might have whooped with anticipation, rushed out into the night and acquired syphilis that would have left me as deaf as Beethoven and as blind as Delius. But my Presbyterian background, and Bessie of course (and most likely being gay) saved me from entertaining that thought.'

As Stanley gazed at the exotic world through the window, he revealed to the group he hoped to join CSE. This brought scowls of derision and the forthright advice, 'Better watch yourself with that bunch of poofs!'

Thankfully, more helpful advice was to follow.

'But I tell you wot,' said the corporal, 'that mob are doing a play right now at the Victoria Theatre, across the padang [playing field]. When they finish their show they could give you a lift to Nee Soon on their coach.'

Filled with steak and eggs and the blithe self-confidence of youth, Stanley made his way to the Victoria Theatre stage door and discovered lots of men in make-up and little groups of backstage workers wearing civilian clothes. He learned later CSE performers were allowed that dress freedom.

Stanley said to one man, 'Hello, is it true that you are all stationed at Nee Soon and you'll be heading back there after the play finishes. If so, is there any chance of getting a lift?'

'No, sorry mate,' came the reply from a rather dour soldier. 'When you think of all the cast of the show and some of the girlfriends–'

The refusal was hardly out of the mouth when another voice crashed into the conversation. It was a nasal-whined magisterial tone that would become instantly recognisable years later to a generation of *Carry On* film fans.

'Now what's going on here?' called out the imperious voice belonging to a grey-haired old man with a grey moustache and wearing a trilby hat. And then its owner turned to Stanley and demanded, 'Corporal, what's your name?'

Stanley looked at the person behind the voice. But on closer inspection he seemed to be a child dressed up as an old man.

'My name's Baxter, and I was hoping to go to Nee Soon, but I was told there wasn't a seat–'

'What? No seat? Rubbish! Yes, of course you can come with us.'

The voice then shouted to the others, 'Give him a seat and let him watch the play first. Nobody wants to see the fucking thing anyway. It's rotten!'

Then this 'old man' turned to Stanley, pointed to a chair and said, 'Here, you might as well sit there.' Stanley thanked him and he replied [Stanley impersonates his new chum with the nasal, wasp-with-adenoids voice], 'Oh, don't be silly!'

'That was my first introduction to Kenneth Williams.'

Williams, the son of an East London hairdresser, was an even less likely soldier than Stanley. Somehow he had survived basic training and was placed with the Royal Engineers as a map maker. He too had been processed at Kalyan before going on to Ceylon and applying for Combined Services. When Williams was auditioned at Nee Soon, he performed impressions of Winston Churchill and music hall actress Nellie Wallace. But in spite of giving of his best, Williams was devastated to hear the shout, 'RTU!' It was only when he produced tears (probably real, given the impact of the decision), informed the CSE people his unit had been disbanded and revealed he could draw posters, the entertainment bosses relented and adopted the soldier orphan child nobody wanted. After some time designing posters, Williams was blessed by malaria (not personally, it laid another actor up in hospital) and the Londoner landed the role of The Detective in the 'creaky old thriller' Stanley was about to watch.

'I sat in the stalls and watched *Seven Keys to Baldpate* – along with about four other people. It soon became obvious that this was clearly another *Ducks and Drakes* situation, a play that was entirely wrong for the Forces who of course wanted Light Entertainment.'

Sergeant Kenneth Williams was just three months older than his new pal but looked 15 years old. If he'd been a boxer he would have been a paperweight but as he reveals in his autobiography,

Just Williams, he immediately took on the role of protector for 'the young, aesthetic 20-year-old called Stanley Baxter'.

When they arrived at the barracks in Nee Soon, in the dead of night of 1 January 1947, Stanley learned the CSE troops were all living in officer quarters at the far end of the camp. Part of the delight in being accepted by CSE was an instant promotion to sergeant and the chance to bypass most of the harsher conventions of army life. Kenneth Williams suggested his new pal should stay the night in CSE's officer quarters.

Stanley said to Kenny, 'I can't go in there. I have to go to the transit camp, and then wait for my audition.'

'Rubbish! We can take you in, there's plenty of room.'

'But I don't want to tempt fate.'

'Rubbish! You'll get through. No point in living in squalor 'till then.'

Brave words, considering *he* had been rejected. (Interestingly, Williams never revealed the story of his audition failure to Stanley. Ever.)

Meanwhile, his ego massaged, Stanley moved into the plusher accommodation while his little Svengali did everything he could to make his new chum at home.

'He was marvellous at that time,' says Stanley, the end of the sentence hinting the lifelong relationship wouldn't always run as smoothly as it had begun.

'He just liked the look of me I guess, which wasn't always the way with Kenny and people. And we became close without it ever being more than friendship.'

The next day Stanley had his dreaded interview to contend with and made his way to the CSE office. His life, as he saw it hinged on acceptance by Flt Lieutenant Albert Arlen, a 'fat, floppy-haired RAF-type with a face like a bloodhound' who was sitting behind a desk. Stanley approached and read for the officer (he can't remember what, an indication of his nervous state at the time).

'He listened and said nothing, then said he would let me know and I was asked to wait in the next room.

'I died. It was all too much. I couldn't bear the suspense.'

Then it all became rather surreal. As Stanley made his way

to the room, a good-looking blond soldier appeared at the Flt Lieutenant's desk and stood next to him. Sitting next door in a cold sweat, Stanley overheard their conversation.

This young Sergeant said to the Flt Lieutenant, in a very butch and rather posh voice, 'Permission to return to unit, sir.'

'What's the matter with you, Brian?'

'Nothing, sir.'

'Nothing? You haven't been your usual self with me. Have you gone off me?'

'Permission to return to unit, sir…'

'Sir? Sir! It was Christian names last night, Brian. And what about the dinner at Raffles? Eh? And what about the silk shirts you liked so much?'

'Permission to–'

'Oh don't keep on, Brian. Look, we'll talk about it tonight. Dismiss.'

'Brian marched off, with the tearful Flt Lieutenant still muttering endearments. And I realised he was raving and had obviously fancied this sergeant. I thought, "Jesus, this is all very different from working with the gunny sacks and the Japs."'

Stanley also quickly realised he just may have found a spiritual home. But that made the fear of failing the audition all the greater. At that moment his fate was decided.

The Company Sergeant Major called out, 'Flight, are we taking Corporal Baxter or are we RTU'ing him?'

'I felt a cold chill go down by back. I was shitting myself. Absolutely terri-fucking-fied. And then the solemn voice came back and said, "We'll take him."'

Thankfully, sad Albert's rejection by lover Brian hadn't tainted his judgement. Corporal Baxter was now an official member of CSE. His days as a touchy typist were over. He was to become a Serious Actor, he would be a producer and director – part of the show team – and he was so truly thankful tears welled up in his eyes.

Then came the added bonus, the realisation he would be living in officer's billets with only two to a room – and he had an Indian man-servant to polish his shoes. It was the life even Riley could only dream about.

Three weeks later, however, the dream threatened to turn to nightmare. The camp jungle drums announced that all straight (as in non-comedic) actors were to be RTU'd. It seems the CSE top brass had had enough of giving house rooms to the hopeful Hamlets and were searching out those who could supply laughs.

The likes of pretentious nonsense such as *Seven Keys to Baldpate* had precipitated the situation. And while the ENSA shows had been free, CSE were charging fourpence. No one wanted to pay good money to see the likes of baby-faced Kenneth Williams gum a moustache to his top lip and pretend to be a 60-year-old – unless it was for laughs.

Stanley seized the initiative. And all claims to be a Serious Actor were jettisoned.

'I thought, "Fuck Shakespeare, I've got to be the all-singing-all-dancing-da-ra-da-ra-dee-ree-dee-dee-ree." And I suddenly announced to Albert Arlen, "I'm not really a straight actor at all, I can do impersonations!"' And he could, of course.

'And speaking at about 300 miles per hour, I bellowed, "I can do light entertainment – I've done church halls since I was six – and I've even written a cod pantomime of *Aladdin*!"'

The Clement Freud-face offered a half smile, which suggested agreement. Stanley's place in the show team was again secured. And so he proceeded to have the time of his life. Camp life, he soon learned, was full of very camp fun.

9
Buggery, Bestiality and Necrophilia

IF BURMA HAD been a squelchy sock in the crusty old boot of Stanley's army experience, then Singapore was a dry, dainty, colourful little cotton number. Literally. Every day, for example, the CSE performers would make the journey across the square from their cosy separate billet to the Gaiety Theatre, at the other side of the camp. En route, they'd pass by the 2,000 regular uniformed troops who'd be parading or drilling. And, of course, there would be howls or derision directed at the CSE boys who would either be wearing strappy sandals, Hawaiian shirts, chic merino wool jumpers or, in the case of Kenneth Williams, soft-linen shorts and ankle socks with little flowers on them.

'Some of the CSE boys even had cigarette holders, it was that camp,' says Stanley, grinning.

'And as we walked past these troops in uniform, all Brasso'd up and shining, we'd hear the calls of, "What the fuck are these supposed to be?" Kenny, of course, would shout back defiantly, "What ya all looking at, then?"'

Even the straight guys in CSE would enjoy camping it up; it was a way to get back at all the fierce RSMs (Regimental sergeant majors) who had previously bitten their heads off. Now they had license to thrill, to parade like peacocks if they so wished. And any abuse thrown their way was caught easily and fielded back. To be ridiculed was to be seen as being different, special. CSE was a world within a world. Yet, Stanley points out the organisation was itself subdivided.

'It was made up of macho, anti-gay guys who drove the trucks and looked after military hardware. We called them the Harties.

'And there were the artistes, many of whom were homosexual,

and those who were more than tolerant. These were the Arties.'

There was much for 20-year-old Stanley to absorb in this new world. Not for him the likes of drilling, sweeping or being shouted at. The ambient noise in the CSE corner was of amateur bands rehearsing or ping pong balls plinking on wooden tables.

Stanley was delightfully bewildered by the paradoxes of this little entertainment world which actually promoted those far less capable of meeting standard army expectations. Such a case was Peter Nichols, the future playwright. He and Stanley became close friends in CSE and remained so. In 1977, Peter would write the delightful *Privates on Parade*. Set in Singapore in 1948, the theatre play, later to become a movie, told the story of the hugely colourful characters in a performance unit. How could Peter Nichols not write about his experiences in CSE? In his autobiography *Feeling You're Behind*, the slim young soldier from Bristol describes his first meeting with his senior NCO (Non-Commissioned Officer) in the mess tent.

The NCO asks: 'Buy you a drink?'

'Yes, I'll have an orange, please, sir.'

'Call me Hank. Here boy! A gin and orange for the new man. Peter isn't it? I hope you'll settle down here.'

'Don't see why not.'

'Don't you? Let me offer you some advice. There are two courses open for you. You can join the men, or you can join the queers.'

'The what, Sarge? Er, Hank?'

'The queers. The fairies. There's your gin.'

'Thanks. Cheers.'

Peter sums up the meeting: 'Not only gin to drink but another language to learn as well.'

The acceptance, in some instances the encouragement, of homosexuality in CSE came as a shock to those who entered the unit. And why wouldn't it? Back in Liverpool at this time Alec Guinness had been arrested and charged with importuning and was fined. (The case never made the newspapers because Guinness gave a false, borrowed from Dickens, name – Herbert Pocket.) Stanley's eyes meantime were opening wider than the Gaiety stage.

'Discovering about sexuality in Britain was groping in the dark in every sense. But in CSE there were just so many poofs. And as such, there was a lot of excitement in realising you are not alone in the world. It's not like nowadays, where you are tripping over gay porn.'

In CSE, Stanley read more Proust (the French-Jewish homosexual and asthmatic semi-invalid) and discovered Havelock Ellis being passed around freely, like partners at a wife-swapping party.

'Kenny and I were fascinated by that whole gay world and read everything we could about it.'

Peter Nichols wasn't gay, although that may not have been the thought of the transit troops who saw him wear his egg-yellow silk kimono embroidered with blue dragons. But he was simpatico with the preferences of his new friends. What he also had in common with his chums was an intellect – and a natural curiosity about the ways of the sexual world.

Peter, at that time a hopeful actor who had also gone through the nerve-jangling experience of a CSE second audition process, writes in his memoir:

> Sexually, we were still in the closet. Afraid of the simple act, we mugged up on the fancy stuff. We'd never touched a naked girl but knew all about buggery, bestiality and necrophilia.

He offers an interesting description of meeting young Sgt Baxter:

> Dark haired with plastic face always awry. A straight actor, producer and writer of cryptic stories and obscure poems. On his wall is a picture of Picasso.
>
> Spent a miserable period of his life as a Bevin Boy near his native Glasgow. He berated mining, miners and all those concerned with the excavation of coal.
>
> Loathes trivialities, excess heartiness and shallow etiquette. Lives for art and for the stating of his beliefs through art. Prefers drama and serious art but is always willing to take part in revues and other entertainments.

Peter adds circumspectly:

> Not yet decided whether I like him or not. But apart from myself, he is probably the most brilliant of those at present residing in this abode of knowledge and female impersonation.

Stanley laughs at his pal's description.

'God, I must have been serious and a bit more intense than I realised. But I suppose we all are when we are young.'

Peter Nichols added that Stanley and Kenneth Williams weren't the easiest of friends: 'Their respect for each other's talent made their friendship a wary one.'

Which means the pair were in constant competition for the spotlight.

'That was pretty much the case then and it continued,' says Peter now.

Stanley expands on the tricky relationship with Kenneth Williams. 'From a position of a slight distance it may have looked as though he had been looking after me. But there was never the arm around the shoulder, certainly not literally. He was very non-tactile. He had a thing about touch and always operated independently. Certainly, there was never the feeling that this was two boys together, no real mates-manship. That was very un-Ken. He simply didn't get that close to people.'

Peter Nichols certainly didn't get close to Williams. But his attitude to Stanley warmed.

'Kenneth frightened me,' he writes, 'and it was some years later before I understood him. But it is with Baxter I have the most in common.'

Stanley liked Peter a great deal. Yet they weren't so close he would discuss his sexuality.

'Some things didn't have to be said. And he was certainly comfortable around gays.'

Over the weeks, the trio would spend endless hours talking over possible show ideas, dissecting each other's work. For the first time since meeting the art school gang back in Glasgow, Stanley found others who could test and stretch his imagination. But they all learned from each other.

'He was also among the first to help me write better,' says Peter of Stanley.

In April 1947, the three clever friends became four. Peter Nichols recalls his meeting with the 'already balding, mischievously smiling Sgt John Schlesinger'.

Former public school pupil John arrived at the camp as part of another concert troupe. He was the magic act. The conjuror with a wicked sense of humour would later go on to become a massively successful film director, creating movie classics such as *A Kind of Loving*, *Billy Liar*, *Darling* and *Midnight Cowboy*. His 1971 film featuring a ménage à trois, *Sunday Bloody Sunday*, starring Peter Finch, Murray Head and Glenda Jackson, was based upon his own experiences.

In May, Stanley celebrated his 21st birthday with his new best friends, Kenny, Peter and John. He couldn't quite believe his luck. Not only was he in a wondrous exotic location with such fun friends, Bessie Baxter and her critique of his life was so far away. And he and his chums could do pretty much as they liked.

'There was almost no discipline at all in the camp,' he says grinning. 'Except when the queens became too outrageous. One morning, as we passed the parade ground, the CSE boys were again wearing white shorts and flip flops and the regular soldiers again made kissing noises at each other, it was all getting very loud and obvious. This bunch of poofs were causing mayhem, so we were given a real dressing down and told to appear in uniform. But of course all our webbing had been lost and there was a frantic search for lost boots amongst mildewed kit bags. "Boots! We can't wear boots! They're horrid and they hurt our feet," Kenny declared.' The return to uniform lasted about a day. As a compromise it was suggested the Arties tone down their clothes; they soon went back to their wickedly colourful ways. And whenever little wars broke out between the artistes and the straights, Stanley points out the gay team always won.

'Who could beat the likes of Kenneth Williams when it came to repartee? And if it came to any physical battle he would win again. It wasn't Queensberry rules of course. He would just dive in with his fists, nails, feet – straight for the knackers. He wouldn't put up with any nonsense. He would go at them like a cat that gone mad. Timid he was not. He had tremendous physical and mental courage.

'Many years later he went to a gay meeting where he was reviled in advance for his right-wing leanings – he was so pro-Thatcher. But he took them on and won, won, won. Regardless of whether his audience were straight or gay, he could always win.'

Stanley's left-wing leanings didn't stop him enjoying the benefits of the Raj, having shoes polished (or flip flops washed), laundry and cleaning done by a bearer. Clean and shiny, on Friday nights he and his chums would take off into town and rather decadently spend their week's wages on a good dinner and several gins and tonics. No beer for these sophisticates.

However, just as the quartet began to take this wonderful life for granted, a large, pink hand grenade was thrown into the camp. The incomparable Barri Chatt had come to town. And there were few who weren't affected by the almighty explosion.

10

To Be Had

ETHEL MERMAN NEVER made an entrance as loud as Barri Chatt's arrival one balmy afternoon in Nee Soon.

Kenneth Williams, in *Just Williams*, describes the creature that was The Barri.

> A group of staff officers were disbanding outside our HQ when Chatt leapt out of a Jeep and performed three pirouettes before a slack-jawed Brigadier, tapped him on the shoulder crying: 'Tell your mother we're here, dear. Put the kettle on!'[9]
>
> Then he disappeared through the swing doors in a cloud of perfume, followed by a supporting cast shouting sibilant greetings and an irate danseuse demanding the loo.
>
> When the officers were told this was a civilian stage troupe sent out from London the Brigadier remarked, 'The city is dammed lucky to be rid of them.' And he predicted dire consequences for the colony.

Chatt was made up to acting Captain for his stint with CSE (it made for easier hotel, shipping, accommodation, booking, etc) but he was more than a drag act sent out to give the troops a laugh.

'He devised satirical dance routines, sharply observed and very funny,' adds Williams.

> He took bows with great panache shouting 'Thank you, lads, thank you. See you at the stage door. There's more round the back.'
>
> The invitation seldom went unheeded. And he'd say, 'Come in, dear, don't be shy. Think of me as your sister.'

It was perhaps an odd thing to say, unless incest was more

common than thought amongst National Servicemen. Regardless, Barri, who wore tight shorts when not on stage, created pure theatre wherever he appeared. Peter Nichols was equally stunned by the 'Yorkshireman with Shaftesbury Avenue sophistication.'

> When he took off his make-up after a show, he put another lot on. He always had a bronze matt complexion under his dyed blond hair. And he never shaved. Pulled the hairs out with tweezers. He would say, 'You must keep up the illusion. It's life, lovies, it's the theatre.'

The sentence was his catchphrase, which Nichols would later appropriate in *Privates on Parade*, with Barri appearing as visiting turn Terri Dennis.

However, back in the late summer of 1947, Barri's performance of Camp Showqueen wasn't well received by everyone. Stanley had no time for it. And he cites his chum Geoffrey Deakin as one reason why.

'Geoffrey was a very ordinary-looking, balding, chubby bloke from the north country who looked a little like Friar Tuck. An intelligent ex-Salvation Army-home boy he had had one affair with another soldier, yet he kept his sexuality quiet. Until Barri arrived.

'Suddenly, from looking very average, Geoffrey became all chiffon hankies and make-up and flouncing about. He went from being a nice, ordinary boy to becoming an outrageous queen wearing huge rings.

'I really preferred the Salvation Army boy and not this creature he had become. When he wasn't speaking in the polari (the gay code, which Williams would use later to great effect in radio show *Round the Horne*, with words such as ecaf (face), vada (see) handbag (money) he picked up in camp) he was actually telling everyone he was gay, saying to the troops, "I'm to be had." Or as he always put it, TBH.

'Even the gay sergeants, never mind the straight sergeants, were saying, "Oh, for fuck's sake, Geoffrey cut it out."'

Stanley's distaste for Geoffrey's new lifestyle grew with every descent (or ascent?) he made into what the Scot describes as 'Nellyland'.

'He could hardly speak without using innuendo, much the same as Barri Chatt. You couldn't say the word 'big' in front of him because he'd grin and say, "Well, you like them big, don't you."

'The poverty of humour was evident. And there is a great poverty of humour amongst that type of homosexual. The gags are all about dicks and arses.

'And yet there is the other type of homosexual like Wilde or Coward, with a brilliant use of language. I certainly get on much better with the Alan Bennett types.'

Stanley didn't abandon Geoffrey to his new life of magnificent mincing.

'Although many of us were very critical we had to side with Geoffrey because we were in his "team" as it were. But transformations like this, from ordinary boy to queen, certainly didn't help with the animosity, the snide little comments we were getting occasionally from the straights.

'I thought, "I really hate this. I really don't want to be involved in this kind of world."'

The Geoffrey Deakin experience taught Stanley he had little tolerance for the more outrageous side of homosexuality, the off-stage wearers of eye-liner and Cupid's bow lipstick.

'I'm ashamed to say it, being gay myself. But it's a fact of life that many people are anti-gay and they think all gays are raving queens because of mincers like Geoffrey.'

Stanley accepts that queens often believe the best line of defence is attack. 'Yes, there are some young men, brought up in the country or whatever, very acceptable young men who suddenly realise they are gay and think that they have to become more like women, to fit the stereotype.

'And certainly older gays who are very effeminate draw them into that. But I hate all that. Why couldn't Geoffrey come out – and still be that normal intelligent person that I'd first met?'

This dislike of effeminate gays never left Stanley. And it would be intensified in time to come, for reasons the actor could never have imagined.

Many years later, when Stanley became revered for his screen and theatre performances of women, several critics were to hint that the performer seemed a little too comfortable in frocks and high heels, the Carmen Miranda outfits or whatever. But he maintains that that couldn't have been further from the truth. He was simply playing at being a woman.

Meanwhile, back in Nee Soon Stanley admits that on the subject of high campery, he granted Williams special dispensation. Although Williams never dressed up in women's clothes or wore Barri Chatt-like make-up, he was often outrageous, 'and certainly nelly'.

'But he was also incredibly intelligent. With a brain like that you could forgive him most things.'

Ironically, Kenneth Williams too couldn't abide the overtly homosexual.

'A young, very beautiful sailor called Leo turned up one day and announced that he could sing,' Stanley recalls.

'Kenny fancied him enormously and was practically doing back-flips. He wanted to help him stay with CSE and I suppose it was rather like when I had turned up at the Victoria Theatre.

'But there was no way he could get Leo in the show because the casting was complete and we already had a tenor. The straights would have gone nuts if we'd let him in. Kenny, however, was determined and set up a special audition, calling in the civilian pianist – who was an old queen – to accompany the sailor.

'And so the pianist said to Leo, "What do you know? What's your key?" And he played, and this voice came out which was very, very impressive. Regardless, we failed to get him in the show.'

The young sailor went on to become the British singing star of the '50s, David Whitfield. The Hull-born tenor who was said to be Elvis's favourite singer, would have an international hit in 1954 with 'Cara Mia', which sold more than one million copies. However, the point of the story is that David wasn't overtly gay.

'If he had been, he wouldn't have appealed to Kenny, who only liked men who looked straight.'

Is this because Williams only liked men who didn't remind him of himself?

'Yes, because for the most part he was trapped in that camp, *Carry On* figure, limited by his body shape and voice. When he later became famous he would still travel by public transport but when someone should yell out, "Oh, there's that little poof!" it would hurt him terribly. He would do what I call his drained face.'

It wasn't only the gay (the word had recently entered the lexicon) Arties who were consumed with sex or talking about sex in CSE. Everyone was at it. The heterosexual soldiers would help out if the gay team were a man short, the married officers had affairs (straight and gay) as often as they had early evening G&Ts and of course the virgin soldiers couldn't wait to be deflowered by the Singaporean Taxi Girls, who offered a virtual guarantee of the clap.

'These were the sort of people I was mixing with,' says Stanley with a wry smile. 'Not at all like the crowd back home in Hillhead.'

Yes, and wasn't he glad of it. Stanley himself did 'a little grazing' in the lush fields of gay sexual opportunity. 'There was no real relationship as such in Singapore, just a series of moments, which was the case for all of us homosexuals until we eventually settle down.'

Yet, he still wasn't ready to admit to himself he was 100 per cent gay. Stanley knew the problems that would create in life.

'But there were so many men who would say to me, "Don't you know about yourself? For Christ's sakes, you're raving."'

How could he be in denial? It was a little easier given that Stanley had certainly not experienced anything like the full-blown passion he'd felt for Bill Henry (whom he never heard from during his army stint. Stanley however was pragmatic about that; what would Bill write of anyway, but trivia from home wrapped up in frustrating expressions of cheerful mateyness?) For now, he would have fun and forget about home, until Bessie's letters arrived, well-written detailed accounts of life back at 5 Wilton Mansions. Alice recalls it was a strange time at home without big brother.

'We'd get the occasional letter saying he was touring Hong Kong or whatever. But not an awful lot.

'Mum missed him tremendously. Probably Dad too, though he never showed it. What my mother would say was, "I haven't had a letter from THAT boy for two weeks. After all I've done for him." She was big on guilt trips.'

All of that was lost on Stanley because he was caught up in the excitement of touring in a CSE revue show, *At Your Service*, put together by Flt Lieutenant Arlen (who had composed the *El Alamein Concerto*).

To say it was a hoot doesn't do hoots justice. This was real-life *It Ain't Half Hot Mum*-style showtime and as camp as a pink Christmas tree. The entertainers took to the stage wearing canary yellow battledress tops and sky blue trousers with a big yellow stripe down the side.

> We're the men of the service, we're at your service,
> Enter-tain-ing you [ten fingers point at audience, ten right feet stamping on the word]
> We'll sing you songs both old and new
> Fun and laughter – if you're blue
> We're men of the service,
> We come from each service, all snappy smart and gay
> So be happy and bright – as we're with you tonight
> We're at your service now.

'I then called out "Salute, smart left turn!" and we marched off, ten bodies piling up in whatever we were using for the wings or backstage, by which time the howls of hairy-arsed derision had to be heard to be believed.

'Luckily, Kenny showed a stroke of genius to save us from disaster. Instead of marching off on the end of the line, he let us go, gave a disgusted gesture and said, "Oh, I can't be doing with all that! I'm not with this lot, you know." Then he launched into a series of impressions of Bette Davis and Suzette Tarri, a cockney comedienne and actress who had starred in radio in the '30s and '40s, which had them doubled up. His stage exit was Harry Champion's 'Any Old Iron'.

'Without at all modifying his camp persona, he had them in the palm of his hands. You could see he had fantastic talent although many, including some of the gays, said that Ken would never make it in the UK, he was far too camp. What could he do? Play fairies in *A Midsummer Night's Dream*?

'But I thought he had a great future as some sort of vaudevillian because he could control an audience – and he had immense stage courage.'

Kenneth however wasn't prepared to send himself up unconditionally.

'I had him play a princess in a burlesque of *Aladdin* which I wrote for the show. He absolutely hated it. Later in his career (1958) he had to drag up when he appeared in Rodgers and Hammerstein's *Cinderella* at the Coliseum, with Freddie Carpenter directing. He hated that even more.'

The drag experience apart, Kenneth and Stanley developed their routines with each performance. Stanley wallowed in the chance to offer a range of performances, from songs to monologues, to take-offs of Highland Scotsmen. He even performed as a feed for a comedian.

Incredibly, he didn't do impersonations – that would have been cutting into Williams' territory. The pair were always rivals as much as friends. And he certainly didn't impersonate Kenneth at that time, even among pals, although his impersonation of his chum was top rate. Stanley knew it would have resulted in claws coming out. (Years later he would impersonate Williams on television and suffer the consequences.)

Meanwhile, Stanley delighted in the chance to direct, to write and produce.

'I suppose I was really learning what the troops liked,' he recalls.

And future audiences. Having polished the show at Nee Soon, the company toured Malaya, going as far north as Penang, then returning to Singapore via Taiping. Stanley loved the touring, the shows, the laughs – either from the audiences or from each other – and the performances.

'It was all the fun of showbiz but without any real responsibility.'

But disappointing news emerged for Stanley, Kenneth and John. Peter became ill with amoebic dysentery and missed the opening tour. He recovered, but was threatened with being RTU'd when he complained about being reduced to a stagehand.

Peter writes in his memoir: 'It seems to me now the officers in charge had never taken to me. Only Stanley's backing kept me there so long.'

Peter accepted his lowly role and the troupe set off to tour again, this time to Hong Kong, on the SS *Empress of Scotland*.

'We sailed into the harbour on the liberty boat and we could see the China Fleet Club where we would be billeted,' Stanley recalls. 'As we got closer, we saw a hoard of sailors stripped to the waist waving to us. I thought, "This all looks very promising."'

And it was. When Stanley and the yellow-striped pals weren't entertaining at the China Fleet Club's little theatre, they were being entertained by the sailors.

'What they say about the Navy is absolutely true,' he says, smiling.

'There were of course a few who weren't interested, but they soon told you in an unoffended sort of way. "Well, I don't actually, Stan, but everybody else will, don't worry."'

Stanley was having the time of his life, with gay flings and trips to the movies, to see the *Ziegfeld Follies* (again), this time with Kenneth. (And he still didn't admit to himself he was a card-carrying member of the Gay Party.)

There was a real scare when Peter Nichols almost died from his dysentery. His chums panicked when they saw his 'cadaverous' body. But the show had to go on in the form of radio, when Stanley and Kenneth made an appearance on ZBW Forces radio, where they played out a dramatic reconstruction of *Nelson's Death*.

'Think of what all this could lead to,' wrote Kenneth. 'Broadcasting experience might lead to overtures from the BBC in London.'

Yet there were signs the curtain was set to come down on the carefree life of Baxter and Williams. The company was due to return to Singapore on the SS *Devonshire* on 25 October, and Kenneth, due for demobilisation, was to stay on board ship as it headed back to Blighty. The chums knew life would never be the same again.

Peter Nichols should have gone home too but hadn't recovered enough and returned to Nee Soon with Stanley. Back at barracks, Stanley felt a deep wrench at the loss of Williams – and many other pals who had been RTU'd.

'All I could think about was when it would be my turn to leave for home. I knew the fun was coming to an end.'

Right on cue, the weather worsened, producing torrents of rain giving way to equatorial heat. And to complete the misery, toothpaste supplies were running out. What could those left behind do to lift spirits? Well, put on a show of course. Stanley set about producing a Christmas set, with Peter now recovered, playing a leading role.

The camp Christmas party turned out to be a mini-carnival. The scratch band played up in the square – three trumpeters, a trombone novice, a comedian on ukulele and a tap-dancer on cymbals. The CSE troops wore paper hats, some carried a candelabra, and Geoffrey (of course) was in drag. A giant conga was formed which marched around the village, as happy and gay as a New Orleans funeral procession. New arrivals at the transit camp took photographs and looked stunned, presuming this sort of thing happened every day. It didn't. It was the end of an era. Peter became ill again, this time with worms, and was shipped home. Stanley too received notice his number was up.

Going home. After two and a half years. And with very mixed feelings. There was a slight sense of warmth at the prospect of seeing his family again but the dominant thought was of the loss of this strange but wonderfully accepting world he was leaving behind.

There was another feeling to contend with: fear. In the short space of six months Stanley had come to confirm – and to a certain extent resolve – his sexual orientation. But then he had also met gay men like Barri Chatt and Geoffrey Deakin and they terrified him. Part of Stanley was afraid he would turn into a Barri or a Geoffrey, 'the faggot from Hell.'

'After watching his transformation, I determined to become a straight actor.'

Did he really mean a straight man? Could he attempt to live without homosexual encounters? At 21, and heading home, Stanley wasn't sure. What he did know was life was about to become incredibly complicated.

11

Poofter Hell

THE FIRST FEW days on the troop ship sailing home to Southampton in February 1948 saw Stanley, for the first time in a year, without a role to play. But rather than drown in a sea of existentialist angst he created one.

'I put up a poster looking for volunteers for a concert party and I was set. I actually ended up doing a fair bit of the show myself. And I can remember I did stand-up comedy – as a cockney. I hadn't realised that I'd picked up this cockney accent. I'd been with the cockneys for so long.'

Stanley would only ever do stand-up again when forced. He feared the very idea of working without a script. But at this time his stage confidence was at its most buoyant.

When the troop ship arrived in Southampton, the memory of merino wool sweaters and soft cotton shorts was completely blown away by the winter winds. Stanley knew he was back in a far less forgiving world as he made his way up to a damp Lancashire holding camp to pick up a demob suit, trilby hat and shoes and socks.

'It was a brown demob suit,' he says, cringing at the aesthetic horror of it all. 'I just wished later I'd taken an overcoat as well. The weather was frightening.'

The excitement of arriving back in Glasgow was numbed by the deluge of freezing rain which greeted him.

'It all looked grey and grimy,' he recalls of the period long before the arrival of the Clean Air Act of 1956, which would banish the impact of the coal fuel and heavy industry.

'I felt alone and lost. The outlook was miserable in every sense.'

When Stanley arrived at 150 Wilton Street, Alice was taken aback to see the change in her big brother.

'He was all terribly posh and he arrived with a "Oh, hello mother, *wonderful* to see you again" – in a Noel Coward accent. "Alice, darling I wouldn't have recognised you. I'd have walked right past you in the street. You're a woman now." And I thought, 'Who is this person?"'

Yet, Stanley had always copied accents?

'Yes, but this was more. I think he had been searching for a new voice, a new identity. He seemed to have found one.'

After the reintroductions and edited tales of the time apart, Stanley was left alone with time to think of all that he had left behind.

'I missed everybody in CSE terribly and I began to get weepy. I had been with these guys 24 hours a day and even on the troop ship I had become pals with people I had been directing.

'The only person I figured I'd hear from again was Kenny Williams. I just knew we'd keep in contact.'

At least he could look forward to seeing Bill Henry. After nearly three years, Bill would be overjoyed to hear the battling war hero had now returned. It didn't matter a jot that Stanley had only ever battled with prickly heat or coming up with a good opening line for a song. Bill, the poet and idealist, would buy into the romance of it all and they'd leap into each other's arms like characters from a Shelley sonnet.

In his dreams.

'I may not have been sure if I were to live my life as a gay man but I definitely knew that I was still crazy about Bill. So I called him up and said, "Can you come over?" He did and we talked 'till all hours. And the same bedtime scenario came about. Or so I thought. I said, "Just stay the night, Bill." He did and I started messing about under the covers. But he jumped up, rather shocked and said, "Christ, you're not still doing this, are you?" I muttered, "What's the matter, Bill?" He simply looked at me almost scornfully and yelled, "Oh, get a woman will you!" I was bewildered by this – he'd had other gay experiences. How could he suddenly decide he didn't want to anymore?'

Years later, Stanley would catch the movie of EM Forster's *Maurice* (1987) and smile knowingly. The storyline sees former private school pupil Maurice Hall (James Wilby) attempt to continue a homosexual relationship into adult life but his former school lover Clive Durham (Hugh Grant) is aghast. Like the character Clive, Bill believed the gay relationship had been of the moment.

Bill however did factor in Stanley's feelings that first night back in Glasgow and eventually consented to sex. But only on the 'Well, if you must – let's get it over with' basis.

'I never managed to work out what had been going on in Bill's head. However, I think sexuality is linear and I imagine Bill was a little homosexual.'

The following day Bill announced they would stay friends and they should push the sex issue to one side. But in the next few weeks, as Stanley began to come to terms (sort of) with the new terms of engagement, Bill dropped a bombshell. He was going off to Paris, to live the life of a tortured artist and join fellow bohemians in a tiny garret.

'Bill of course pushed aside any references to the fact that his extremely wealthy father, with a chain of pubs in Glasgow, was sponsoring this suffering artist phase.'

Regardless, Stanley was now officially alone. Cousin Alma was living in Leeds and the closeness with Alice, now 17 and quite grown-up with boyfriends and plans to go to teaching college, seemed to have evaporated.

Bessie wasn't a stranger to Sonny Boy's dark moods however and perhaps she even felt a little guilty, having challenged him about his new accent. As a pacifier, she went out and bought him a gramophone. Stanley then promptly purchased as much mournful, melancholia Sinatra as he could afford, songs such as 'I Couldn't Sleep A Wink Last Night' and 'I Fall In Love Too Easily'.

'I'd play them until I was greetin' really. I think this demob period was my real adolescent angst.'

Stanley did a couple of acting stints with the BBC's Auntie Kathleen and found a new, close friend in handsome young Glasgow-born actor, John Fraser. (John, who was also gay, would find major acting success playing lead roles in the early '60s in films such as *Tunes of Glory* and *El Cid.*) But Auntie Kathleen was children's radio, not at all where Stanley needed to be. He desperately needed to become a straight actor, to join some form of repertory company and learn the acting craft.

However, Fred was still determined his son would go on to become a teacher of English. And war broke out.

'My mother and father argued about my future and he pulled out the stats highlighting the average income an actor in Scotland earned. When she made to protest he yelled, "Don't you interrupt me this time, Bessie!"'

Fred, having won the battle, surrendered shortly afterwards when he saw how distraught his son was.

'With great resignation in his voice my father said, "Oh, well, you'd better go and try it."'

Stanley thanked the heavens and put a plan in motion. He had a read about Michel Saint-Denis (the acclaimed French director and drama teacher who had opened the London Theatre Studio in 1936, and worked with the likes of Olivier and Gielgud) and his famous Young Vic Theatre School, the off-shoot of the Old Vic. The young Scot determined to go to London and audition for the man regarded as one of the greatest acting teachers in the business, who would later work with the Royal Shakespeare Theatre.

'That was the world I wanted to be part of.'

By coincidence, in April Stanley heard that a Glasgow theatre/dance company were off to Reading to stage *A Midsummer Night's Dream*, in which Shakespeare was wrapped up in swathes of tartan.

'The company was looking for an actor to play Bottom. I got the job and it paid about tuppence.'

He deserved far more considering the job involved dancing around the stage in a kilt looking like a camp version of a very young Harry Lauder. But the job had two positives: his train ticket south was paid for and Stanley met young dancer Bruce McClure. The pair hit it off immediately. Bruce, a tall good-looking Glaswegian with a gift for clever one-liners delivered with an endearing slight stutter, would become a lifelong pal.

There was the Young Vic audition to get through but Stanley knew that would be a formality. After all, he had been acting since the age of seven, had become a radio actor, worked with Unity Theatre – and had spent the past two years entertaining audiences across the Far East.

Wrong.

On the cold April day, Young Vic directors Pierre Lefevre and Glen Byam Shaw said they liked Stanley's audition piece, Pirandello's *The Man with the Flower in his Mouth.*

It was perhaps an apposite piece for a young man searching for an identity, the tale of a unnamed, anxious Man who, while struggling with the point of existence, is determined to grasp all that life has to offer. 'I'd kill myself,' says The Man, 'but the plums are just ripening.'

But then the directors tossed in a hand grenade.

'How many radio broadcasts have you made?'

'Well, about 100 or so... before I was called up...'

'What? 100? Oh no, we can't have that. Well, you see, you are too, too... well-*formed* for us. We like to take on people so much... rougher... Of course, we can't refuse you a second audition after that performance, but don't hold out a lot of hope.'

Yet, Stanley did hold out hope. He felt he'd auditioned well and buoyed, took off to East London's Marchmont Street, to share the news with Kenneth Williams. The pair hadn't been in touch, but both revealed later they'd missed each other terribly. Kenneth, he learned, had returned to his old job in a drawing office – and was as miserable as every sin ever committed.

'Kenny lived above his dad Charlie's hairdresser's salon with Mum, Louisa, a couple of cor blimey cockneys. I could see where Kenny had a problem in ever becoming an actor. Charlie couldn't have been more non-theatrical and often declared he hated all Kenny's poofy friends.

'That night I turned up, Charlie revealed he'd recently been to see one of those restoration comedies, *The Relapse*, and gave me his version of the play.

He said: 'And they were all poncin' about wiv their 'ankerchiefs, waving and shouting, "Oh, your bumship!" and stuff loike that, Stan. And at the end all the audience are shouting 'Bravo, bravo!"

'Bravo? What a load of rubbish! Two days later I go round the corner, to the Odeon, to see the most beautiful film oive ever seen. It was called *Son of Lassie.*'

Fred Baxter may not have embraced the stage in the way Bessie had but he never suggested, as Charlie did to his son, that he was about 'to descend into poofter Hell'.

Yet, in spite of Charlie's scorn, Stanley managed to change the course of his pal Kenny's life.

'Stanley Baxter came down from Glasgow,' Kenneth writes in his autobiography:

> ...his visit altered everything. I waxed nostalgic for the old days...
>
> 'In a way I wish I was still acting.'
>
> 'Well, what on earth are you doing as a draughtsman?'
>
> 'It's my old job, and my father thinks there's no security in a theatrical career.'
>
> 'Security? You don't take up a profession like an insurance policy. You've got talent and you enjoy acting. You don't enjoy maps.'
>
> 'No, but I don't know how to get into the theatre.'
>
> 'Write letters. Write to every repertory theatre in the country. Tell them you have had experience, mention CSE, say you're willing to be a stage manager and do small parts. No good sitting on your arse moping about the past.'

Kenneth's backside shifted as suggested and by the end of the month he had a job in rep (Small Parts) in Cornwall.

Now back home in Glasgow, a 'cautiously optimistic' Stanley awaited news from the Young Vic. The letter duly arrived and Stanley then travelled south again, for the second audition.

'This time I chose to do Mercutio's Queen Mab speech from *Romeo and Juliet.*

Queen Mab was the fairies' midwife, who assists with the birth of people's dreams: 'Delivers the fancies of sleeping men.' But the dreams Mab delivers seem to arrive with a price; they take the dream to extremity. 'Soldiers dream of cutting foreign throats.' Was Mab a warning? As Mercutio says, 'Dreams are the children of an idle brain.' Be careful what you wish for?

Regardless, Stanley didn't consider any of that. He dreamed of the moment he could become a professional actor. Indeed, it was all he lived for, But Mab didn't certainly do Stanley a hellish amount of good.

'The directors went through the motions. I went home and

waited for the rejection letter.'

It arrived a few days later. The Young Vic confirmed Stanley was 'too formed'.

Disaster. Dejection. Despair. Tears. More tears. 'I thought, "Oh shit! What will I do now?" My father reminded me I could still go to university but that thought only made my heart sink even deeper. I was lost. Again.' News of Kenneth Williams' early success served only to illuminate his own failure and Stanley took to wandering the cold streets of the city centre, his countenance as heavy as his new tweed overcoat.

However, one Saturday as he wandered down Union Street, Stanley bumped into Alan MacKill, the actor he'd worked with at Unity Theatre. When Alan asked how life was going Stanley's eyes welled up. Alan made a suggestion. The Citizens' Theatre Company (the outfit which Stanley had tried to join pre-army) had moved from the Athenaeum to a new home in the Gorbals district in the south side of the city, based at the Royal Princess's Theatre – where Stanley's dad had taken him to see his first panto. (Rather paradoxically it was based in a part of the city better known for slum housing, endemic poverty and razor gangs.) More importantly, the Citz, headed by James Bridie, were looking for actors to play smaller parts in August, in a play called *Ane Satrye of the Thrie Estaitis*. Stanley's heart leapt a little. The Citz may not have been the Young Vic but it was set up to become Glasgow's version, to offer Ibsen and Bernard Shaw at bottom drawer prices. His eyes began to dry, and then sparkle.

'Alan MacKill then said to me he'd put a word in for me with the wonderful director Tyrone Guthrie, who was coming back to Glasgow with the *Thrie Estaitis*.

'I said, with massive understatement, "Oh, I'd be so grateful if you would!"'

Stanley parted from his pal so high on anticipation he didn't need a tram home, he could have floated to Hillhead on a passing cloud. The dream was alive once again. Yet, during the audition-waiting days, again the fear developed. What if the Citz, like the Old Vic, felt he was 'too formed'? And there was a further complication. The *Thrie Estaitis* was a 16th century medieval morality play, spoken in Lowland Scots.

'*Ane Pleasant Satyre of The Thrie Estaitis* in Commendation of Verteu and Vituperation of Vyce As Follows...' was how it was billed when King James v saw the premiere in 1539.

'I was sent a copy of a speech to learn and immediately thought to myself, "Oh, Jesus, shit... how will I ever get through this? It's pissing incomprehensible!"'

12

Ménage à Deux

BETTE DAVIS WROTE in her autobiography, *The Lonely Life*: 'It has been my experience that one cannot, in any shape or form, depend upon human relations for lasting reward. It is only work that satisfies.'

The rather depressing comment came on the back of a long stint in the '50s when major success eluded the Hollywood legend – until she was rediscovered in the 1962 to-become-a-classic, *Whatever Happened to Baby Jane?* But had Stanley read those rather bitter words in the spring of 1948 (although penned in 1962), he would have concurred. Who did Bill Henry think he was anyway? Career was all that mattered. And in many ways, the Citizens' Theatre Company was the perfect vehicle. The face of this brave new acting world linked up stiff upper English lips with coarse ginger Scots hair, ageing worldly thespians and angry young men, all of them evangelical about producing great theatre.

The Artistic Director at the Citizens' in 1947 was John Casson, the son of Dame Sybil Thorndyke and Lewis Casson. Some of his stellar actors included future film and theatre legend Duncan Macrae, Roddy McMillan, whom Stanley had worked with in Unity Theatre, Fulton Mackay, who found fame later in life in the '70s TV series *Porridge* and Gudrun Ure, who would become *Super Gran* in the '80s TV series. Stanley was excited at the prospect of working with the troupe, but even more so at the thought of being directed by the great (later Sir) Tyrone Guthrie, probably the most famous theatre director in Britain at that time.[10]

All Stanley had to do to become a straight actor was perform a speech in a language which hadn't been spoken for 400 years.

Nervously, he treated the script for the *Thrie Estaitis* as he did a trigonometry exam, committing it to memory. Reading for the director he proclaimed the near-gibberish 'Sal stand ye back an hold ye coy...'

But it was well-read gibberish.

'After a few lines Colin White, the manager of the Citz, who had quite a posh English accent, cut me off and said, "Yes, that's fine. Can't understand a word of it but I've heard three others and that sounds like the best."'

Oh joy! Acceptance. Affirmation. Now, he was going to be a Straight Actor. Okay, he was little more than a spear carrier (playing Corrections Varlet) with a dozen lines but Stanley was on £6 a week and £2 extra for living away from home. Bessie Baxter was delighted, but she had the good sense not to rub it in to her disappointed husband, who again produced the actuarial tables to reveal how desperate an actor's life could be. And, of course, Bessie didn't want Sonny Boy's head to swell – even though a slight increase in circumference was justified.

Rehearsals would start in August and the heaving and sobbing season was now officially over. But it wasn't only a career lifeline Stanley enjoyed. Just as he focused on career and on pushing matters of the heart aside, Bill Henry called with an invitation asking Stanley to join him in Paris, the most romantic city in the world. Clearly, Bill had come to his senses and realised Stanley was so much more than a pal. (It turned out that, for Stanley, all those months learning French in Millport hadn't been wasted.)

On 17 July, Stanley and his stiff brown suitcase arrived at the Gare du Nord train station and discovered the colourful, vibrant city he'd long dreamed of visiting. He was in for a truly fantastic time.

Or so he thought.

On meeting, Bill dropped a bombshell on Stanley's head from Eiffel Tower height. He announced he had a new girlfriend living with him.

To soften the blow, Bill announced that the young lady in question was very easy-going and that three certainly wouldn't be a crowd. Stanley felt it all a bit bizarre, but then he was still in love and would have followed Bill anywhere. And so the three shacked up in the little garret in Montmartre.

'This is why I now hate Paris,' he says, the harshest of memories still resonating.

'You see, the Hungarian girlfriend, Magda Karachone, quickly realised that there was more than chumship to the relationship. She became pretty foul and dismissive, and I became more and more upset by her. Eventually, I went storming out into the night and Bill followed me. And we had a big argument about whether she knew about me and him, and he tried to play it all down. But I couldn't see reason. And to get back at him for this rejection I really hit him where it hurt.'

He kicked him in the politics.

Stanley shouted, 'Anyway, why are you cooking over a little Bunsen burner and always looking for something to eat?'

'Because we're poor, of course.'

'No, you're pretending to be poor. I've seen those food parcels arriving from Jordanhill.'

Ouch.

'I knew that Bill was basically heterosexual, but I felt hurt and neglected. To placate me he took me out one night, without Magda, to the Folies Bergère and this show became a backdrop for discussing sexuality. He asked me if I found the women on the show exciting and I said I did, that any kind of musical theatre appealed to me. But this wasn't the answer he was looking for. I think he'd hoped I'd get randy and get a French girlfriend.'

Bill was being a selfish bastard as it happens, happy enough with two people devoted to him. Tea or coffee whenever he fancied a sip. But neither tea nor coffee could bear it. Jealousy reared its head again and again and soon after the Folies night out, Stanley, in a fit of pique, dramatically announced his departure.

'I said, "I can't stand this! This isn't even a ménage à trois! It's not even a trois. It's more like a Bette Davis movie!" (Actually, it was rather more like John Schlesinger's *Sunday Bloody Sunday*.) Regardless, Paris in July was now cold and unwelcoming. Sartre's existentialist nightmare describes Hell as being trapped for all eternity with two women – and the one he was attracted to was a lesbian. Stanley's Hell saw him stuck in a tiny room with a frighteningly jealous Eastern European and a fickle lover. He had to go home. And Bill didn't even coax him to stay.

'To add to the injustice of it all, on the train carriage from Paris three Lancashire women sat next to me who all talked like Beryl Reid and chatted to me endlessly about their first-ever foreign trip. I was bored shitless.'

Never mind. He'd get to lampoon those Lancashire hot pot voices hundreds of times later in his career.

Back in Glasgow, Stanley again sought solace in Sinatra and wrote poetry about the sad adventure:

> This is man's real damnation, the thin, drizzly rain.
> Not the icicle's east descent or the desert's firey pain
> It's never the great big kick up the arse things that finally get you down
> It's the sullen drip of suburban leaves that are not in and not out of town.

'Kenneth Williams read it later and loved it,' he says of the consolation.

Stanley still missed his CSE pals. But at least he had work to look forward to. That would become his love. And so it was a positive and determined young actor who turned up in Edinburgh in August for rehearsals.

Stanley took to Tony Guthrie immediately. Guthrie, who wore polo-necked sweaters, an improbable bank manager moustache and a constant smile on his face, spoke in staccato, which was 'wonderfully effective' for getting his point across in a no-nonsense manner and the ideal delivery for his crisp one-liners. More importantly, he liked Stanley. But would Edinburgh like Guthrie's production? The play was certainly attracting major media attention, given that it was the showcase for the Second Edinburgh International Festival and performed at the specially adapted General Assembly Hall of the Church of Scotland. Yet, while many assumed this medieval morality play would be impenetrable to modern-day audiences (it certainly was to most of the actors) it somehow, incredibly, became a huge success.

On opening night, 22 August 1948, the critics loved it. 'The

Fourth Estate has been taking a great deal of interest in the *Thrie Estaitis,*' said *The Scotsman.*

'It's unsuitable for children!' exclaimed the Catholic Church in *The Daily Record*, which boosted ticket sales even more.

The play's run ended in September 1948, Duncan Macrae took off to film Ealing's soon-to-be-classic *Whisky Galore* (alongside Gordon Jackson), while Stanley arrived back at the Citizens' looking to establish his place in this colourful world. And he could have been forgiven for thinking he'd walked into the Arrivals lounge at Luvvieland. Dame Sybil Thorndyke and Sir Lewis Casson were visiting and Dame Sybil was, as always, effusive and exuberant. The lady, whom relatives referred to as Auntie Gush, never described a production that wasn't 'marvellous!' or an actor's performance that wasn't 'wonderful!'.

'Noel Coward came up with that great line [Stanley offers up a Coward impersonation]: "Nobody loves anybody – like Sybil loves everybody." And it summed her up perfectly. But she was lovely and she helped create a great atmosphere at the Citz.'

There were others rather more grounded, such as Assistant Stage Manager (ASM) Jimmy Gilbert, a former pilot who had spent a couple of years at RADA (the Royal Academy of Dramtic Art in London) and was also a songwriter and singer. Almost straight away Stanley and Jimmy became great friends.

Stanley found another new friend very quickly in Moira Robertson, a 22-year-old former wardrobe mistress and now actress.

'I was officially introduced to Moira by Kenneth Miles, another ASM at the Citizens' and occasional actor,' Stanley recalls.

'I think Kenneth was an old boyfriend of hers but whether it ever got to nookie or not I never thought to ask.

'But regardless, I liked her. I admired how fashionable she looked. She was far more bohemian than me and could be very amusing.'

Stanley felt immediately at home at the Citz, yet his dressing room door was not being battered down with offers of same-sex companionship.

'The Citz wasn't like CSE at all,' he says, his face illustrating the disappointment he felt.

'At that time it was a totally heterosexual company.'

Yet the lack of kindred spirits at least offered the chance to start a new life free from temptation, to avoid being cast permanently as a homosexual man. Besides, what choice was there if he wanted to avoid being marginalised, considered an outsider for the rest of his life and perhaps even sent to jail? One morning, when a vivid reminder of his past life rang the Baxter doorbell, in the form of his army pal Reggie Short, Stanley *knew* he had to live the straight life. He would take Bill Henry's advice and forget about 'messing about'.

'It was great to see him,' he says of his splay-footed pal from Bradford. 'We had been great mates and the fumble we had was forgotten. It had to be forgotten. Reggie wasn't gay – and I didn't want to be.'

Stanley went on to enjoy himself in the Christmas romp, *The Forrigan Reel* by James Bridie, despite it being a rather unsuccessful airy-fairy Scottish farce. But his *Macbeth* experience in January 1949 was less fun.

'Such a rotten wee part. I think I was one of the Thanes. And like most *Macbeth*s, it was stricken with bad luck. Macrae broke his foot in rehearsals when he tripped over a set of bagpipes and attempted to play the part in a plaster cast. John Casson had to take over.'

As spring approached, Stanley saw even more of Moira, taking her along to 5 Wilton Mansions to meet the family. Alice recalls meeting the actress.

'She wasn't like me, she was a very quiet, refined girl, and I didn't find it too easy to communicate with her. And of course we were the sort of family who used aggressive humour, putting each other down quite a lot. I would have a dig at Stanley but Moira would interject and defend him. You'd find yourself saying, "That was a gag, Moira." However, she was a nice, sweet lady. I liked her very much.'

Marion Irving Robertson was the daughter of a successful but very down-to-earth building contractor from Dumbarton, a little town 20 miles from Glasgow on the Clyde coast. Moira had gone to The Glasgow School of Art and *looked* like she had been to art school. Incredibly chic with hooded eyes, she could have passed for Bette Davis' better looking younger sister. Moira had even been friends with the love of Stanley's life, Bill Henry, and his girlfriend, Betty Low. Small world? Yes. And she was at Glasgow's Park Theatre alongside Stanley's actor friend and future film star John Fraser. The globe seemed even smaller when it transpired Moira had once been a pupil with Stanley's randy old voice coach Percival Steed – and he had indeed touched her up. Moira was not a lady with a powerful personality but nonetheless, she was someone people warmed too. She had never been quite sure of her direction in life, wavering between art and acting; but being something of a little rich girl in Glasgow terms, her affluence afforded her considerable choice.

Yet, in spite of her lack of focus and rather whimsical ways – or perhaps even because of them – Stanley liked her. She was clever and elegant, a brilliant seamstress and a good artist – certainly not a typical West of Scotland girl. Whatever the reason, the pair developed a closeness that meant when they weren't working, they enjoyed a movie or dinner together. However, Moira seemed determined to take the relationship to the next stage.

'Moira chased Stanley,' says Alice. 'There's no doubt about that. For obvious reasons, he didn't find it easy to get serious although you could see he liked her. But she kept calling for him and my mother wasn't too happy about this. In fact, she showed her disapproval of Moira right from the start.'

Stanley agrees. 'My mother didn't think any woman was good enough for me but there was more to her criticism of Moira. Early on she used to say, "That woman's following you around like a wee dug!" And she was right. There was a sort of obsession.'

Dick Mabon recalls meeting Moira with Stanley at this time.

'She was a lovely woman, but she seemed very fragile. What I felt though was that Stanley was very good to her. Very fond of her. Of course, I had little idea at that time that she would one day break his heart.'

Stanley dropped more than a few clues to his young lady friend that he wasn't a rampant heterosexual, but Moira seemed to brush them under the carpet. Still, it wasn't an issue. Work was all important and that same month Stanley and Moira made their first stage appearance together in Kenneth Woolard's *Morning Departure*. This submarine drama had a double set on stage, the (very realistic) inside of the sub on one level and the HQ above.

But there was nothing realistic about Stanley's performance as Lieutenant Oakley.

'I was very bad in that,' he admits. 'It was a straight role of an English officer. I realised I simply couldn't play straight leading men. I was never any good at playing straight juveniles either. I'd rather have played fucking Othello than chinless wonders. Having said that, I don't even think Olivier would have surfaced from beneath the deep in *Morning Departure*.'

While Stanley can now reflect he wasn't a fabulous straight actor, he didn't take well to Dick Mabon's suggestion his chum's submariner had plumbed the depths of acting.

'I told him he was awful,' says Dick. 'And he got very annoyed. I said, "Look, Stanley, straight theatre is not your *métier*." And I was right because he did go on to have a great career in comedy.'

Could Stanley play a straight role in life in the spring of 1949? It seems he tried very hard. In April, Stanley wrote to Kenneth Williams and claimed he had fallen in love. With Moira. In the *Kenneth Williams Diaries*, Williams reveals that he was not entirely convinced of his friend's newfound emotional state – but neither was he totally dismissive.

'Silly boy,' wrote Williams. 'Nice, though.'

'I don't remember writing that to Kenny,' Stanley says now. Perhaps selective memory has kicked in? What's undeniable however is his career trajectory was rising; if he stuck to comedy.

In May, when he appeared as a burglar in F Brooke Warren's *The Face at the Window*, a Sweeney Todd-like melodrama featuring dead bodies and bank robbers, Stanley couldn't help but get laughs, even where there were none in the script. The next production saw the company move down to Ayr on the west coast for the summer season and Stanley and Moira had lots of fun together. It's hard to know if the invigorating sea air – or simply timing – resulted in Moira's declaration; she wished to have a full-blown sexual relationship with her leading man.

Stanley was up for the challenge – since the Cathy Scott days he'd wondered what sex with a female would be like – but at this time, seaside landladies took a very dim view of guests, particularly theatricals, 'abusing the facilities'. And so the young 'lovers' stole their moments wherever they could. Mostly on the dressing room floor of the Gaiety Theatre at the end of the first act.

'Five minutes, Mr Baxter,' bellowed the stage manager as the couple writhed around, bits of clothing next to them on the floor.

'Just coming,' Stanley replied, while he and Moira suppressed giggles.

'Well, it was a big first, me losing my heterosexual virginity on that floor,' says Stanley, smiling at the understatement. 'And I guess I had come to really like Moira. The more I got to know of her I realised she was a lovely woman, a woman of enormous heart.'

Stanley also loved the idea of having sex with someone who loved sex. Especially with him. But as for Moira's motivation? Was it just sex? Not a bit of it. She had pushed aside question marks against Stanley's sexuality, partly because she adored her boyfriend and recognised his talent. And if Stanley had been telling Williams he loved Moira, he was probably telling her also. Yet, her willingness to leap into this potentially problematic relationship probably had a little to do with her sense of rebellion, the idea of being part of a risqué demi-monde.

'That's true, yet at the same time she had a real edge of vulnerability.'

Just how vulnerable Moira was Stanley would discover later, but for the moment, the relationship sort of made sense. And the sex was 'fine – not rockets going off or anything'.

'I was apprehensive about getting involved for all the obvious reasons. But I had all sorts of excuses for developing a relationship. It was partly a feeling of "I'll show them", that I could be as heterosexual as the rest of them.'

He was determined to play the role of Straight Man for all it was worth.

13
Life Gets Glamourouser

AS STANLEY CONTINUED to play the heterosexual on the theatre floors of the West of Scotland in the late summer of 1949, his small parts were growing gradually into much larger ones. The young actor was wowing audiences in the likes of Paul Vincent Carroll's *Vineyard Street*, opposite Gudrun Ure and Duncan Macrae. *The Scotsman*'s critic predicted: 'Baxter is on the verge of an illustrious career.' It wasn't a comedy role, as such, more of an oddball part. But Stanley showed he could shine – so long as he wasn't restricted by straight characters.

The 23-year-old's comedy skills were ever improving, thanks to studying the likes of Duncan Macrae. Yet Macrae, who had worked with Unity Theatre, was not a role model in life. He was regarded as one of the best actors of his generation by John Casson, however his biographer Priscilla Barlow said he was horrid to young amateurs once he became famous. He could be a delight to work with and yet capable of telling an entire theatre company – as he once did in Ireland – that they were all rotten. Macrae also didn't have much time for young acting hopefuls, unless they were attractive and female. And although he was a conscientious objector during the war, he was delighted to be awarded honorary officer status when he agreed to a stint in ENSA in 1945 (the predecessor of CSE) and loved to wear uniform – especially when it meant he could kick soldiers out of officer-reserved train compartments. The man was riddled with inconsistencies, yet while he and Stanley were not obvious soul mates they got on 'well enough' in a range of productions. Certainly, Duncan Macrae came to be very thankful Stanley was around come panto time.

James Bridie's elitist endeavours and silly romps such as *The*

Forrigan Reel had seen the Citz company haemorrhaging money to the point Glasgow Corporation threatened to cut off their subsidy. Bridie was no fool. He knew that to avoid closure of the theatre a transfusion of undiluted populism was required. And so he came up with a plan to revive an old Royal Princess's Theatre tradition of using a 13-letter-titled panto (it was part of Glasgow folklore). Bridie, under the pseudonym of AP Kellock, took the rhyme about the lost treasure of Tinto Hill as a loose connecting theme for a series of sketches interspersed with music and layered it with an 'updated' view of Scots history. And so *The Tintock Cup* was created. But the script just didn't work. John Casson tried to make 'feverish cuts' to bring about cohesion to the book but failed, and everyone in the theatre knew they were facing a box office disaster. However, Stanley reckoned he knew how to fix it.

'I don't know where I got the nerve but I stepped up to Casson, told him it wasn't right and said boldly that I knew all about light entertainment.'

Well, he had been to lots of variety shows with Bessie. And he had his CSE experience to call upon. John Casson thought for a moment and declared, 'Would you like to be my assistant producer?'

'Would I!' said Stanley.

With comedy writer Alex Mitchell on board (a Macrae recommendation) Stanley came up with the ideas. Since there was no reliance on a traditional panto storyline, he packed the piece with balletic comedy, singing madrigals and lots of sight gags, with the idea being just to keep hitting the audience over the head with laughs. CSE was coming to the Citz. Thus was born the classic theatre sketch *Polly of the Palais* (the Palais being a local dance hall) which included such immortal, and later much quoted dialogue as:

> 'Are ye dancin?'
> 'Naw, take ma pal. A'm sweatin.'

And how about the line which features two young ladies speaking of their would-be dance hall suitors:

> 'He said he was a champ dancer. Whit he meant was he was a damp chancer.'

A few pieces from Stanley's Rangoon days were also resurrected to help with the pace. In another sketch Stanley teamed up with young actor Dougie Campbell, playing punch-drunk boxer Joe McGurk being interviewed on American television, halted at regular interviews by interviewer Campbell to make mentions of the show's sponsors. It was a clever satire on the fight game and the constraints of commercial backing. But would the Citz audience, used to high-brow entertainment, take to the comedy low-ground mixed with satire? Stanley knew he faced being crucified – or deified – depending upon the result. When Bessie Baxter saw the dress rehearsals, she was convinced her son was facing a box of iron nails and a big wooden cross.

'This will never last!'

'But it's just a light romp.'

'A light romp? It will never work! Have you not got another play in rehearsals?'

'No.'

'No? Well, it's terrible! Terrible! And while you're at it, get rid of that Alex Mitchell.'

Stanley believed he had the content right, but he was worried. Bessie, after all, had spent half her life in the theatre.

However, on opening night on 20 December, from the moment he and Douglas Campbell appeared from the stalls – not the wings – as Broker's Men (the standard panto double act in which one character is even dafter than the other, a comedy version of the 'heavies' who evict people from their property) and began to create havoc, sounding off horns and rattles, the audience were in hysterics.

Before Macrae made his show-stopping entrance wearing a cheap, long, black, sequinned evening gown and hair piled up with even cheaper blond curls singing, 'I'm Polly from the Palais, you'll see me doon our alley,' (shades of Barri Chatt) the audience *knew* they were in for a great night.

Thereafter, each sketch seemed to go down better than the previous one. *The Two Windie Hingers*, for example, featured the Glasgow ladies who lean out of their neighbouring tenement windows and chat, offering up idle social commentary. The fact their elbows are supported by bed pillows indicates the time scale of their conversations. One lady looking down at the street, comments: 'Look, There's Sandra McGuffrey. I don't think Sandra McGuffrey is a very glamorous name, do you?'

And her friend calls back: 'I've heard glamorouser.'

Huge laughs.

'Whit's that she's got on her hauns?'

'Oh, my – gloves!'

Even bigger laughs, highlighting how Glasgow hated any sign of pretension, yet also indicating the current poverty level. And it wasn't only the audiences who loved it. The *Evening Citizen* bought the script and published it in serial form.

No one really knew what the show was about, but it didn't matter. The city loved it. And they loved Stanley. There was great critical praise too for Macrae, whose Dame was described as 'superb'. (And in fact his performance was noted by other theatre companies.) Even Bessie loved it (Fred Baxter did too), although she never actually said that, given she'd predicted wanton disaster.

'I made a point never to listen to her criticism again. I thought, "Anyone who thought that show would be a flop knows fuck all about showbiz."'

Meanwhile, Kenneth Williams had been following the panto fortunes of his Scots chum and in late January 1950 travelled north to Scotland (for the first time ever) to see what the fuss was all about. Alice recalls his arrival at 5 Wilton Mansions.

'This creature arrived on our doorstep, so outrageous and so camp. He said that, as he hadn't any work on, he would come and stay. And Mum immediately loved him, even though she was highly strung and he would forever be winding her up.'

On the Wednesday after his arrival, Kenneth met up with Stanley and Moira. Clearly, he failed to see Cupid hovering above the couple with his bow string pulled back. And he was irritated by Stanley telling him not to be camp.

Part of Stanley was delighted to see his little chum but another part of him was even more delighted to see the back of him when he left. Stanley was afraid his obviously gay army pal would blow his fragile cover.

'He was so loud,' he says in soft voice.

Meantime, the panto, initially planned for a five-week run, showed no sign of stopping. After an incredible 15 weeks it was still rammed each night. It was only pulled in April because the Citz feared losing its Corporation grant – this time, perversely, *because* of box office success. But at least the Citz management would have been thankful to the likes of Baxter and Macrae for the almighty success?

'Oh no they fuckin' weren't!' says Stanley.

'Director TJ Honeyman was quoted in the *Evening Citizen* saying, "The success of this extravaganza has actually been an embarrassment to us." He said the show, which ran for an incredible 15 weeks, was against the (elitist) policy of the theatre.'

But the success was certainly acknowledged by Glasgow's main theatre venues. Macrae was snapped up by the Alhambra Theatre to star in next year's panto. Stanley was offered the chance to move to the same theatre, although Macrae would still be top dog. And he too was offered a fantastic new pay deal. But he chose to hang on for a headlining role. And once Macrae revealed he was off, the Citz reacted accordingly and the pretender to the throne was given a salary increase, to £18 a week.

Yet, while Stanley was being lauded as a comedy star of the future, he still wasn't entirely sure that was the direction he wanted to go in. Yes, he loved the loved the laughter, but he maintains part of him still wanted to earn his dramatic wings. Stanley was in denial, as it happens. When he walked on stage to attempt the dramatic roles, comedy followed as close as a shadow. In the second half of April 1950, Stanley appeared as Launcelot Gobbo, Shylock's original servant before he changes his allegiance to Bassanio, in Shakespeare's *The Merchant of Venice* and *The Scotsman* declared, 'Launcelot Gobbo can rarely have had such a comical interpretation that that of Stanley Baxter.'

The *Evening Times*, meanwhile, singled Moira out for attention, playing Jessica, lover to Fulton Mackay's Lorenzo. But it's not surprising she was especially convincing. Producer John Casson had demanded realism from his performers and Moira (a wild bohemian free spirit – or simply overly impressionable?) took him literally. Many years later she confided to Stanley that she had employed method acting to get into her part.

'She had a one-off fuck with Fulton Mackay,' he says with a shrug.

'She said, "It was all John Casson's fault. He said to me, 'Now look, you really can't get into this romance unless you fuck each other.'" And so we did.'

'I felt a wee bit miffed when I heard this. At first. And then I thought, "Well, my God, she's since had to put up with a lot from me. I shouldn't complain about her."'

Stanley, incidentally, doesn't rate method acting.

'Acting is about *pretending* to be someone else, not *being* them. Method acting is complete bollocks.'

In July, British theatre giants Howard & Wyndham, who were theatre owners, producers and ran a national management company, came calling with an offer that would treble his salary. But Stanley still had no intention of leaving a theatre he loved – and in which he was still learning. And he wasn't sure about moving on to variety full time. But he couldn't resist a fantastic comedy radio opportunity.

The Scottish Home Service (the BBC) in Glasgow had tried to match up young affable Glasgow comic Jimmy Logan, who had been born into a vaudeville family and would go on to become a variety star, with a feed called Eddie Fraser to bring a cutting edge to radio with new Light Entertainment Show, *It's All Yours*. But the live studio audiences may as a well have been dead. Jimmy admits in his autobiography, *It's a Funny Life:* 'I was about to commit suicide.' BBC bosses – and Jimmy Logan – knew they had to take drastic action. But rather than sack the pair, the BBC promoted Eddie Fraser (a tactic which would seem strange to anyone without an idea of how the Beeb worked) to Head of Light Entertainment. Now, Eddie the boss needed to replace himself on air with someone very good – or the show was doomed.

Rikki Fulton, a 27-year-old laconic comic actor from the East End of Glasgow, *knew* that man was him. Eddie and Rikki had worked together in local theatre many times over the years and a few weeks after Eddie had settled into the boss's chair, they bumped into each other in the BBC canteen. Rikki writes in his autobiography, *Is It That Time Already?*:

> He looked at me very directly, his watery blue eyes twinkling and said, 'I mean, there's a question of *It's All Yours* – I'll need someone to take my place, won't I?' I smiled and nodded my head. I had an idea what he might be talking about. 'Well,' he said, 'I've given it a lot of thought and I think – I know – the young man who could fill my shoes.' I couldn't believe it. I was really excited. Then Eddie said, 'The young man who will take my place is – Stanley Baxter.'

Rikki was bereft. He knew he had a great talent and the fact he would later become a Scots comedy icon, a TV comedy star in the likes of the BBC's *Scotch and Wry*, a massive panto star and a formidable straight actor confirms this.[11] But here was this rising star being put in place by the upstart that was Stanley Baxter. It was the moment Rikki first believed Stanley to be his nemesis and developed the enmity that was to last a lifetime.

But why did Eddie Fraser favour Stanley rather than Rikki? Rikki didn't subscribe to the view Stanley was simply the hottest ticket in town. He argues it was a personal revenge attack by Fraser and trashes the radio boss in his book, resorting to deeply personal attacks. Unfortunately, the paths of Stanley and Rikki were destined to cross again. Meanwhile, Stanley, oblivious to what was going on behind the scenes, simply enjoyed the return to radio and a salary of £22 a week.

The matching of Logan with Baxter proved to be perfect. Ratings soared. Listeners, in this era before television in Britain had any real impact upon people's lives, loved the invented characters and catchphrases such as 'Sausages is the boys'. Yes, this now sounds nonsensical but in austere post-war Britain sausage meat was heralded as the ultimate earthly delight.

'It was a lovely show to do,' says Stanley of the 180 broadcasts. 'Jimmy and I got on well right from the word go.'

A young Billy Connolly, not quite eight years old, was one of the fans of the radio show.

'My Auntie Margaret, who lived in our house, talked about

Stanley all the time when he was on his radio show. I'd listen in and I thought he was like Bob Hope. He was cosmic. All the comedians I knew of prior to this had been English or American. Now, here was this guy being funny in my own accent. Stanley just blew me away.'

Billy adds: 'By the time I was 12 or 13, after I'd been to variety theatre and seen Stanley, I'd decided I wanted to become a comedian.'

The success of *It's All Yours* meant Stanley was now working seven days a week; not that he minded. It was life, luvvie. It was the theatre. And radio.

Stanley didn't have much time to see Moira outside of work, but in August they appeared together at the Edinburgh International Festival in James Bridie's *The Queen's Comedy*, a fantasy play about the Greek siege of Troy and the relationship between men and the gods who determine their lives. The audience loved Stanley's campery (now with a girlfriend he could take the chance and wear a pink frock). But they didn't quite get his appearance in his old favourite, *Rope*, when he appeared as murderer Charles Granillo. This was a serious piece featuring two psychopaths. Yet Stanley got laughs. Could he have stopped himself from providing them? Probably not. Regardless, Citz theatre bosses gave in to the fact their young star had comedy bones and decided they would create a vehicle especially for him.

That vehicle was the Christmas panto *Red Riding Hood* (another 13-letter title). Stanley played Granny McNiven and Moira played Red Riding Hood. The critics loved it. Stanley even came out on top against Macrae's Dame, playing across the river. The *Evening News* writer Scott Hall declared of Stanley: 'He is fresh, brisk and new as a new penny. And work is plainly his main pleasure.' Not a great line, but certainly true. And no one knew this better than Kenneth Williams. That's why when Williams received a letter from Stanley on 23 December he was shocked to the core. Williams' diary account of the day simply says: 'Stanley wrote to say he is going to marry Moira.'

14
The Get Out of Jail Free Card

STANLEY WAS HAPPY to have the world think Moira was his girlfriend. It suited him. And since he was having sex with her he wasn't, in his head at least, living a complete lie. But his head also contained the information which suggested his heart still lay elsewhere. He was still very much in love with Bill Henry. 'There was a long time of lust and longing,' Stanley admits. 'I used to almost faint at the thought of him.'

Bill was now back in Glasgow, but Stanley saw almost nothing of him. Bill kept his distance. Stanley had to move on, focus on the future. And he had a bright and attractive girlfriend who thought the world of him. It was an accommodating relationship. Or so he thought. The little bohemian girl wasn't so carefree after all. She wanted the ring of respectability.

'Things were fine until just before Christmas 1950 then I realised Moira was so serious that she wanted to get married.

'But I couldn't entertain such a thought and I felt the relationship simply had to stop, so I broke it off. However, Moira was very, very upset. I kept getting those sheep's eyes every time she passed me in the theatre and she appeared to be heartbroken. Then one night she invited me up to her little rented flat at 65 Clouston Street for my favourite spaghetti and I was seduced back into bed again.'

The appetite sated, Stanley reckoned the only way to break off the relationship once and for all was to be entirely honest with Moira and underline his true sexual prediliction.

'I told her my preference and said, "That's why I am breaking off the relationship. This would be NO life for you, married to someone who is essentially and primarily homosexual!"'

Moira's reaction was surprising, even to those who knew how liberal she was.

'She looked up at me, shrugged and said, "Oh, I don't care about that at all. That doesn't worry me. Oh, you mustn't let that worry you."' And I said, "Well, it does worry me. I don't think you know what you're talking about and I don't think you realise that the future will be bleak for you and difficult for me."'

Stanley again informed Moira the relationship was over. And for good. Suddenly she raced to the front window of their second storey flat, opened it and climbed out onto the window ledge, yelling, 'If I can't have you then I won't settle for anyone else!'

Stanley was terrified. His heart raced as he rushed towards her and pulled her back. 'I tried to keep things calm and said, "Okay, okay, well if you want to get engaged, we could try it for a year or so and see what happens."'

Just after the window ledge moment, Stanley was handed a Get Out of Jail Free card. Moira wrote him a very sane and balanced letter. It said, words to the effect of, 'I'll let you off if you don't want to marry me.'

This was *the* defining moment of Stanley's life. He had his chance to make a clean break, to move on alone. And he turned it down.

'By that time, I had so many tender feelings for her,' he explains.

'I thought she would be still be heartbroken. But of course I should have been stronger. It was real weakness on my part.'

It was more than weakness. It was absolutely selfish. Kenneth Williams certainly thought so. Williams' feelings about the union ran far deeper than his *Diaries* comment suggests.

'Kenny thought I was making a terrible mistake,' says Stanley. 'And he was losing a friend.'

Williams believed Stanley to be taking advantage of Moira and a traitor to the cause. And why shouldn't he? After all, the pair had spent endless hours discussing sexuality, preferences and honesty. Kenneth asked Stanley about the future he could expect to have if he married Moira Robertson. Stanley asked the same question of himself – but pushed the answer aside.

Did Bessie Baxter have any idea of Stanley's true sexuality? If she did, she never let on. And she never knew of the window ledge incident. But she did mention several times there was 'something wrong' with Moira, that her emotional balance wasn't quite right. On 15 January 1951, the engagement became national news, yet this didn't really register with Stanley. After all, marriage was a long way off. And in any case his immediate thoughts were concentrated on making the panto a success.

It turned out to be a stormer – in fact the panto was so successful the run was halted by the Citz management on 22 February with the theatre again terrified it would lose the Corporation grant. Stanley went right into the next Citz production, a straight role in *Retreat from Moonshine* by Murray McClymont, but the critics indicated he should retreat from the serious parts.

The Scotsman of 14 February wrote:

> Nobody excels like Mr Baxter in portraying outraged innocence or conveying peevish innuendo; but if he has a good mind to his future, he will economise in the eye rolling business and develop other notes in his register.

Stanley toured with a seaside show in the summer and, feeling rather guilty about leaving Moira behind in Glasgow took her shopping in London in August. The pair met up with Kenneth Williams, who almost had to be hospitalised, his nose was so far out of joint:

> We traipsed up and down Bond Street looking for blouses for his future wife Moira, who is with him. I can see that my relationship with Stan has become, or is rapidly becoming, bifurcated. I think she is rather boring, which is a pity for she is terribly sweet, but it's just that most women do bore me.

Arriving back in Glasgow, Stanley was met with earth-shattering news. Fred Baxter had suffered a coronary thrombosis.

'Of course, he was the perfect candidate,' says Alice. 'A sedentary job all his life, virtually no exercise and although very quiet and controlled on the outside, highly strung on the inside. He wanted to move out of town to where he could have a little garden and potter about but Mum wouldn't move away from the friends and shops she knew.'

Stanley recalls his mother being 'terribly worried' about his father. Thankfully Fred recovered, however Stanley's career ladder looked shaky. John Casson, the mumbling actor-producer who had hired Stanley, quit for a new life in Australia. Oxford graduate Peter Potter arrived from Salisbury Playhouse and the Citz star would come to rue the day.

Just before panto rehearsals began, Stanley met up with Bill Henry, by chance, as they walked in the West End of the city. The pair got to filling in the time blanks since they'd last met: Bill revealed he had married and was working in one of his father's pubs. And then he quizzed his friend about his own personal life.

'Is it true you are getting married to Moira Robertson?'

'Well, yes, I am.'

'Why?'

'Well… love!'

'And he looked at me for a moment, shrugged and said, "Well, we always called her the Poor Little Rich Girl when we were together at the School of Art."

'And I went a bit, "Mmm," about that.'

Bill had either been making a clumsy attempt to convince Stanley he was making the wrong choice or was simply being disparaging. Regardless, the pair parted with Stanley feeling crushed. He would have expected his one true love to have been generous enough of spirit to wish him well. But what he really had hoped was for Bill to tell Stanley he loved him, and he should forget all this nonsense about getting married.

'I was still in love with Bill. I just couldn't get over him. But I was so troubled by his comments I thought I would have nothing more to do with him.'

However, Stanley was to have little say in the matter. A short time later he learned that Bill had died of a heart attack. He was just 26. Stanley was inconsolable when heard the tragic news. Bill Henry, he felt, had been the one person who really understood him. He had been the one who indulged his teen fantasies. He had been his first and only love.

By way of coping, Stanley tried to recall how cold Bill had been to him about Moira, about how he had played with his heart and brought along that bloody Magda Karachone woman. Now, none of that mattered. Bill was gone and he would never forget him.

Thankfully, in December, the demands of work concentrated Stanley's thoughts. The panto, *The Happy Hap'ny* was a *Tintock Cup*-like revue format featuring a collection of sketches, songs, satire and madrigals – all glued together with high energy performances and clever Alex Mitchell writing.

Stanley's 'Dame' was a bridge-playing society hostess, a frightfully awful straight-talking socially-destructive female who would go on to become Rosemary Gusher and feature in many of Stanley's future television sketches. *The Happy Hap'ny* featured Roddy McMillan, Andrew Keir, close pal John Fraser and a 21-year-old from Essex, Joan Sims, as the Principal Girl.

'She was lovely, lovely woman,' says Stanley. 'A great mate.'

The show was even more successful than *Riding Hood*, the queues around the Citizens' so long that teams of buskers turned up to entertain them. And to top it all, Stanley was voted Comic of the Year by Glasgow daily newspaper *The Bulletin* (which ceased production in 1960).

But these were also unhappy times at the Citz. The new boss Peter Potter, a one-legged former RAF pilot (he'd lost the leg in battle) with high-flying ideals had joined from Salisbury Playhouse – and hated Stanley's populist panto. The tall gangly Potter's Eton-Oxford background and high-brow theatre experience didn't sit well at all with the sensibilities of the Baxter-inspired Glasgow humour. Just as importantly, the Scots actors were sidelined on Potter's arrival.

'When he saw fit (which was often) he invited English actors to join the company,' says Duncan Macrae's biographer Priscilla Barlow. 'This was enough to alienate certain members of the company and a discernible schism appeared.'

And when the programme for the 1952 season was drawn up, and an English Lear recruited in the form of the relatively unknown George Colouris, Stanley found himself with small parts. That was his cue to take up the Howard & Wyndham offer. In February,

The Daily Record revealed he would have equal billing with veteran comic George Lacy in the *Half Past Eight* variety shows.

'I didn't want to leave but I had no choice. In fact, I took the new job with some anxiety. How would I do starring in a Number One theatre, with changes of programme weekly? It was a helluva mountain to climb.'[12]

Yet Stanley had more to think about than his career. When he and Moira had become engaged the year before, Stanley reckoned it would be at least a few years before the couple arrived at Wedding Central. Now he realised he had boarded a runaway train.

15
Bob Hope or Bill Holden?

HOLLYWOOD GOSSIP COLUMNISTS came up with the phrase 'Lavender Marriages' to describe couples who chose marriages of convenience, such as Rock Hudson, Barbara Stanwyck and Rudolf Valentino. Closer to home, the likes of Alec Guinness, Laurence Harvey, Wilfred Brambell, Alan Bates, Laurence Olivier and Vincent Price all covered themselves with the patina of marital respectability. Stanley chose to wear the same cloak.

'I had tried not to get married. But not that hard. I have to be honest and admit in a way it suited me. It was a great cover.'

There was another reason for boarding the Dumbarton train headed towards Moira's parents' home on the Saturday morning of 5 March 1952. Sonny Boy desperately needed to cut the umbilical cord. Since returning from the army, his mother's constant demand to 'Try harder!' had worn him out. She wanted to know the detail of every role he took on. She wanted an input into his performance. She wanted to be involved in the panto ideas he had been coming up with. Bessie was entirely aware however there was no real romance between her son and Moira. But her main reason for wanting Stanley to stay single was the fear marriage might dull his desire to get to the top. Yet, Bessie wouldn't have wanted Stanley to stand Moira up on her wedding day. It would be cruel, and of course the Baxters would be talked about across the land. But as the train sped west to Dumbarton, Fred Baxter, knowing his son was unconvincing in the role of Happy Groom, attempted a last-minute derailment.

'This is a very big step you're taking, Stanley. We hope you've really thought about how important it is.'

Stanley nonchalantly countered, 'Oh, not nowadays. If it doesn't work out, you just get divorced and you move on.'

Fred replied with a very heavy voice, 'No, it's not as easy as that.'

'And he was so right.'

The wedding took place between Stanley Livingstone Baxter and Marion Irving Robertson in Moira's front parlour overlooking the Clyde. (There was no best man; you didn't need one if the wedding took place in a private house.) The following Monday, The *Scottish Daily Express* wrote of the 'quiet wedding':

> Stanley Baxter and his wife Moira were secretly married in the drawing room of the bride's house in Dumbarton. She then went to their new Glasgow flat to cook spaghetti for his supper.

Their new home, a large ground-floor flat, at 73 Clouston Street, was just a few doors along from Moira's previous flat. But what the *Daily Express* didn't know was that when Stanley arrived home, with the sound of Saturday evening theatre applause still ringing in his ears, he broke down in tears. The honeymoon night – predictably – was a disaster.

'I sat on the edge of the bed and sobbed my heart out,' he admits. 'Moira asked me what was wrong and I said something about the emotion of it all. But it was because I knew I'd made the biggest mistake of my life.'

What could he do? He had to get on with it, focus on finishing the last ten days of the panto season – and his last ten days at the Citz.

Stanley at least had now made the decision to go into 'illegit' theatre, the world of variety and entertainment. His talents, he conceded, owed more to Bob Hope than Bill Holden.

'I had, sort of, come to terms with the fact I was a comedy actor.'

Stanley had a couple of months off before joining Howard & Wyndham, time for the newlyweds to take a well-deserved holiday in Spain. But on arriving back in Glasgow on 27 March 1952, all energising benefits of the break disappeared in an instant.

Alice was waiting at Stanley's door to announce Fred Baxter had died, aged 63, from a second coronary. Stanley was so stunned he could barely breathe.

'Yet, I had to go straight off and do a radio comedy at the BBC, a new show called *Listen to Speedie*. I had to go through with it. But I suppose the whole surreal experience had an odd effect on me, the getting on with it, the working on the laughs while I was grieving.

'I then went back home and found I had raging tonsillitis. I guess it was shock really. And I was still in bed when the funeral happened.'

It must have been shock. Stanley had had his tonsils removed as a four-year-old.

'A day or two later when I'd recovered, I went up to the family home. Still depressed by it all I asked my mother if there was anything of Dad's I could have to remember him by.'

Bessie's reaction was sadly typical.

'She said, "Och, I've given it all away," in this matter-of-fact voice. And then added, "Well, maybe there's a pair of cufflinks or something."'

That's not to say Bessie was unaffected by the death of her husband. He was her rock. He allowed his wife to romp in the clover of a fairly carefree life. And while she may not have loved Fred Baxter, she did care. Feeling rather alone, Bessie turned her attention on 22-year-old Alice, in an attempt to groom her for stardom.

'I had to say, "Mum, you're too late! You didn't bother about me when Stanley was growing up."'

Stanley meantime regretted not spending enough time with his dad. He certainly never had his metaphorical fishin' trip, his *On Golden Pond* moment.

'Bessie wouldn't have tolerated that,' he sighs. 'It would have cut her out of the picture.'

Bessie, however, could at least take delight in watching Stanley's career move steadily forward. He and Moira did a radio series together, *The Baxters,* in which he played the role of The Professor who translates broad Glaswegian into English. This Alex Mitchell-written character would later evolve into *Parliamo Glasgow*, one of Stanley's most successful sketches.

In April 1952, television came calling for the first time. The BBC invited Stanley to join the London-based talent showcase, *Shop Window*. Sadly, the audience didn't buy into the idea. But the actor sensed television could be the future of comedy. He told an interviewer he loved the intimacy:

> The opportunity for putting over changes of facial expression can be very satisfactory. I believe that whatever talent I have is three quarters on the visual side and so might be suitable for television.

Stanley would have to wait another seven years until he would discover how insightful he had been. (There were just over 40,000 TV licences bought in Scotland in 1952, as opposed to well over 1,100,000 radio licences. A year later, Queen Elizabeth's Coronation would see a surge of TV sets in the nation's living rooms, bringing numbers in Britain to over the three million mark.)

To highlight how young TV was, the week Stanley left the Citz saw BBC Scotland record its first live broadcast of a dramatic play *The Old Lady Shows Her Medals* by JM Barrie. The television producers asked the actors to speak their lines sotto voce, so as not to upset sound levels. But those at the back of the stalls couldn't hear a word. Stanley took great delight in hearing Peter Potter had to come on and make an apology.

But before embarking on his 22-week variety season, Stanley and Moira took one last break, again in London. They didn't meet up with Kenneth Williams, however, who was working out of town. (It was a pity for he could have told Stanley all about his recent trip to Collins Music Hall, where he saw an 'appalling' show featuring a tragic-looking Barri Chatt.)

At least Stanley's own fate looked a great deal more secure when on 30 May he opened as a headline act in the *Half Past Eight Show* at the Theatre Royal, a Number One theatre of course. It was a fantastic achievement for a 26-year-old. But although the £75 a week contract – on top of the £20 a week he earned for *It's All Yours* – seemed a lot of money, Stanley reckoned he was worth more.

'I found out I had to pay for my scripts, although I wrote some of them myself every Sunday afternoon, and I had to buy my own costumes.'

What Stanley did appreciate was the cutting edge ethos of the Howard & Wyndham shows. Gone were the days of Harry Lauder's kilted kitsch; these new shows were a little raucous and raunchy, with heaps of satire. Instead of streams of gag men, the audiences demanded well-written sketch material performed by actors who could deliver with ease. Stanley and Co. were the New Wave comics of the moment. *Scottish Field* magazine put the shows in context:

> This was the first time Glasgow comics were working from scripts especially written to suit the local audience and the individual talents. And it was tough.

Each week the programme changed and the new, sharp, contemporary material had to continually please a new crowd.

'We'd work all week and then I'd spend every Sunday at 73 Clouston Street writing my stand-up comedy spot for the following Thursday, sitting there going through joke books looking for ideas. There was no time for socialising. I don't know how I did it. Then I went on to fortnightly runs the next year and it was slightly better. But I was channelling everything into work. Ambition was all.

'Fortunately, I began working with George Lacy, an English comedian with a lot of material who provided doubles for us.' Stanley was to later discover a darker side to George, but for now he enjoyed sharing his bag of laughs.

'George wrote up a Guy de Maupassant short story in which he played an ageing courtesan and I played a randy young Scottish sailor. Boy, did I enjoy looking at myself in the mirror in that matelot outfit.'

The summer season played to capacity audiences and Stanley – sailor-suited or otherwise – thoroughly relished working life, pushing himself and others to the limit.

'No matter who I was working with, if their timing was out, I would give them notes at the end of the show. One comic complained. He said, "Stanley, it's the last night of the season! What can I do about it now?"'

In September 1952, Moira returned to the Citz for an appearance in James Bridie's *The Golden Legend of Shults* and she got good notices. However, Stanley reckoned his wife's place was in the home.

Moira never questioned the decision, even though it later proved to be very, very wrong.

'I didn't think that she was ever going to make it very big and I suggested she give it up. I shouldn't have done, but I did. It was all very selfish of me and a bit macho. She now had to be a housewife, which she found very frustrating. And although she was a good cook, she wasn't very good at washing. The pulleys were always full of stuff.'

Moira was more Dora from *David Copperfield* than Glaswegian domestic goddess. She may have worshipped Stanley but she never got herself worked up if her husband's white shirts weren't dry in the morning.

'At the time my main concern was, "Who's going to make my dinner at night when I come in if I haven't got my mother to do it?" I was working hard all day, performing at night and I needed shirts to be washed. I know it all sounds terribly old-fashioned but men had those expectations in those days,' Stanley recalls.

Many years later, in 1979, Stanley revealed to the *Daily Record* another reason why he suggested Moira quit acting: 'I believed that no one in our family should be anything but a star, so I encouraged her to quit.'

Meanwhile, in November 1952 Stanley focused on playing Buttons in *Cinderella* at the Theatre Royal Glasgow, his first traditional panto. He shared top billing alongside 'two cosy queens' called Terry Bartlett and Colin Ross, who played the Uglies; Cinders was Nicollete Roeg (the rather unimaginatively-named sister of movie director, Nic Roeg).

The panto was bigger and flashier than the Citz efforts but no more demanding to work on. Unless of course you take into account the 'queen of queens', Freddie Carpenter. Freddie, an ex-Australian dancer wore a dyed-red toupee on his head, a wicked sneer on his face and made Kenneth Williams look butch. Freddie was one of the biggest bitches in the business and was said to be the inspiration behind several stage and film productions' queenie directors. He commuted regularly to New York to see the top musicals and had worked in America before becoming a top choreographer with Howard & Wyndham.

'We got on fine-ish, and we used to entertain him a lot at 73 Clouston Street, but God help anyone who didn't get on with him because he could be a sadistic bastard. He would usually choose one girl, almost always the Principal Boy, and work to reduce her to tears. It was his favourite sport.

'As you may expect, Freddie was devoted to doing pantomime as glamorously as possible, but he wasn't mad about comedy. He really wanted to be doing lavish musicals. So when you suggested slapstick, he would go, "Oh my God, you mean making a mess on my nice floor?'"

Stanley loved his first *Cinderella*, in spite of Freddie Carpenter's waspishness.

'Buttons is the only male part worth playing in panto. You can't fail, it's actor-proof.'

The show ran well to great business but across the river at the Citizens, the company's new 13-letter panto, *A Glaikit Spell,* favoured less well now that their favourite son had joined the big league. However Stanley wasn't sticking out his tongue in the direction of Peter Potter. He had his own theatre worries to contend with.

16

Stage Frights

GEORGE LACY, A married gay with a troubled spirit, had been generous enough on stage to begin with. But he was now showing all the signs of a man on the edge of a nervous breakdown. Stanley believed George was becoming paranoid, that George was imaging his young co-star was stealing the limelight. But just because you're paranoid doesn't mean your stage partner isn't grabbing all the attention.

Stanley's laughter count was way higher than that of the older performer and he was attracting more column inches in the papers, but it wasn't deliberate. And he wasn't prepared to put up with George's ever-increasing huffs. The young entertainer suggested to H&W boss Stewart Cruikshank that he push George stage left. Needless to say, Lacy was apoplectic when he heard the news.

Who was to replace the fragile Lacy? Jack Radcliffe seemed a perfect choice. He once billed himself as 'Scotland's Greatest Comedian' and underlined his self-confidence by often asking unruly audience members to fight outside. This unusual tactic resulted in management changing Radcliffe's show title on the bills to *Any Time You Like!* Radcliffe accepted the stint with Stanley gratefully. And even though H&W management wanted the younger talent to be top of the bill, Stanley says he balked at the very idea of it. But it wasn't only about keeping the older star happy.

'I didn't have a backlog of material, whereas Jack was a walking library. But I made more of the material than most of his feeds. I think I made it a nearly equal comedy.'

The partnership worked and the *Half Past Eight* shows ran again for an incredible 18 week stretch. Over at the Citizens' however, Stanley noted that Peter Potter left amidst serious concern that the theatre had lost its direction. But Stanley didn't gloat. His attention at the time was more concerned with another newspaper story.

Recently knighted actor Sir John Gielgud was fined £10 at West London Magistrates' Court for 'persistently importuning male persons for an immoral purpose'. When apprehended by police, the actor gave his name as Arthur Gielgud, 49, a clerk. The star pleaded that he was 'tired and had had a few drinks' and that he was not responsible for his actions. However, the incident threatened to wreck his career. Stanley was horrified to read *Sunday Express* columnist John Gordon fulminate 'moral rot' and urge 'decent people' to ostracise such 'social lepers'. Thankfully, theatre audiences proved more charitable and Gielgud was staunchly championed by Sybil Thorndike and Ralph Richardson, with whom he was appearing on stage. Yet, while the Gielgud story angered Stanley, it caused him to breathe a sigh of relief he'd married. Marriage to Moira was far from ideal but there was no way he'd ever wish to endure the humiliation suffered by his fellow actor. There was no way Stanley would ever put himself in that position.

At the end of the *Half Past Eight* season of '53 however, Stanley faced a more immediate crisis. His next panto, at the King's Theatre, Edinburgh, was *Aladdin* and although the script flew like a magic carpet, and his costumes were great (for some of the stage outfits the actor took off to the Ladies section of a department store and sneaked into a changing booth while Moira stood guard outside), the panto came with an added villain.

'To my horror they brought George back,' he recalls. 'Freddie Carpenter was being a little bastard.' Freddie reckoned George could be good for business. George Lacy, as you would expect, didn't want to work with Stanley but he needed the work, and the director played on this. And so what if the turns didn't get on? Well, that could be funny.

But George didn't think so.

'This time, George became even *more* paranoid about me. When he was off-stage he would get thick tape and strap it around the tannoys in the dressing room so he wouldn't hear my laughs.'

Things got so bad that George's Widow Twankey and Stanley's

Wishee Washee never actually met on stage; George wouldn't appear in the same scene as his stage partner, which of course made a nonsense of the book. Surprisingly, and fortunately, the critics never picked up on it. Thankfully, Stanley at least had a pal in his corner during the run's hostilities. Bruce McClure had been granted his wish to become a Genie.

Moira at this time was also in Edinburgh – and back on stage. But it wasn't that Stanley conceded Cinders should surrender the domestic drudgery and go to the ball – on this occasion it made financial sense. Director James Gibson had offered his wife a part in Edinburgh's Gateway Theatre production of *Hame* and it meant they could rent a flat together. Moira hadn't been protesting to get back to work. She wasn't the sort to go against her husband's wishes. But Stanley recalls she beamed when offered the job. He should have recorded that joy and encouraged her to continue working. It was a decision he would deeply regret.

However, Stanley wasn't focused on Moira's comeback. He was dealing with a new drama every day in the form of George.

'As the run progressed, he became even more surly. It was taking some of the magic away from the show.'

And then he truly lost the plot. On the last night in February 1954, the older actor took the curtain call and created a scene that could have come from Shakespearean tragedy. He stood at the front of the stage and began to denounce Stanley to the audience. George gave his greatest performance of the season: 'I have not come here from radio, to be treated like this!'

This final diatribe had the effect of Stanley feeling truly sorry for his co-star.

'I suppose it must have been tough for an old man to have to listen to someone else getting laughs like that – as his were getting less and less. The ego can be so easily bruised, especially in comedy. I hope I was as generous with him as I could have been.'

Poor George had to be carried off screaming into a taxi. It was life, luvvie. It was the theatre, although not perhaps the theatre Stanley had anticipated.

Life in variety theatre would prove to be even more dramatic. In the new *Half Past Eight* spring season of 1954 Stanley wasn't happy with his partner. Again. Jack Radcliffe didn't throw Lacy-like tantrums but nor did he have George's subtlety. Radcliffe, says Stanley, was as filthy as a Glasgow chip shop doorway at 6.00am on a Saturday. Working with the street fighter comedian meant dumbing down. Drastically.

'George Lacy, little bastard that he was, brought more style to the show than Jack Radcliffe ever did.'

Journalist Gordon Irving wrote that the Baxter–Radcliffe mix wasn't right:

> Young Stanley's plan of attack for making audiences laugh is more sophisticated, I guess because he has come from a legit background at the Citz. And he seems to regard himself as being in a different and slightly upper-class category of comedy than the robust Scottish style of Radcliffe.

Stanley wasn't going to take on JR over his lack of subtlety – he would have lost that battle – and crying to H&W wouldn't work twice. Thankfully, in June a delightful new challenge appeared on the horizon which refocused his mind.

Stanley landed a small part in a new Scottish film, *Geordie*, the tale of a puny Highland boy who, thanks to a weightlifting correspondence course, porridge and the cold fresh air which flowed over his bare feet as he hung them out of the bedroom window each night, becomes an Olympian. Stanley would have three days off from theatre to play The Postie, alongside Bill Travers in the title role and the wonderful Alastair Sim as a mad-hatterish Highland laird. It was a seminal experience.

'I suddenly thought, "This is what I have been gearing up to all my life. The acting games at Millport as a kid, with the cousins and Alice, had been about me playing a mini-film director." While watching the others come down the hill on a bike, I'd always imagined there was a low loader [camera] in front of me. So when it came to the actual filming, I thought, "I've done all this before! Duck to water!"' A rather precocious duck, at the age of ten, to understand film equipment. But then Stanley had spent a great part of his life at the movies, absorbing the process.

Regardless of the size of her son's small part, Bessie Baxter was simply jubilant, telling the world that her Stanley had now made it into films. And of course the little movie went on to become a massive success in Europe and North America.

Back in Glasgow, life was pretty much based around the Alhambra and any socialising involved Stanley and Moira having a few friends home for dinner after the show. Although that's not to say 73 Clouston Street was an open door. Jack Radcliffe hadn't been forgiven for not being what Stanley hoped (although why Stanley thought Radcliffe would jettison his fruity material was anybody's guess) but the likes of Molly Urquhart, Fulton Mackay, musician Arthur Blake and Freddie Carpenter – with some great tales to tell – would come to dinner. Veteran English panto Dame Dougie Byng also regaled guests with tales of the West End cabaret in the '30s and Bruce McClure was very much a regular.

'Bruce was very extroverted, but not camp. He was another gay who hated effeminate men. And he was just terribly funny.'

Another new invited chum was young dancer-choreographer Lionel Blair, who worked with *Five Past Eight* for two seasons.

'Stanley was great to work with,' he recalls. 'Although he wouldn't put up with mistakes.'

Relations with Moira were now 'fine', although two years into the marriage sex was dwindling. Moira wasn't entirely unhappy with the situation. After all, she was with the man she adored. And wasn't marriage about compromise? It certainly was for Stanley. Very occasionally he had little encounters with kindred spirits he'd meet through friends or in the gay-friendly tea rooms of Glasgow, but he made a point to stay away from good-looking gay chorus boys around the theatre.

'They could be dangerous,' he said. 'They were forever gossiping. So you kept schtum and you kept them at a distance.'

When one of the Glasgow chorus boys was charged with importuning it was a further reminder of the vulnerability of the gay community.

But Stanley's focus was, as always, on work, and in November he found himself battling with H&W again over their choice of co-star. Stewart Cruickshank decided Stanley would co-star with radio pal Jimmy Logan at the Alhambra in a brand new panto.

Stanley stamped his foot as hard as he had done in the Bevin Boy colliery days.

'I complained to Freddie Carpenter: "This is madness! I'm all run in to reprise Wishee Washee from last year."'

Was it about a new panto, or did Stanley not wish to compete with a contemporary, one who was very talented? He argued the theatres should feature a young/old double act.

Freddie passed the buck and Stanley flew to London to convince Stewart Cruikshank he was right. He was so nervous of taking on the boss that he spent the flight time locked in the toilet. But he won his argument: Jimmy and Duncan Macrae would run at the Alhambra and Stanley and Alec Finlay – as Dame – would play the Theatre Royal, and H&W would pack both.[13] He was right, as it happens. The box office for both theatres was great.

Stanley was certainly becoming used to getting his own way. In February 1955 when he moved over to the King's, Edinburgh, to join the now renamed *Five Past Eight Show*, he was consulted about his new partner. Harry Gordon was a veteran comic from Aberdeen who had successful panto stints in Glasgow playing Dame alongside the likes of Will Fyffe. Stanley and Harry liked each other (mercifully) but audiences were not so keen on a night at the theatre. A really hot summer meant that people stayed outdoors as late as possible in the evening and Stanley – still a much bigger name in Glasgow – had to get used to the sight of empty seats in the house. He recalls taking his concerns to Harry's dressing room one day.

'Harry, the weather's broken! It's pissing down out there. So we should have a good house tonight?'

'No, no, not necessarily. No, no, it's no' like that.'

'Why is that, Harry?'

'Ye dinnae ken Edinburgh, Stanley. If it's too hot they'll no' come in. They'll be away playing gowf in the meadows. And if it rains, they'll no' leave the hoose!'

Exasperated by this bizarre logic, Stanley asked, 'So when *do* they actually come to the theatre, Harry?'

'When it's just threatening.'

At least the rising star could delight in the laughs he created when audiences did show up.

Stanley himself laughed aloud a few days later when he heard through the grapevine how Kenneth Williams, appearing in Orson Welles' production of *Moby Dick*, had greeted new cast member Gordon Jackson:

'I'm Kenneth Williams, the only one in the cast worth knowing,' he said, his sucked-cheeks-face perfectly straight.

Yet, this astonishing immodesty didn't prevent Williams and the Scot from becoming lifelong friends.

Stanley meantime put his heart and soul into *Cinderella*, working on the script with Alex Mitchell from August. And he liked his Buttons, played by cockney theatre star Reg Varney.

'Reg was very good in it but he didn't seem too happy at this time. He was furious that the man who had been his feed in theatre had now become huge in television, Benny Hill.' (Reg would find fame much later in 1969 as a cheeky bus driver in ITV sitcom *On the Buses*.)

But at the end of 1955, after four years with Howard & Wyndham, Stanley reckoned he had had enough. He says it had nothing to do with not being paid as much as Jack Radcliffe or Jimmy Logan, nor the growing awareness that there was a bigger audience out there; on Sunday nights at 7.30pm, 28 million people would sit down to watch *I Love Lucy* and then the variety show, *Sunday Night at the London Palladium*. No, part of Stanley was fed up being matched up with the Jack Radcliffes and the George Lacys of the variety world. He also wanted more control; after all, he was now co-writing, co-producing and often directing, as he had done in CSE days. But there was something else going on in Stanley's mind. Although he'd walked out of legit theatre and skipped lightly over the river to variety, part of him (the rather more delusional part?) reckoned he *still* had something to offer as a straight actor. He felt he could prove to the critics he had what it took to play straight drama. The Gemini Stanley wanted the best of both worlds.

17
Fruit-flavoured Mother-love

STANLEY ENTERED STEWART CRUIKSHANK'S Glasgow office with his gun drawn, ready to shoot his variety and panto career in the head and move to London to seek his fortune. He explained his decision wasn't at all about money (now well into three figures a week), but that he needed stage success in a different (more serious) form. The Howard & Wyndham boss's cold eyes betrayed his panic at the news – the potential loss of box office was frightening – but he kept calm.

'Cleverly, Cruikshank thought for a minute about what I had said and then suggested an idea. He said, "Suppose I got a senior British impresario to present you in serious plays in Scotland. Would you agree to that?"

'Of course, the idea was about spiking my guns, hoping if I did straight plays in the summer, he'd at least have me available for panto in the winter.'

Stanley's guns returned to their holster and Cruikshank hired top London theatre producer Henry Sherek to create six plays. Stanley could not fail to be impressed. Sherek, the multi-lingual son of an international theatrical agent, was high-brow. He'd produced the plays of TS Eliot and had been production manager of the 1934 film *Waltzes from Vienna,* featuring Danny Kaye.

'The plan was we would play in Edinburgh at the Lyceum and the King's Theatre in Glasgow, changing plays fortnightly.'

The demands on an actor to learn a new play in such a short time were Herculean. But that didn't matter. This was a new bold adventure Stanley could immerse himself in, and he also had a say in choosing the plays he felt would work for him.

After buying a car to transport Moira, their belongings and

their cat back and forward from Edinburgh, Stanley kicked off the series of plays with *Harvey*, the Broadway hit about the man with a giant rabbit for a pal that became a film success for James Stewart. Stanley's Elwood P Dowd was a great success, perhaps helped by the fact *Harvey* was comic fantasy, and Elwood walked a fine line between sanity and insanity. The great box office business rolled on in plays such as *The Lass wi' the Muckle Mou'* and in March 1956 critic Alexander Reid of *Scotland's Magazine* wrote:

> *The Whiteheaded Boy* by Lennox Robinson and performed by The Stanley Baxter Company is a brilliant study, right on the mark, showing the mark of comic genius.

'Comic genius.' Stanley may not have acknowledged it but he was still in the laughter business, albeit wrapped neatly in the kudos of legit theatre. But it meant he could mark this experience up on the CV – and yet remain in denial about his limitations as a straight actor.

The other bonus was in leaving behind the Jack Radcliffes of variety. Now Stanley could work alongside real acting talent such as young Glasgow actor Ian Bannen, in *Festival Fever*. (Bannen would pick up an Oscar nomination for his film work in *Flight of the Phoenix*.) The Bannock, as he was called by friends and indeed signed himself, hit it off with Stanley straight away.

'He was a very, very nice guy,' says Stanley of the late actor, 'except he was a bit devout as far as the Roman Catholicism was concerned and we couldn't agree on religion, considering I was an atheist.'

Perhaps they wouldn't have agreed on the principal of homosexuality either. In 1971, Stanley's old chum John Schlesinger cast Bannen in the role of the homosexual doctor in *Sunday Bloody Sunday* (after Alan Bates pulled out over other filming commitments). But Bannen then withdrew. Screenwriter Penelope Gilliatt claimed the actor never felt comfortable with the part and anxiety adversely affected his performance during the early filming. Yet, while Bannen may not have been comfortable playing a gay man, he wasn't averse to socialising with them. He came to dinner at

Clouston Street several times during the Sherek season, meeting a clutch of Stanley's friends, gay and simpatico. And the evenings were a delight. But one invited star guest proved to be incredibly hard work.

Singing legend Eartha Kitt was appearing at the time at the Glasgow Empire, a theatre with a frightening reputation for performers (Des O'Connor fainted on stage in expectation of being barracked). Whether or not the theatre's reputation had impacted upon Kitt, the tiny American was terrified when she slinked on in front of the Glasgow audience. Then when she heard a shout for a request of the famous 'Monotonous' she thought it was a heckler describing her show. The singer crumbled and left the stage. Her assistant however had met Moira, who was at the show (Stanley and the American star shared the same agent) and this proved to be fortuitous.

'The assistant grabbed Moira, who was a huge fan of Eartha Kitt, and said, "Oh please come backstage Mrs Baxter, you seem to understand sensitive people – and Ms Kitt is very upset at drying [forgetting her lines] Could you speak to her?'"

Moira, the last person to ignore a personal SOS, approached the star's dressing room, knocked and entered – and found her curled up, cat-like, on a chaise longue.

'Moira rushed to comfort her, saying the singer was in the wrong venue for a star of her sophistication and how wonderful she was. And gradually Eartha warmed to Moira.

'The sheer kindness worked and Eartha went back on stage for the next two nights. Then, on the Thursday night after one of the Sherek shows, I went to the theatre with my company to catch her second act. We all loved the show and I went backstage afterwards to add my own reinforcement. So I knocked on the door and walked in but she didn't turn around, still taking her make-up off in the mirror, with that fixed, feline stare.

'And I said, "Miss Kitt, I think you met my wife when she came in on your first night. I'm here with my company, and we'd all like to say how much we enjoyed you."

'Total silence. And still smearing the face. I thought, "That's rude!" So I said, "Well anyway, that's all I wanted to say. Bye bye."

'And I was just walking through the door, feeling so insulted, when she said briskly, "No, no, wait a minute. I did see your wife. And I got on with her very well indeed. What are you doing for dinner?"

'So I called Moira, and we went to the Central Hotel for dinner with the lady, and Eartha slithered into the dining room, wearing her leopard-skin trousers. Of course, immediately everyone turned around to look at her. But she became very upset. "See! They are all looking at me. They hate black people. They're racist!"

'I tried to calm her down, saying, "Look, Glasgow is one of the most non-racist cities ever. It's down to two things. One, they don't see many black people here and two, most importantly, you're a star. That's why people stare."

'She said, "Do you really think so?" And I looked at her. "Look you've really got to get over this. Come and have dinner with Moira and me tomorrow night, back at 73 Clouston Street."'

The following night, somewhat reassured, the singer did indeed turn up at the Baxters' home.

'She walked in, took her coat off and curled up in front of the coal fire. Then she did something very strange. She picked up a newspaper and began reading out loud to us, as if she was proving to us she could read. [Stanley takes on Kitt's abbreviated vocal style]: "Two nights ago, Harold MacMillan went to Chequers..."

'I thought, "This is surreal!" To break the ice, I mentioned I had a book of Cecil Beaton photographs, and she was in it. I showed her the book, which was glowing in its praise. But she accentuated a negative, she noticed the line describing her as, "a small, but incandescent star". And she said, "Small? When was this book published? Ah, three years ago."'

Stanley and Moira spent the night walking on eggshells as Eartha spent most of it staring into the flames in the fireplace. Still, Stanley could take comfort from knowing he'd never meet the extremely self-conscious and neurotic lady again.

For the penultimate play in the Henry Sherek season, *Who Goes There!*, Stanley chose to play a lesser part. Alexander Reid of *Scotland's Magazine* believed it to be a 'heart-warming display of rather un-actory generosity'. In fact, Stanley was stepping backwards into the spotlight.

'That's the case,' he admits, offering the performance of a pained smile.

'I think I was influenced by Olivier's time at the Old Vic when they were staging *Peer Gynt*, and Olivier chose to play the Button Moulder. And of course you couldn't take your eyes off Olivier, because it was him.

'I thought that like Larry I'd appear modest.'

The plan backfired, yet the Sherek season had been a success, thanks to each play allowing Stanley to be funny. But while his professional life was running smoothly, in the summer of 1956, and his 30th birthday, the actor couldn't resist the gay life.

'I couldn't put up with the very long periods of not being with men,' he says. 'Thankfully Moira was very understanding. If there were someone I were interested in I could bring them home. And she was very good about letting them go to bed with me. She would go off to our bedroom and let me take the one opposite.'

Moira didn't have to turn a blind eye very often.

'Not nearly enough,' he says, with a twinkle of the eye. 'It was still a very fallow period for a homosexual. I'd have to make do with the odd lover, sometimes someone in the business or a married man who didn't want to be, who would swoon into my life for a one night stand – and then a few months later another might appear.'

Stanley says he had no option but to bring his one-nighters home.

'If it didn't happen in the family home, where could it happen? Would it be in some public lavatory or somewhere I could be arrested?'

The fear of jail – and the subsequent public ridicule – still hung over the head of every gay man in Britain, underlined in September 1956, by the Liberace story.

The flamboyant entertainer brought a libel action against the *Daily Mirror* columnist Cassandra (AKA William Connor). Liberace's arrival in Britain had prompted the journalist to describe him, rather astonishingly, as:

> A deadly, winking, sniggering, snuggling, chromium plated, scent-impregnated, luminous, quivering, giggling, fruit-flavoured, mincing, ice-covered heap of mother-love.

In case readers missed the point, Connor added:

> He is the biggest sentimental vomit of all time. Slobbering over his mother, winking at his brother, and counting the cash at every second, this superb piece of calculating candy-floss has an answer for every situation.

Liberace claimed Cassandra was effectively labelling him a homosexual. The case would take three years to go to trial, but meantime gay entertainers feared they would wander into the sights of such 'literary assassins who dip their pen in vitriol and murder reputations', as Liberace's lawyer David Jacobs later described Cassandra.

Stanley knew he simply had to hide his predilection. And this was the reason he made one of the strangest professional choices imaginable.

18

Five-buck Blow Jobs

THE SUCCESS OF the Sherek season suggested Stanley should go off and enjoy a stint in legit theatre, at least in comedy plays. Instead, he took a job selling Brigadoon Scottishness to second-generation Scots, desperate to keep the shortbread tin image of the Auld Country alive in their tartan-bunnetted heads. Stanley agreed to join *The White Heather Club*, the haggis and heather show which toured the likes of North America and New Zealand. It was a bizarre choice. He had no time for tartan kitsch and he even hated whisky and the sound of the bagpipes.

'Yes, but this was a chance to see the major cities of Canada and America and be paid for it.'

There was another reason. Perhaps the principal reason. The three-month trip beginning in the autumn of '56 was a chance to escape to Funland. He couldn't take Moira along – the producers wouldn't pay for partners – and Stanley wasn't at all unhappy about that; Moira was though.

'To take a wife along would have been so difficult,' he says unconvincingly.

On arrival in Montreal, the troupe were met by agent Neil Kirk, a New York-Dundonian.

'He was an old ex-comic who would talk about the good old days of theatre in the '20s when "You could sit at your desk and the actresses would give you a blow job for five bucks, Stanley."

'I thought, "Lovely. What a rich life people enjoyed in the '20s."'

The *White Heather* tour proved to be a punishing schedule.

'But the hardest part of the performance was the after-show commitment, socialising with the Caledonian committee who'd organised that particular night. The committee members' wives were invariably vast ladies wearing white bombazine dresses with tartan sashes over their huge tits. And inevitably, their kilted husbands with hybrid accents would bear down on me with a half a glass of whisky, with me having to say, "I'm sorry, I don't drink whisky. Could I have a gin and tonic?" "What? Gin and tonic!" Of course that was an insult to these exiled patriots.'

At times, the bombazined ladies got well bombed and asked for a wee peek at what Stanley was wearing beneath the Anderson kilt. But the star's sporran remained unmoved.

The notion of seeing the North American cities didn't work out either – there was so little time and Stanley made a promise to himself he would return. And while the travelling tartan circus played to sell-out audiences, and Stanley was on a percentage of the box office, he made very little money.

'There was a lot of fiddling going on,' he says, rolling his eyes at the recollection. 'Perhaps Neil Kirk had a lot of five-buck blow jobs to pay for.'

Back home he returned to panto, concluding his second stint in *Cinderella*, this time at the King's in Edinburgh, again alongside 'nice' Alec Finlay. (On the west coast the Ayr Gaiety was also staging *Cinderella* – with one of the Uglies played by the irrepressible Barri Chatt.)

This time Stanley's Buttons was played by the then rock 'n' roll singer and later tartan warbler, Andy Stewart.

'Freddie Carpenter didn't have much time for Andy, but I argued his case and the panto was a success.'

The New Year of 1957 brought about another chance to go off adventuring; Stanley was going back into the army. The War Office was having a difficult time of it with uprisings in the Middle East and Cyprus and it was deemed that the troops were in need of some jolly good entertainment to take their minds off the possibility of their minds being blown off their shoulders at any given time. And so former CSE turns were invited to complete a final tour. Sadly, Williams, Schlesinger and Nichols were not invited to relive the salad days – that would have been fantastic – but Stanley chose to go regardless. He loved the idea of heading a concert party to tour Jordan, North Africa, Malta and Cyprus, where the Turks and Greeks where vying for control. (He loved Cyprus and would later buy a villa there.) And as a little morale booster, although he had left the army as a sergeant, Stanley was asked to go back as Honorary Brigadier Baxter.

More importantly, he wangled it so that Moira could come along too as a working actress. Guilt from the *White Heather* tour had somehow formed in his head and Moira was in raptures at the prospect of touring with her husband.

'She never asked to go. She never tugged at me. And by this time she had sort of settled into being a housewife.'

Sort of.

Back in Glasgow in September, it was back to real work with the new *Five Past Eight* season at the Alhambra. But now his heart wasn't in it. It was all about repetition and predictability, churning out the same sketches, feeding or being fed the same lines, and yet trying desperately to come up with new gags, new ideas that would bring out the best in the performers. What helped Stanley through the year was lining up with radio pal, Jimmy Logan (this wasn't panto and Stanley felt they could work in variety, and he was right). Jimmy even pushed Stanley to go off-script for the first time.

'Although I could work an audience with looks and whatever, I hadn't done improv. But it was all part of the learning curve.'

Stanley and his new stage side-kick had great material to work with, thanks to a new writer, Glasgow journalist Stan Mars (real name Stanley Marshall). One of his sketches involved three wee boys from Glasgow who had been arrested for stealing flowers – and the boys chose to defend themselves in court.

'For example, the po-faced judge said to one of the kids, "What is your occupation?" and the reply squeaked back, "Child." Whoosh!'

Stan Mars also created a sketch based around the three boys, *The Hameless Ones*, with a laugh of recognition guaranteed thanks to an infamous American cult of that time, *The Nameless Ones*. But the best idea of the season came from Stanley. He came up with the conceit of playing a couple of '50s Glasgow wide boys, Francie and Josie, two inherently stupid loafers who wore Teddy Boy suits and Tony Curtis hairstyles and waxed lyrical about life.

He suggested he play the more stupid of the two, Francie. Jimmy would have none of it at all

'Jimmy was very generous on stage but he always liked to be the boss. And this wasn't his idea – so it was out.'

Jimmy's dismissal of the Francie and Josie idea would lose him a potential fortune. Stanley would later develop the idea with Rikki Fulton, who would then transfer it onto STV with variety star Jack Milroy. The spin-off theatre shows were phenomenally successful for three decades to come.

> JOSIE [to the audience]: 'I'd like to thank you for the opporchancity to expose wurselves to you.'
> FRANCIE [sarcastically to Josie]: 'You're a rerr dancer.'
> JOSIE: 'It's in ma' blood.'
> FRANCIE: 'It's a pity your blood doesn't go down to your feet.'

The lost opportunity apart, Stanley and Jimmy could do no wrong on stage. Meanwhile, Kenneth Williams' return to Glasgow wasn't so much fun. Williams, still sore from working with Tony Hancock on *Hancock's Half Hour* (Hancock eventually forced him off the show) sought comfort in his CSE chum. With Stanley working, he went to the cinema with Moira. And became irritated when Moira fell asleep.

Two days later however, Williams had had more than enough of the city and left on the first train to London. Williams' hissy fit and unannounced exit was one of many Stanley would endure over the years. Stanley explains why his army chum flew the coop so abruptly.

'I had to give him a bit of a row when he made an arse of himself – again – after he took Moira to the terribly fashionable 101 Club in Hope Street, while I was busy working.

'She said he was just so loud, so camp, demonstrative and demanding attention – in a public place and in the middle of Glasgow.

'Moira was so embarrassed. [And Stanley, by association.] I ticked him off that night when they came home and the next morning there was a note on his pillow. "GOODBYE."'

It was a pity Williams left because Stanley could have used a chum to talk to about the trials and tribulations of being married. Should the gay affairs continue? And what were they doing to Moira?

'I don't know how she really felt in her heart of hearts.'

He didn't try to find out. He didn't really want to know.

Stanley certainly couldn't share secrets such as this with pals such as Jimmy Logan.

'You don't want to talk about your sex life to someone who is heterosexual, unless they are a psychiatrist – and at that point you are in deep trouble.'

That day would come. In August 1957, Stanley and Jimmy appeared in a gala variety night to celebrate the launch of STV, the first commercial TV station in Scotland.

In November, it was time to prepare for panto, and Stanley discovered that he was to be reunited with former Citz favourite Duncan Macrae in *Mother Goose* at the Alhambra, alongside tartaned kilted singing star, Kenneth McKellar.[14] By rights, Stanley should have been awarded top billing but Freddie Carpenter became the Wicked Queen again (in Stanley's eyes) when he demanded Macrae play the lead, Goosie. Stanley was having none of it, flapped his wings hard and maintained he should be the bird.

'I fought like hell to get it. I knew that whoever played Dame would get to play it the following year when it moved to the King's in Edinburgh. Eventually, I persuaded Freddie telling him I knew exactly what I could do with it. He said [camp voice]: "Very well, we'll let you." Duncan, however, was not at all happy about me playing Dame.'

Off-stage, Stanley and the rather camp, exotic Macrae got on well together. But in *Goose*, the egos clashed like bent cymbals. No wonder.

'I had given him an invented character to play I had dreamed up and it didn't do him any favours. To make things worse, normally he was eccentric, so undisciplined, but in this panto he was murder. I remember once saying to him during a performance, "Why are you speaking? You're cutting into the gags?" He said, "Ah yes, but I have my own theory. Don't let them laugh, don't let them laugh, and *then* let them laugh."

'I said, "No, you don't let them laugh so long they don't *want* to laugh."'

Stanley certainly didn't learn from the great Macrae.

'No, no, no! He was a warning. Sometimes a fuckin' nightmare. And his curtain speeches were legend. You never knew what was going to come out. I remember standing behind him on stage on the day that George Bernard Shaw died. "He was our greatest playwright and his parting is a great loss to the world of theatres," said Macrae in sombre, dramatic voice. "In fact, a dead loss!" I nearly fainted.'

Despite the stars of *Goose* flying off in different directions, and Norman Wisdom, who Stanley would meet some years later in New York, playing at the King's with a new musical, *Where's Charlie?*, the panto did good business. And Stanley picked up the best crits, from the likes of *Evening Times* writer Jack House: 'Stanley is a comic all the year round now. *Five Past Eight* for one half the year and panto for the rest.'

But the 31-year-old comic was now bored rigid of variety's character-driven little playlets. He no longer wanted to share a bill with the plate spinners, the magicians and the dancing poodles. He needed to raise his game – and he needed a new challenge. The New Year brought one – but again, not the kind he was hoping for.

19
The Scots Cain and Abel

DICK HURRAN HAD once been a hoofer, a song-and-dance man who had played at the infamous Panopticon Theatre in Glasgow's Argyle Street. This was a theatre so wild its shipyard worker audiences would show performer displeasure by firing rivets at them using elastic slings.

Perhaps that's why the new Alhambra boss wanted to create a very different world. The man from Surrey arrived at the theatre with the idea of bringing Las Vegas to Glasgow. Hurran's idea of entertainment was an English big name wearing a sparkly jacket appearing in front of a huge velvet backdrop studded with more lights than Blackpool, sporting a giant sparkly violin.

Hurran also loved dancing girls. Lots of them, preferably wearing fish-nets and feathered head-dresses. But all of this meant that the Scottish turns ended up playing second fiddle to the violin-decorated scenery. In the spring of 1958, Stanley, already jaundiced of course, began to see the writing on the velvet-covered wall.

'*Five Past Eight* was turning into a succession of spectacular settings brought in from Las Vegas or Paris, and Scots comedy, the backbone of it all, was being reduced. The likes of Max Bygraves and Matt Monro were drafted in and paid fortunes.'

The days of sketches featuring the likes of windiehingers were gone. Stanley, at 32, had another reason to be deeply troubled.

'The press were saying to me, "You could be the next Jimmy Logan." But I was alarmed because I felt Jimmy couldn't do what I could. And I wanted to do more sophisticated material.'

Stanley determined this would be his final variety season. But he had he had a much bigger problem to contend with than sparkly violin and velvet backdrops. Rikki Fulton was brought in to co-star.

It was like asking Cain and Abel to play together nicely in the backyard. Two years older and a little behind Stanley at this point in terms of success, Fulton came from a similar lower middle-class Glasgow background and had worked his way up through rep theatre and onto the Howard & Wyndham stage. An intelligent man with an instinctive ear for what makes good comedy and blessed with brilliant stage timing, Rikki and Stanley should have become best of pals. Instead, thanks to the *It's All Yours* selection, Rikki's enmity had never evaporated. Stanley worked hard to make his new partnership work. But it was torturous.

'He threw cold water on everything. He wouldn't go for the ideas I suggested yet, at the same time, he wouldn't give me a hard time to my face. What he'd do was really pick on Stan Mars. I hated that bullying aspect of his personality.'

Rikki's reputation as showbiz bully would carry right through his career. Yet, such was Rikki's love of saying no, he even rejected Stanley's idea of the pair playing Francie & Josie, the act Jimmy Logan had rejected but was to make Rikki a star in Scotland.

'At first, he said he didn't want to pay for the Teddy Boy suits, that they would be too expensive for an act that may not work out. And I rallied and said, "Well, I'm afraid that's a risk we will have to take."'

Rikki eventually agreed. But Stan Mars' Francie & Josie scripts were ripped apart.

'Rikki, you see, fancied himself as something of a writer. When Stan would deliver a new script, we all had to sit round and do a read-through – and of course authors are incredibly sensitive about their stuff – but Rikki chose to forget this.

'He would start to pull faces, tutting, flicking back pages and saying in that morose voice, "Oh God, is that *all* you could come up with?" And poor Stan Mars would be sitting there, his knuckles getting whiter and whiter. Later, Stan would come into my dressing room and say, "I'm going to kill that bastard..." And I'd say, "Don't worry, Stan. We're going to do the script as written. It's perfect. And when he hears those laughs he'll change his mind. He's just doing it to wind you up."

'All the time, I was becoming aware of having to comfort a

writer because a comic wanted to show power. The irony was that Rikki wasn't even second top on that bill. It was David Hughes, the pop idol [who had a series of '50s hits, such as 'Till the End of Time' in 1951], who went on to do opera very successfully.'

Stanley was right about the Francie & Josie scripts. The characters were adored and Rikki would go on to form a new Francie & Josie partnership with the genial Jack Milroy. Jack, fortunately, was prepared to push aside his partner's obvious faults and make the act work, allowing Rikki to adopt the superior position.

'Jack realised of course that there was a lot of money in carrying it all on.'

But there were other reasons why Rikki Fulton behaved so badly, not just in the 1950s but throughout his career. He had long-term psychological problems. Rikki revealed in his autobiography *Is It That Time Already?* he had been seeing a psychiatrist since he left the Navy in 1945 and he had an abnormal fear of dying. Not surprisingly. Rikki recalled almost drowning in 1942 when HMS *Ibis* was torpedoed and he spent five hours in the water. He wrote of the nightmares he later suffered, having watched friends die around him.

'I couldn't count the number of legs I saw as they floated in whatever direction the sea demanded.'

He described how he'd tried to climb aboard a raft, only to be punched back into the water by desperate sailors.

Yet, while Rikki didn't criticise Stanley to his face, he played out his bitterness in some very odd ways. He would never allow his second wife Kate to mention Stanley's name in the house. He would insist that she cut all references to Stanley out of the *Glasgow Herald* (his favourite newspaper) before it was passed to him for reading in the morning.

'He was a most unfortunate creature. And we know he was talented. He did some quite wonderful sketches, apart from France & Josie. And he was also a very good writer. Yet, he had bile in his soul. He was a man utterly, utterly without warmth.

'For the sake of the stage partnership I invited Rikki and his wife round to 73 Clouston Street to the dinner parties. But we could never be friends.'

Stanley believes part of Rikki's fight against the world was related to his sexual preference.

'Well, he totally, totally, bottled up his homosexuality. I can remember the chorus boys he chased around the room, and he would later chase my TV producer David Bell around the table, although David wasn't interested.

'Rikki was clearly hell-bent on pursuing gay affairs but then that part of him got totally suppressed. And if you totally suppress these things you pay a terrible price. You are as sick as your secrets. And Rikki made his sexuality a huge secret.'

Of course, Stanley kept his own sexuality a secret. But the two situations, he says, are quite different.

'Keeping something back from the world at large is fair enough but it shouldn't be a secret amongst people with whom you are intimate friends. If you try and kid the whole world – including pals – that you are something you are not, it's going to catch up with you.'

There has to be some shared experience?

'I think so. But the man was clearly so difficult it would be so hard for others to get close to him. And he claimed to be a devout Christian so perhaps that's why he couldn't be honest about sexuality. Anyway, I vowed never to work with him again.'

Rikki never revealed his antipathy towards Stanley to the public. He was professional enough to make sure that the successful on-stage relationship was not contaminated.

Bessie Baxter was thrilled to see Stanley and Rikki work so well together, cutting their great reviews from the papers. Of course, she didn't tell her son this to his face. Nor could she find the time to be kind be kind to Alice, who was set to marry handsome young lawyer Andrew Warwick. Bessie declared she liked Andrew – until she discovered he was a Catholic.

'My mum thought Catholics were wee, snotty-nosed boys,' recalls Alice.

Stanley's support at the wedding meant the world to Alice.

'When we came out of the church, I said to him, "Well, what did you think?" And he smiled and said, "Great theatre. Loved the props."'

Sybaritic theatre managers, egotistical actors, bigoted, demanding mothers... the West of Scotland was closing in around Stanley. And the news that Kenneth Williams had broken into films with *Carry On Sergeant* (playing the 'perfect' part of a toffee-nosed intellectual who resents authority – and picking up a nice fee of £800) provided added impetus. Stanley simply had to go south. The performer arranged a meeting with Stewart Cruikshank.

'I told him I had made up my mind to leave Glasgow and he was very angry. He tried to stop me going, even resorting to threats. He said, "If you go and it doesn't work you can't necessarily expect me to take you back again." I thought, "Oh fuck!" But I had to make the jump. It wasn't just courageous, it was desperate.'

Billy Connolly highlights how worrying Stanley's move south was.

'It is very difficult to move when you are successful. I've had years of it, when you may be famous in the place where you come from, but you go off somewhere else and suddenly you are a nobody.

'You see, there is part of your brain saying, "What the fuck are you thinking about? You're moving out of your comfort zone." And then you're faced with the challenge of trying out new material. Your brain then says to you, "You know this old stuff works. What the hell are you doing being inventive?"

'But Stanley was bold enough to move on. And when my time came to think about that too, in the '70s, Stanley was the trailblazer I had in mind.'

Billy adds: 'I love Scotland. And I love to go back there. But at the same time you mustn't stay there too long. The Presbyterian darkness will get you. In the end it will fuckin' nail you. It gets everybody.'

In November, Stanley began rehearsals for *Mother Goose* at the King's, Edinburgh, with Jack Anthony taking over from the ousted Macrae. The run went well but as the final curtain came down Stanley suddenly felt the incredible weight of the decision he had taken. In the New Year he would be bringing down the curtain on his Scottish variety career. Was he being a trailblazer – or a buffoon?

20

Padding, Tits and Wigs

QUENTIN CRISP ONCE described wartime Britain as 'one giant paved double bed', evoking a world of sexual abandonment. But the London that Stanley was to encounter in the spring of 1959 was more of a narrow, uninviting, cot for one.

Homophobia was fed by post-war austerity, Cold War hysteria, the Burgess and Maclean spy scandals and the appearance of queer-baiting tabloid newspapers. Even drag acts disappeared from the theatres and there were frequent purges of 'queens' from the merchant marines. Gay men fled to Amsterdam, then the most liberal city in Europe, as they had fled to Paris in the 1890s and Berlin in the 1920s.

Although an inquiry had been set up in 1957 to consider changes to the law on homosexuality (precipitated by the case of journalist Peter Wildeblood, who was jailed for 18 months in 1954 after he admitted his sexual preference), it would be ten years before same-sex relationships would be legalised. In short, Stanley was not crossing the border into the Kingdom of Carnal Delights.

'I figured London may offer a little more sexual anonymity than Glasgow. But that was about the limit of my expectations.'

But the move south was mostly about career ambition and in February the Glasgow Dick Whittington stuffed his life savings of £3,000 from the Bank of Scotland into his bag, paid Moira's mum back the £1,500 they had borrowed to buy their Clouston Street flat (with interest) and packed their belongings – and Moira's cat – into the car.

Stanley was journeying in the faint direction of hope but unknown to him he had a Fairy Godmother waiting, in the form of Jimmy Gilbert. In recent years his old Citz pal had enjoyed rapid career success having written a massive West End show, *Grab Me a Gondola*, then moved into television. Now, Jimmy was a producer with the BBC in London – with a remit to make a new satirical TV series, *On the Bright Side*. And when he heard Stanley was leaving Glasgow, Jimmy believed Stanley could not only provide real talent but help develop clever ideas.

'There had never been a successful revue on television before and so I worked on a format,' says Jimmy. 'My belief was a good revue would work, if you had the right people. I knew what Stanley had achieved with *The Tintock Cup*. I knew he was immensely talented and clever.'

When Stanley heard of the offer he was taken aback. It all seemed too good to be true. And Moira seemed happy, loving their new rented home, a swish apartment in Boydell Court, St John's Wood, where porters parked the residents' cars. But had she truly leapt at the idea of leaving Glasgow and friends and family behind?

'Moira didn't ever leap anywhere,' he says softly. 'She wandered, like Ophelia through *Hamlet*, but she would have moved to the ends of the earth for me.'

So too would Bessie Baxter. Denied the front row seat from which she could watch her son's life play out, Bessie was reduced to odd visits to London.

'My mother loved our new flat,' says Stanley. 'It had a chute on a landing that plummeted all the rubbish down four floors. But she had to point out the very trendy but totally impractical black bathroom suite. "Stanley, you can see every hair and piece of soap…!"'

Stanley could cope with soap marks given he was working on a great show with a great cast. It featured Betty Marsden, who had appeared in radio sketch/variety series *Beyond Our Ken* the previous year with Kenneth Williams, Amanda Barrie who would go on to become a *Coronation Street* icon and another young sprite, Una Stubbs, of *Summer Holiday* and more recently TV's *Sherlock* fame. Richard Waring was also in the line-up. And one of the writers (another fantastic talent, suggested in fact by Duncan Macrae) was a man Stanley would come to depend upon, the very clever and often wicked, Ken Hoare. *On the Bright Side* was to be recorded at Shepherd's Bush, but rehearsed in a church hall near Baker Street. Stanley was in his element. The show allowed him to stretch himself in a way variety theatre in Glasgow never had. Not only did he get to work to a clever, skin-tight script but to do impersonations professionally for the first time.

'While I had been impersonating people all my life, at school behind the teachers' backs sort of thing, never professionally. Now Jimmy Gilbert said I could impersonate Sir Brian Horrocks, who fronted a popular show, *Men of Action,* all about brave wartimes heroes.'

On the Bright Side aired on 3 June 1959, 45 minutes of classic live, black and white television and the reviews were great. *The Guardian* writer Nancy Spain appreciated *OTBS*'s clever – and all new – idea of running bits of film, news footage etc, on a screen behind Stanley as he spoke at a podium. 'I really like this Hegelian inversion,' she wrote. Yet while Stanley delighted in the chance to impersonate, he was loath to drag up.

'Stanley never dragged up in all the time he worked with me on the show,' says Jimmy Gilbert. 'And I agreed with his decision. I thought the later London Weekend Television (LWT) shows overdid the drag for him. He has a far better and wider range than the drag suggests.'

Fed up with panto frocks? Emotional scarring from being dressed up as Mae West at the age of seven? Fear of being perceived to be effeminate? 'All of those,' says the comedy actor. In later years, Stanley would organise a post-panto party for the Glasgow cast, his way of saying thanks to his co-stars. And it would always be fancy dress (he loved the idea of actors wearing their own costume choice). But Stanley would never drag up for the wrap parties.

'Usually I would be an athlete or a footballer,' he says, smiling. 'Something as butch as I could think of, in contrast to all that padding, tits and wigs.'

Despite the success of *On the Bright Side*, Stanley took nothing for granted. His life continually revealed sharp contrasts of undeniable confidence and raging fearfulness. And he had moments of worrying he would be 'chased up north again'. The fear was understandable. Few Scots had made the journey south and survived.

Rikki Fulton, talented as he was, hadn't made it in London. Yet, Jimmy Gilbert recalls he was hearing of interest in Stanley from ITV. The BBC at this time didn't have the kudos it developed later and Stanley himself says journalists were asking if he planned to move to ITV and work on a hit series such as *The Army Game*.

Stanley however came to love the capital. While it wasn't a king-sized bed of sexual opportunity, nor was it the little single bed in which he'd once attempted carnality with maid Cathy Scott. He took to finding new friends, thanks to other gay friends. 'But I didn't have so many, gay or straight. There was John Franco, the choreographer, who I sort of got to know socially.'

Homosexuals still had to be ultra-discreet. In June, the Liberace libel trial came to court and the performer won out against the *Daily Mirror*. His very clever lawyer David Jacobs had done his homework. Jacobs knew that Cassandra was legally able to describe Liberace as 'mincing' etc. Although pejorative, it wasn't claiming he was absolutely gay. However, describing him as a 'fruit' was. ('Fruit' was an American slang word for homosexual.) And if Cassandra was claiming Liberace to be 'a homosexualist' (the word used by the judge in court) he'd have to be able to prove it. Cassandra's QC couldn't. Liberace was awarded £8,000 in damages, the equivalent of £500,000 today. But Stanley didn't smile when he read of the result.

'It was a hollow victory. Liberace had had to deny his sexuality in order to win the judgement.'

Meantime, Moira continued to play a supporting role. Looking back, Stanley can't quite believe how inconsiderate he was of his wife.

'I didn't even say to her, "Are you all right on your own all day?" I have to admit I was so obsessed about making it south of the border I never gave it a thought. And when I got home, I'd give her all the news about who-said-what-to-whom, and ask her to take me through my lines for rehearsals and she appeared to be happy enough with all of that.'

Stanley's concentration on his career was at least paying off and several work offers appeared on the table. Two were West End shows, *The Gazebo*, a comedy playing at the Savoy Theatre and

The Amorous Prawn, a musical comedy set to tour Britain and then run at the Saville Theatre. The third, *Two Way Stretch*, was a comedy film starring Peter Sellers, The neat role on offer was that of the Reverend Basil 'Soapy' Fowler, whom we discover is not a man of the cloth at all, but a crafty conman. Of course, Stanley couldn't turn down his first major film offer, playing alongside class acts such as Bernard Cribbins and Lionel Jeffries. But that's exactly what he did. And his part was hoovered up by Wilfred Hyde-White.

'Don't think I didn't think hard about it,' he says, pre-empting the question. 'It was a very important part. But then I figured I would be just one of the many big names.'

Ah, the quest for success was contained by the ego. And fear perhaps. Either Stanley wasn't prepared to be judged up against Peter Sellers or he figured he was good enough for the starring role. He's still not sure of how he truly felt at the time although it's probably more to do with the latter. But there would be many occasions in later life when the Scot would be offered terrific supporting roles – and turn them down flat.

Meantime, he chose to star in the West End theatre production *The Amorous Prawn*, written by Anthony Kimmins and directed by Murray MacDonald, a farce about a general's wife who converts his Scottish HQ into a hotel in order to fleece visiting Americans. Stanley would be playing the very safe – and funny – role of Corporal Sidney Green, a crafty cockney (although the actor decided he would use a Scots accent – not wishing to take too many chances, despite absorbing cockney during his CSE stint). Stanley knew the writing would be strong enough. Anthony Kimmins had adapted celebrated farces such as *While Parents Sleep* and wrote and directed some of George Formby's best comedies. He had been George VI's speech writer, so he clearly had a sense of humour. But there was another reason for picking *Prawn*. The show would be directed by Murray MacDonald, the brother of Citz director Tom Honeyman (the name change, an attempt to accentuate Scottishness).

Stanley was asked to share a stage with Evelyn Laye, known to her friends as Boo. The blonde singer had been a great success on the London stage in the 1920s and in the 1947 movie *GI War*

Brides. Yet, Stanley didn't fear the competition. In fact, the director had asked Stanley to mentor the 60-year-old star.

'Boo was becoming a little forgetful, and she needed extra time in rehearsals. And she knew very little of comedy timing. So I would give her notes."

The actress was happy to take them.

'Listen, Boo. Why are you not waiting for the second laugh? With that line I can get two laughs with the expressions I do.'

'Oh, darling, have I got it wrong? Oh, please tell me what to do.'

'Well, here's what you do – don't speak until I look back at you...'

'When I think of the cheek of it! The Scots comic coming down and telling the great Evelyn Laye she's buggering it up.'

Stanley's gentle chiding however ensured that the pair became close chums and he reckoned the tour that was set to follow the six months in the West End should prove to be great fun.

'I was in a little dressing room next door to her and the wonderful thing about working with Boo was she would knock on the wall and call out, "Darling, come in and meet..." and I'd go in and be introduced to one glorious name after the other, such as Alice de Lissier, and Sybil Thorndike, whom I'd known from the Citz.

'One night she knocked on the wall and Boo called out, "Darling come in and meet Gloria Swanson." I did of course, excitedly, and Gloria was quite ebullient, saying to me "Oh, you were wonderful!" Then turning to Evelyn, she said, "Boo, don't you think he looks like Bill Holden [her matinee idol co-star in *Sunset Boulevard*]."

'Of course, my wee head swelled. And to return the compliment I said, rather stupidly, "You look so much younger than you did in *Sunset Boulevard*." And she replied, with some grace, "Of course I do, darling. I was playing an old has-been in that!"

'Oh dear!'

The Norma Desmond moment apart, Stanley's confidence was growing. And when Murray MacDonald had a slight heart attack, the 33-year-old actor was asked to take over the director's reins. Stanley was delighted to. And it wasn't too much of a stretch. He'd directed in Singapore, and was a virtual director at the Citz during panto time.

'I wish I'd gone on and directed more.'

Although he didn't always get his own way with *Prawn*. When departing resident camp chef Derek Nimmo left the play, Stanley had the idea of bringing in a young Scot, Angus Lennie (who would later find fame as Shughie McFee, the camp chef in TV soap *Crossroads*). But Murray MacDonald, on his return, argued the move was cooking up trouble.

'Murray said that Angus was *too* camp. "Look, Stanley, we've already had too much trouble with Derek Nimmo, who was too homosexually orientated!'"

'And I protested, "But Derek is straight!", which of course he was. Anyway, I lost the battle and Angus was elbowed.'

This episode indicates that London theatre wasn't as gay-friendly as it would become. Yet, Stanley enjoyed the West End success and funnelled £5,000 worth of it into a house in Islington, at 2 Bewdley Street.

Moira liked her new home although she still spent her days 'doing God knows what', until she eventually found work with a local milliner. Outside of work, Stanley and Moira made new friends. Paul Anstee ran a local antiques shop and had several celebrity chums.

'One night, Paul invited us to dinner at his home and he mentioned that "Johnnie Gielgud might turn up". Paul was assumed to be one of Gielgud's lovers, so we sat expectantly through dinner.'

But no sign of Johnnie. Dessert was served and the assembled group looked up at the clock. Then the host suggested perhaps his friend had gone to the cinema. More time passed and it wasn't until coffee was being sipped that the doorbell rang and in walked the absent guest. Acting colossus John Gielgud had indeed gone to catch a movie, queued for almost an hour with the rest of the punters and then just as he was about to buy a ticket the cinema attendant yelled, 'Sorry, house full!'

'Now, you couldn't accuse "Johnnie" of megalomania, could you?'

Stanley was then introduced to the acting great.

'I had already spoken a little bit to everybody else, and he said suddenly, "Oh, you're Scots. Oh, I wouldn't have known that, but then I'm very bad on accents."'

Stanley adds, grinning: 'Perhaps my Percival Steed pronunciation threw him.'

Stanley didn't detect great natural warmth from the acting great.

'That wasn't the first word that springs to mind. He seemed slightly aloof and nervous. Charming, yes, but full of more gaffs than Prince Philip.'

At the end of the year, *The Amorous Prawn* was pulling in great audiences while Kenneth William was soaking up praise for his West End revue show, *Pieces of Eight*. But Williams was far from singing the praises of his camp co-star Fenella Fielding and complained to producer Michael Codrun 'about her lack of professionalism and comic timing'. Was the complaint fair? It's true Williams often complained about his co-stars. Stanley would later decide for himself how easy it was to work with Ms Fielding. But for the moment, he focused on becoming an even bigger star.

21
Kommandant Baxter

IN THE SPRING of 1960, Stanley was delighted to hear a second series of *On the Bright Side* had been commissioned, although it meant giving up the tour of *Prawn*. Jimmy Gilbert said his star couldn't do eight shows a week and then give his all at *On the Brighter Side* rehearsals the next day. Stanley argued the case but surrendered (eventually) to the producer's argument. Jimmy Gilbert was proved correct. In June 1960, both producer and performer were nominated for their first BAFTA, which they won.

An added delight meant Stanley could raise a couple of defiant fingers up to Stewart Cruikshank and to the *Daily Record*. The Scottish tabloid had taken a fairly critical stance since Stanley 'defected' to London – and then committed the most heinous sin of all – using an English accent. One comment piece ran: 'Stanley Baxter would do well to remember how his success came about. He seems to forget he is in fact a Scot.'

'I had decided I wouldn't play any Scots characters for the first two series, to show my range,' Stanley recalls. 'The *Record* hated this.'

But there was another, less obvious reason – even to Stanley – why the actor had jettisoned his own voice. At a pre-recorded interview with Ned Sherrin for BBC radio to promote *On the Brighter Side*, the producer became irate at Stanley's accent continually shifting between English and Scots. 'Can we go again, Stanley?'

'I thought, "You can go as many times as you like and it's still not going to be right." The problem was, I just couldn't do it as myself.'

His voice softens, and darkens: 'Looking back, I realise I just didn't want to be me.'

That was worrying. And so too was the fact Moira hadn't really developed a life of her own. The part-time work with the milliner didn't seem to hold her interest. And Stanley noticed her little eccentricities, her remoteness, her rejection of life's boring rituals of cleaning, cooking, laundry, had become more pronounced. But he didn't tackle the issue.

In the New Year of 1961, Stanley was still all-consumed with work. Theatre impresario Peter Bridge picked up the rights to *On the Bright Side,* with the plan to open in the West End, tour the provinces during the spring and then take the show back to London. But although it opened on Valentine's Day, Stanley and comedy queen Betty Marsden were far from being sweethearts.

'She had become an egotistical monster in rehearsals,' he maintains. 'Going out live on TV she was shitting herself trying to remember the script and that kept her in line. But in theatre it all changed. She had this small coterie of faithful followers who were all faggots. And when the *OTBS* tour began, all these queens came out of the woodwork, supplying her with comedy lines and telling her how to perform.'

Despite the mini-drama going on, Stanley was relaxed enough to surprise the director – and himself – when he agreed to drag up for one sketch, playing a Lady.

'But Betty went up in arms at the very idea of me doing drag. I think she thought I was stealing the spotlight.'

Future *Rowan & Martin's Laugh-In* girl Judy Carne slotted in well to the cast but when Richard Waring moved on, Stanley and Jimmy scouted for a replacement. They had heard good reports about a chubby young man who 'did voices' and after watching just a few minutes of a radio show studio recording they knew they had found their star-in-the-making. The chubby young man was 31-year-old Ronnie Barker. Barry Cryer, who'd written for the TV series, recalls seeing the theatre show.

'Stanley was obviously the star, but he admitted, "Watch out for this one [Ronnie]. He's stealing it all." Stanley spotted it right off.'

Stanley believes Ronnie Barker wasn't just a comic genius.

'In rehearsals, he would whisper an idea in my ear and say, "Why don't you use that line? It will get a huge laugh!" He was a very, very generous man.'

The provincial tour of *OTBS* would include a stint in Glasgow on 27 February – and how exciting was that! The conquering hero could return home with a hit TV series to his credit, bringing the brilliant stage spin-off with him. The Scots fans would worship at the altar of his very being.

Not quite. Sure enough, it was a box office triumph, with the Glasgow public throwing money at their local hero's new show. But they were to be very disappointed with the content.

'The week before we arrived, Rikki Fulton had been enjoying a massive success at the Alhambra with the panto, *A Wish for Jamie.*

'His was a show that could have ran and ran. But Howard &Wyndham took it off because *On the Bright Side* had been booked in. (Rikki Fulton hated having his hit show pulled; another bullet loaded for another day.)

'This resulted in people turning up to the box office to see *Jamie*, told it was Stanley Baxter, assumed it would be the same sort of light comedy thing and eagerly bought tickets. But instead it was this would-be sophisticated and intelligent *soi-disant* theatre, a slightly pretentiously intellectual revue with some very outré musical numbers and sketches.

'I remember one sketch with David Kernan, Una Stubbs and Amanda Barrie walking about under umbrellas, looking really avant-garde and one very bored man in the front row yelling out "Oh, for fuck's sake, do something!"'

Manchester was a little kinder to the show, but just before Newcastle Stanley developed serious throat problems. It was not however (not this time) a little dose of hypochondria and attention seeking, induced by the Betty Marsden friction.

'Kenny Williams said I should go and see showbiz throat specialist Johnny Musgrove. Before I got there Kenny told him I was addicted to a decongestant, Fenox. Then when I arrived at Johnny's office he took my Fenox and threw it across the room into the fireplace, shouting, "I never want you to take that filth again."'

Such drama. Williams loved that tale, which Stanley revealed to his chum later.

'Musgrove then opened my nostrils and burned inside them, boring through bone. I was terrified, but he was so reassuring I trusted him. And it worked. I never took Fenox again.'

The OTBS tour was postponed. Johnny Musgrove told Stanley not to speak for three months. But Stanley had been pestered to do an interview for the *Scottish Daily Express* and he agreed, reluctantly offering up a very croaky voice to Ramsden Grey.

Sadly, it turned out to be the actor's first stitch-up article. Stanley, off the record, confided he'd knocked a couple of years off his age for *Who's Who* (on advice from Boo Laye) and the next day the headline on Grey's page ran 'HOW I LIED TO *WHO'S WHO* BY STAR STANLEY'. The copy underneath made Stanley out to be a vainglorious cheat.

'Nowadays, you expect newspapers to sensationalise but back then, because I had been used to nothing but praise, it was like a dagger through my heart. And I had trusted him.' He adds, with a grinning acknowledgement of his own over-sensitivity, 'I simply couldn't take it.'

By April 1961, the voice was on the mend and Stanley agreed to appear on television in a new sitcom pilot for a *Ten of the Best* series of ideas by two very clever comedy writers, Ray Galton and Alan Simpson. It was a great opportunity given the writers had previously created the brilliant *Hancock's Half Hour*, which had grown from a BBC radio sitcom to a TV series. Kenneth Williams featured alongside Tony Hancock and Sid James, Williams' range of character voices proving to be massively popular.

The actor liked the idea of *Lunch in the Park*, playing a straight(ish) role alongside Daphne Oxenford, who had been the voice of the BBC's *Listen With Mother* – 'Are you sitting comfortably, then I shall begin...' – and an early *Coronation Street* star, playing Esther Hayes. Stanley and Daphne played a couple of civil servants who sat and had lunch. And it was a chance to show he could star in a rather serious role, albeit black comedy. But it didn't work. (One of the ten did catch on, *The Offer*, which would become *Steptoe and Son*.)

'Who'd have believed it? Two men sit about and whinge and it becomes massive.'

Yet, Stanley wouldn't have accepted regular sitcom work had it emerged.

'How could I control the scripts and maintain a standard?' he says, in imperious voice.

The ego was becoming rather more visible. But for the moment Stanley could be choosy, although *OTBS* didn't play well in London. Given the poor reaction to the show during the tour of the provinces, the producers cut away at the rather clever material, leaving the broad comedy. But in jettisoning the clever stuff over the provinces, the revue landed on London's cognoscenti in a rather lightweight condition. The critics hated it.

Stanley's throat trouble flared up yet again. Was this really a severe attack of angst, precipitated by the bad notices?

'Well, maybe. But I was over-using the voice because I had to sing in this show and it was tearing up the vocal chords.'

He isn't convincing at all. Meantime, Stanley went back to specialist Johnny Musgrove who confirmed his condition was, to an extent, psychosomatic.

'Now, look here, chum,' said the throat doctor, 'what you are suffering from is *Globus Hystericus*. It's a hysterical condition which means that if you keep thinking about a part of the body it becomes useless. In fact, this is a condition more common in women than men.'

When Kenneth Williams got hold of the story he reached for his embroidery kit and told his chums, 'Bax is suffering from a condition normally suffered by pregnant women!'

'Kenny added that little bit of spin, just for the laugh. He really was a little bastard.'

Stanley's throat, and his ire, was soothed however when he heard producers from Independent Artists, a subsidiary of Rank Films, were enquiring about him. Julian Wintle and Leslie Parkyn reckoned he would be exactly right for a starring role in a new film, *Very Important Person*. The comedy-drama POW film was a vehicle for the hugely imposing Scots actor, James Robertson Justice, and co-starring Leslie Phillips.

Stanley had been earmarked to play the part of Jock Everett, the aggressive, no-nonsense Scots boy who couldn't stop tunnelling. (It was a part big enough not to pass up; he wasn't going to make the same mistake he'd made with the Sellers movie.) However Stanley feared he wouldn't get the Jock role because he didn't look Scots, all too sadly lacking in pasty face, ginger-hair and bandy legs. Bespectacled with an air of seriousness, Stanley looked, and sounded, like an English university lecturer. (The Caledonian parts would often go to his red-haired Citz pal, Roddy McMillan.) Indeed, from the moment he met with the producers and director Ken Annakin at La Pastoria, a little Italian restaurant off Leicester Square, it seemed Stanley's chance of film stardom were fading faster than a Scottish sun tan.

'Annakin didn't like the look of me. He seemed not to consider I could *act* the role of Aggressive Scots Boy.'

Leslie Parkyn was in Stanley's corner, as was Julian Wintle, but it all looked a lost cause. However, just as Annakin was about to call for the cheque, Julian Wintle revealed something Stanley was to seize upon. Wintle mentioned that Jock Everett makes his escape from the POW camp by impersonating Camp Kommandant Stampfel. Wintle said he had flirted with the idea of having the same actor play the Kommandant and the Scots boy. In effect, the chosen one would also play a third role in which the Scot does an impersonation of the German.

Stanley could barely contain his excitement. Now, he desperately wanted this role. But he didn't show it. Instead he played a bluff and shocked himself in the process. 'Well, I would seriously consider doing this film – but ONLY if I could play both roles.' Annakin was certainly impressed with this young fellow's nerve and offered a shrug by way of approval.

But what Stanley didn't know was the director had a secret plan. When filming began at Beaconsfield Studios, Annakin shot out of sequence; Stanley's first day on the lot saw him dressed up for the role of the Kommandant. What the actor was unaware of was that if his Stampfel didn't look convincing on film, he would be dropped from the project. Annakin was giving himself time to recast. Thankfully, the director watched the rushes and saw his actor was entirely convincing, not only as the German officer but as the young Scots tunneller doing a passable impression of the man. What sealed the part for Stanley though was Annakin wasn't the only man to be convinced.

One American head of Pinewood on a set visit took Annakin aside after seeing Stanley strut around the studio in uniform and demanded, 'Who's the actor playing the German Kommandant?'

'Stanley Baxter, sir.'

'No, I know Stanley Baxter plays the Scot who impersonates the guy. But who is the actor who plays him for real?'

'Stanley Baxter.'

'You mean that's the *same* guy?'

'I was thrilled when I heard that,' Stanley reminisces, 'that's what made it my favourite film.'

On a personal level, Stanley loved working with co-stars Justice and Phillips.

'James was exactly as he appeared on screen, a big personality, larger-than-life with a heart of gold. He had never been on a stage in his life and he said he had no intention of doing so.' (His career began after he was called in as an adviser on falconry for a film about Tudor England. Clearly, producers were captivated by this character when he spoke.)

JRJ was also wickedly funny during the six weeks filming in the summer of 1961.

'In one scene, James is captured by Nazis and has to strip. Stark naked. And the macho crew had a great laugh at this social equaliser, when the great big star reveals his weapon is not as large as would have been expected in such a significant frame. But Robertson took the teasing. And came up with a counter attack.

'"Yes, but what you imbeciles don't understand is the coefficient of expansion!"'

Leslie Phillips was as he appeared on screen: 'A bit of a smoothie. But I liked the man a great deal.'

To Stanley's delight – and perhaps more importantly to Bessie Baxter – it was announced that *Very Important Person* was to have its UK premiere at the La Scala picture hall in Glasgow's Sauchiehall Street. With her son's name in lights, Bessie could now take up her rightful position as the Queen Mother of Scottish Showbiz. It had all been worth it: the late night bus trip to Milton of Campsie church halls, the parental responsibility arguments with Fred, the irritation she suffered listening to Gordon Jackson's mum point out his stream of movie successes. Sonny Boy was coming back home – as a star. Independent Films spared no expense in turning

Glasgow into Little Hollywood for the evening. Meeting Stanley at Central Station was a very large limo which had a very large *VERY IMPORTANT PERSON* banner on top. The Baxter family, sister Alice, cousin Alma and all the aunties, were in raptures.

'Oh, the thrill when I saw this limousine,' Stanley recalls with twinkling eyes. 'And the very idea of going back to my hometown as the star... I was stunned.'

At the cinema pre-screening, Stanley, to his own surprise, made a speech.

'I stood up and said I remembered the days when I'd come here as a child and seen ladies sit at tables with little shaded lamps where they would take afternoon tea and watch the screen.

'I said, "And now, to think that I will be up there on that screen is pretty terrific." I felt really, really proud.'

Moira didn't attend the glitzy *Very Important Person* premiere. Surprisingly, Stanley can't recall the reason for her absence.

'Maybe I had decided it would be better if she didn't come. Perhaps the timing...'

Moira had been prepared to surrender her own identity since the day they first met. And she never asked for it back. Stanley now regrets he didn't bring her back to Glasgow with him but imagines at the time his Brylcreemed head was full only of his own success, wallowing in crits by the likes of the *London Evening Standard*'s Alexander Walker who described the actor as 'the new Peter Sellers'. And who wouldn't be affected when their name is up on lights outside two major London theatres? While The Empire, Leicester Square, showed *Very Important Person*, over at the Phoenix Theatre his name was displayed in giant letters for the final London stint of *On the Brighter Side*. And to top all that, Rank then came in with the offer of a three picture deal, beginning with another Ken Annakin directed film, *Crooks Anonymous*, starring alongside Julie Christie in one of her first appearances, Leslie Phillips and Wilfred Hyde-White. The Scots actor felt he was soaring skyward.

However, during filming of *Crooks* in early 1962, Stanley flew too close to the sun. And his fall to earth was spectacular.

22

There's Nothing Funny About Stanley

STANLEY RECKONED *CROOKS* would in effect become The Stanley Baxter Showcase and open the floodgates to major success. The plotline certainly indicated real fun potential. Gorgeous stripper Babette (Julie Christie) tells her boyfriend and petty thief Captain Dandy Forsdyke (Leslie Phillips) he must go straight or she'll keep her clothes on where he's concerned. And so he enrols in a rehab group, 'Crooks Anonymous'. The head of the rehab group, Montague (Wilfred Hyde-White), informs Forsdyke he will be watched over constantly by his assistant, Brother Widdowes. Dandy does well – until temptation taps him on the shoulder – and the urge for one last big steal becomes too much.

As well as playing Brother Widdowes, Stanley was cast as a series of incidental characters; his eight roles would equal Alec Guinness's famous multi-tasking in *Kind Hearts and Coronets.* Stanley was elated. This was the chance to enter the Hall of Greats, to declare himself the face – and the voices of British comedy. Clearly, Rank Films saw Stanley as having the potential to go all the way. And life certainly looked wonderful. Until one night of madness in Holloway, just a three-minute drive from his home.

To offer context, back in Glasgow Stanley had become part of a small gay theatre fraternity and enjoyed the very occasional frisson this offered, with Moira readily accommodating. But if London *was* starting to swing in the early '60s, he was the last person to feel the motion. Despite achieving fast success, his was *not* a life of Jaguar E-types, coffee bars, Cuban heels or bacchanalian orgies. (The Scot still looked like a time-locked academic with his sports jackets, tidy haircut and wire-rimmed spectacles.)

Stanley certainly had had little opportunity to indulge in sexual dalliances. He worked almost constantly. And fame had come with a price. There were a few coffee bars doted around the capital that catered for gay men. And there were the saunas. Yet, he could scarcely look for kicks in such semi-public arenas where he might be recognised.

As mad as it sounds, when Stanley's sexual antennae picked up signals from the cottaging world (the name based on the cottage house design of the toilet buildings), he deemed the occasional meetings of complete strangers in subterranean public toilets to be his best bet. It was crazy, of course. Just because the partner was a complete unknown didn't mean Stanley wouldn't be recognised. The actor says he didn't find any thrill in the dangers of cottaging itself, as the playwright Joe Orton had at the time. And Stanley knew it was risky to use a public toilet as a pick-up place. But it did offer a brief encounter in privacy. And he reckoned the risk was very slight. Yes, Gielgud and Guinness had been caught out. But Stanley pushed that to one side; that was some time ago. And the arrest of Beatles manager Brian Epstein for the same offence was still in the future. That's not to say Stanley wasn't anxious when he entered the public toilet looking for a quickie, but his libido was overriding his brain.

'A few weeks before the arrest I had taken the chance and gone to these same toilets in Holloway, met someone, gone back to their place and it had all gone quite successfully.

'I was in the mood for something like that again and I went into the public lavatory. But there was no one there.'

Yes there was.

London's 'Finest' were waiting to pounce. As part of a Home Office purge on homosexuals at that time it was deemed the streets – or rather the underground lavs – should be strictly off-limits to those looking for sexual release. British society hadn't moved on since 1533 when the Act of Henry VIII classified sodomy as an illegal act. Stanley had been aware of stories going around at the time of the police slipping powder compacts into men's trouser pockets, to use as evidence they were homosexual. And a few years earlier, police in Edinburgh rounded up suspected gay men, put them on a train to London and told them if they got off and came back they'd be beaten up. But on that fateful Monday night of 15 January 1962, the young actor could not have known the Met were waiting to grab the first gay man who walked into the Madras Place toilets.

'I had gone down the steps and realised I was quite alone in this public lavatory. I stood there in the dark – there was no light in the place – and cursing my bad luck that there was no around. But I was still feeling quite randy and thought I would just have a wank.

'Suddenly, two plain clothes detectives emerged from the darkness and started grabbing at me, grabbing my fly. I tried to put it away and as I did so they told me I was under arrest for soliciting.

'I yelled that there was no one else there! But they told me they were taking me down to the station in Clerkenwell. I said, "I've got my car here. I can drive." The policeman said, "No fuckin' chance. You're coming with us. We'll drop you back at your car." And they took me to the police station where I was fingerprinted and booked to appear the next morning.

'But what I didn't know at the time was that a couple of men had been arrested recently in the toilets and every gay in the area knew to stay away – except me, who was out in Buckinghamshire filming.'

Released from the police station, a distraught Stanley was dropped off back at his car. The two-mile drive home to Bewdley Street was one of the longest journeys he ever made.

'It was horrendous. I cried when I got home. And, of course, I had to tell Moira what had happened.'

As a child, Stanley had never even gone close to breaking the law. Steal sweets from a shop? Not a chance. Tell lies? Never. Stanley's worst crime had been in once telling tales to the teacher about other naughty boys. And the fact he remembered that story shows how it played on his conscience. Fred Baxter's Presbyterian indoctrination had worked wonders; Stanley Livingstone Baxter was not a man to break the law. But then he grew older. And he realised he wanted (needed) same-sex relationships. Yet, he knew it was illegal. He knew every time he met a kindred spirit he was guilty of a crime, of being a homosexual.

The next morning after being charged, the 35-year-old felt his

The wedding of Bessie and Fred Baxter in Glasgow, 1924.

Stanley's beret sets him apart from his cousins, and little Alice in the pram.

Three year-old Alice, who would go on to become a comedy feed, with seven year-old Stanley.

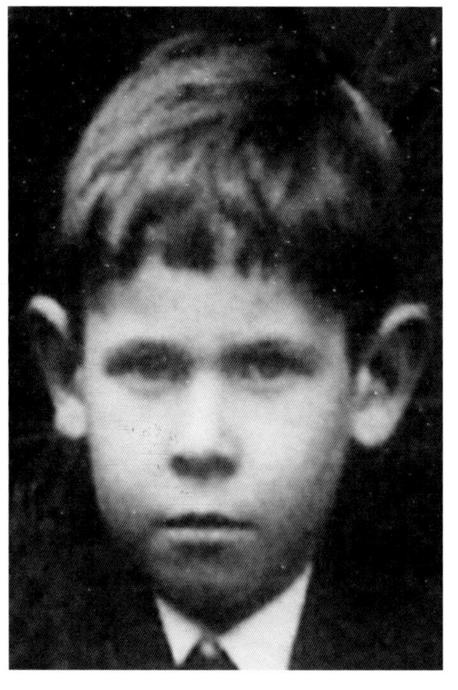

The nervous five year-old is revealed in Stanley's first school photograph at Hillhead School in Glasgow.

The McCorkindale sisters couldn't prevent themselves from dressing up.

The irrepressible Bessie Baxter set to unleash another performance on Scotland's West Coast.

Fred Baxter, insurance actuary and the grounded, sensible voice of the family.

Stanley dressed up to take on North America as part of the *White Heather Tour.*

At the Citizens Theatre in 1948, ready to reveal his talent to the world.

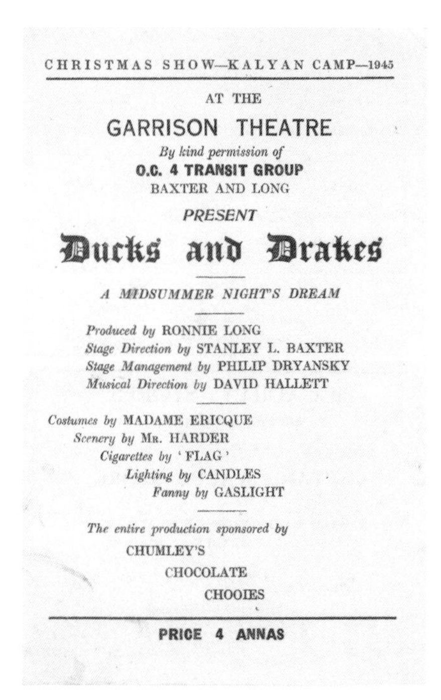

CHRISTMAS SHOW—KALYAN CAMP—1945

AT THE

GARRISON THEATRE

By kind permission of

O.C. 4 TRANSIT GROUP

BAXTER AND LONG

PRESENT

Ducks and Drakes

A MIDSUMMER NIGHT'S DREAM

Produced by RONNIE LONG
Stage Direction by STANLEY L. BAXTER
Stage Management by PHILIP DRYANSKY
Musical Direction by DAVID HALLETT

Costumes by MADAME ERICQUE
Scenery by MR. HARDER
Cigarettes by 'FLAG'
Lighting by CANDLES
Fanny by GASLIGHT

The entire production sponsored by
CHUMLEY'S
CHOCOLATE
CHOOIES

PRICE 4 ANNAS

Stanley's own Forces Production, *Ducks and Drakes*, in Kalyan Camp, India, 1945.

Starring in *Voyage Ashore*, part of the Henry Sherek Season in Glasgow.

Alice's wedding, with her big brother giving her away.

Kenneth Williams returns to Glasgow for some fun time with Stanley and Moira.

Stanley and Moira on honeymoon in London in 1952.

Stanley and Kenneth Williams enjoy one of their happier nights out.

Kenneth Williams and Stanley Baxter in what appears to be a photo-booth picture – the greatest of friends, but a fall-out was never far away.

The cast of radio hit *It's All Yours*, with Jimmy Logan (centre).

Bessie Baxter, Stanley and Alice Baxter celebrate at the premiere of *Very Important Person* in Glasgow, 1961.

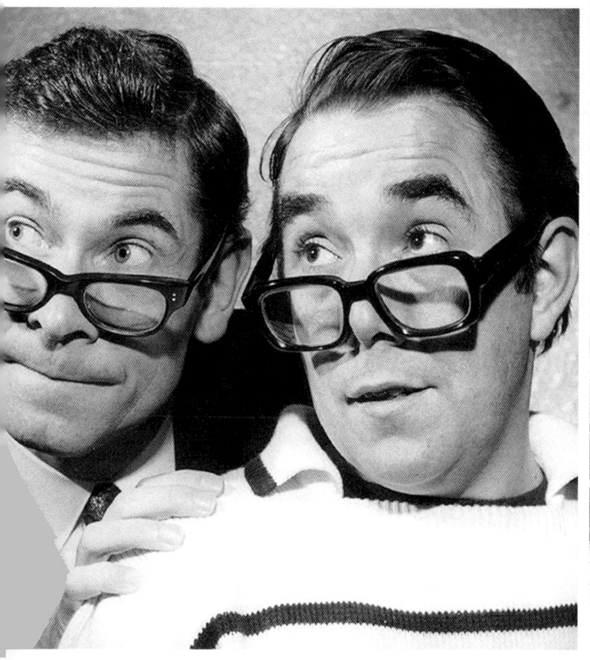

ınd Ronnie Corbett play the Ugly Sisters in *Cinderella* at the King's Edinburgh pictured by Duncan Dingsdale, in December 1967.

Stanley's submarine commander character on stage was never totally convincing.

tanley stars in *Very Important Person* with ›bertson Justice and Leslie Phillips.

ınley and best friend, television director David Bell.

Above: A rather eager to please Stanley meets the wo
he has impersonated so many times at the 50th annive
celebration of BBC Scotland.

Left: Stanley Baxter and Angus Lennie star in *Cinderella*

Happy at home in panto, starring in *Aladdin* as Widow Twankey.

Stanley as George Formby, a chance to have fun with ris

soul leave his body. He wanted to lie down and die. He wanted to be anywhere but in London. But he had to turn up for filming in Beaconsfield, if for no other reason he couldn't wreck the movie's tight schedules. Yes, every nerve end in his body was exposed like bare wires, but he was also a professional. Bessie Baxter had brought Sonny Boy up to believe the show had to go on. The drive via the West End out to Buckinghamshire however was horrendous. The newspaper billboards at Piccadilly stood to attention like the Praetorian Guard of the nation's morals and screamed out 'FILM STAR STANLEY IN MORALS CHARGE'.

When he arrived at Beaconsfield, Stanley was close to tears. But director Ken Annakin had heard the news on the radio and quickly realised immediately he had a basket case on his hands. Annakin helped soothe the totally terrified Stanley by making light of the situation. The director laughed as he suggested the Scot had adopted the role of criminal too readily. It helped a little. And the rest of the cast were entirely supportive. But Stanley knew all too well his career was hanging by nothing thicker than the width of Babette's knicker elastic.

'I thought, "Christ, I'm starting to make it in the business. I've had a hit TV series, a hit theatre show and I'm on my way to becoming Alec Fucking Guinness. Except that I'll be totally fucked. And all because I had to have a night of release."'

If he was to have any chance of survival, Stanley had to find a legal superman who could save the day. Or at least his agent, Ronnie Waters, would. Waters made some calls to the showbiz world and was given the same name by several people. As a result, he recommended his client speak urgently to David Jacobs. Jacobs was the lawyer who had taken on the *Daily Mirror's* Cassandra on behalf of Liberace and won. Ronnie Waters however didn't sing the praises of the top London solicitor. He never thought to mention how successful Jacobs had been in defending other gay men, and in representing stars such as Garland and Dietrich. He simply told Stanley that Jacobs was the man to represent him. Stanley trusted that to be the case. But when he met the solicitor at his offices in Pall Mall, the actor discovered something about his brief that sent a shudder down his spine. It wasn't the realisation the six feet two-inch David Jacobs was gay; at least he could be assured of empathy. Stanley's lawyer wore make-up. And he revealed he also wore it in court.

'The thought of appearing before a jury represented by a brief who looked like Quentin Crisp caused me to quake in my boots.'

Jacobs was an upbeat, ebullient character, but paradoxically this made Stanley more worried. He wanted his lawyer to be seriously worried, to view his case as the most important ever, and *then* to deliver slivers of hope. But Jacobs was jovial, funny in fact.

'I wasn't sure about him at all.'

The pair met and spoke often. But Stanley's fears increased even more when he discovered just about everything about David Jacobs pointed in the direction of Gayville. The lawyer drove around London in a pink and maroon Bentley. The greying hair on his 52-year-old head was dyed black and always coiffed. Jacobs had a list of gay clients and indeed had a live-in male partner. Stanley wondered how Jacobs himself managed to avoid police prosecution, given he was so obviously gay. But for the moment, his concerns, naturally, were for his own survival.

'I thought, "This man is raving. How will he represent me? What do the police, the courts make of this man? Will they be prejudiced against me before I even meet the magistrate?" My worries were building by the second.'

A few days later Stanley made his appearance in court. It was simply to plead his case and the only two words he uttered were 'Not guilty.'

'When I'd gone up to court to plead, David Jacobs told me to say nothing. That's standard advice to all clients. Yet, while the media knew this, the next day the newspaper line was, "During all the accusations the actor stood there and said not one word in his defence."

'It's fair to say I wasn't in love with the press.'

Stanley returned to filming in Beaconsfield and did his best to lose himself in the world of comedy conmen.

'If I hadn't been working, I'd have gone off my head.

Stanley spoke to David Jacobs a couple of times in the weeks ahead, trying to glean some, any little bit of reassurance. David

Jacobs, as always, was upbeat, but without attaching logic to his countenance. Stanley's mood darkened.

A few weeks later, his case came to court. Any fears Stanley had in his head were compounded when Jacobs immediately requested a continuance. Stanley stood in court and panicked, assuming the lawyer had no defence and was simply prolonging the inevitable.

'I was guilty. Not of importuning, because there was no one there to importune, but of being gay. How could I get past that? The police were out to convict another poof and as I walked out of the court, not knowing when I'd have to go back, I knew I was fucked.'

In between times, there were few people Stanley could talk to. He had since lost touch with Jimmy Gilbert and given Peter Nichols was straight, Stanley felt he couldn't chat about the case with him.

'Moira didn't want to hear about it, and what could she say anyway to pacify me? As for Kenny, he would have been sympathetic but he was too negative to talk to. And there was a chance he'd have predicted doom, that I should contemplate the possibility of my career ending, that I was facing oblivion.

'And that's what I was facing. If I were found guilty of a sex charge, been proven to be a homosexual, the film company would have used their Indecency Clause to drop my contract. Television would have kept away from me like I had the plague. My career was over.'

Three weeks later, David Jacobs and Stanley returned to court to fight for his life. It had been three weeks of absolute hell. He slept very little, ate even less.

'I don't know how I got through it. I couldn't drink to ease the fears because I worried I would have ended up a drunk. And I was aware of how difficult this case was for David Jacobs. He knew the police could say what they like and the magistrate would most likely believe them.'

It was true that Jacobs had no real defence, Stanley was guilty of being homosexual, he had in fact gone into the toilets to seek male company. But Jacobs was also as diligent as he was shrewd. After the continuance, he had commissioned a series of photographs to be taken in the Madras Place lavatory, which showed the council building to be in darkness. Bulbs had gone out, it seemed, and the local council hadn't replaced them (or someone had removed the bulbs in recent times and replaced them with broken ones).

Jacobs had two points to make, Stanley recalls: how could the police charge the actor, this much-loved respectable personality, this very funny television star, with committing a sex act with another man when the damp, dingy, mildewed-tiled dungeon of a toilet was empty? Just as importantly, the pictures illustrated that in such a black hole, not only could you not see your own hand in front of your face, you certainly could not see someone else's hand performing a self-gratifying sex act. Jacobs' argument was simple – how could anyone be offended when no one could have seen what – if anything – was going on?

The police had to confirm, extremely reluctantly, there was no one else in the toilet. Stanley's heart heaved and then breathed a sigh of relief. Could he be home and dry? David Jacobs then spoke to the Prosecutors in whispered tones and walked over to Stanley to deliver the result.

'I've spoken to the Prosecution and they have agreed to drop the charge of importuning.'

'What? That's fantastic! A result!'

Tears formed in Stanley's eyes. Tears of joy. This was the moment he had been praying for (even though a devout atheist). And it's as well he was sitting down at the time because there's a real chance he would have collapsed.

'Hold on a minute, Stanley. It doesn't mean you are off the hook.'

'What? But they've dropped the charges!'

'They've dropped *that* charge.'

Stanley's face lost its colour. He lost the will to live. Again.

It had turned out to be a pyrrhic victory. David Jacobs informed Stanley that the prosecution had now substituted a lesser charge of Indecency. London's finest were not prepared to give up without a fight.

This in itself was bad news because if Stanley had been tried on the importuning charge he would have gone on to appear in a Crown Court before a public jury. This sounded even more scary to Stanley, but given the cold facts of the case, David Jacobs had surmised there was a real chance this was the theatre in which Stanley could perform best. As an actor he could have protested his innocence. He could have proclaimed he was not a homosexual, as Liberace had done, which was accepted. And Jacobs could have argued Stanley could not have been found guilty of picking up men in public when it was revealed there were no men to pick up (which explains his confident demeanour throughout).

David Jacobs reckoned the police to be entirely capable of lying in the Magistrates' Court, and said they had spotted someone leaving the toilets. Such was their determination to rid the city of queers they would have stopped at nothing. But would a Crown Court jury take the word of the police so readily, or would they side with this young actor who seemed so likeable, and funny? The prosecution had realised this and backed off on the charge of soliciting. Now, however they were trying to kill Stanley off with a different gun.

He was being charged with indecency, and this lesser charge would be heard by a local magistrate. And Jacobs pointed out that acquittal was extremely unlikely because the local magistrate would most likely side with the local police. It didn't matter that no one but the police saw Stanley about to commit an indecent act in public.

'On hearing all this I thought, "Jesus Christ, I'm finished!"'

Stanley went home and if he felt he'd already reached his darkest point he was wrong.

'It made no difference to me that importuning had been dropped for indecency because I knew the public wouldn't make a distinction. All they would think is Stanley Baxter is a pervert. And I would still have a criminal record for committing an act of indecency, which would stay with me for the rest of my life.'

A life, he reckoned which was now worthless. He admits he thought of bringing it to an end.

'I was going to top myself,' he says, his voice solemn.

'I thought, "My career will never survive this. And if I don't have a career, what do I have?"'

Days dragged on and Stanley's despair worsened. It wasn't

enough to tell himself he had been unlucky, or that the police policy was inhuman, that he'd been part of a witch hunt. Stanley's mind became a silent movie screen that continually displayed one word in giant lettering *GUILTY*.

But then one day, astonishingly, his mood lifted. As the Scot sat in his little office at 2 Bewdley Street he found an inner strength he never even knew existed.

'It sounds bizarre but what got me through was listening to the music from *Gypsy*. I played that record over and over and over again. Somehow, I'm not sure how, it gave me the conviction to keep going.'

What also helped was a growing support system. The cast of *Crooks* became ever closer and Jimmy Gilbert offered to appear in court as a witness for Stanley, citing that he had shared a bed with his pal while on Citizens' Theatre tours and no proposition ever took place.

Back in Glasgow, Bessie Baxter, now living with cousin Alma, was distraught. Here was a mother who had bathed in the glow of her son's achievements for so many years. Now, the glow had turned to toxic radiation as she suffered the sneers from those looking down from the moral high ground.

'My mother had a really hard time,' says Alice. 'Yet she held her head up and if anyone mentioned Stanley she would defend him to the hilt. But overall, it was something that wasn't spoken about. We just hoped it would go his way.'

Stanley didn't speak to his mother during the three months of court appearances. It would have been too painful, too awkward to make conversation about everything but the subject that really mattered.

All Stanley could do was hope that David Jacobs could come up with a solution. The actor and the lawyer spoke often; Stanley had to call almost daily, just in case Jacobs had thought of something. Jacobs would say he was working on the case, to try and remain upbeat and that he was working on a plan. And one afternoon, with Stanley continuing to film *Crooks,* Jacobs called to say he had conceived one.

The plan was revealed on the third occasion in court. The lawyer cranked up his delivery to full Shakespearean levels and suddenly morphed into the young Macbeth about to take on the Thane of Cawdor. Rather than make appeals to the court, Jacobs demanded it be considered that Stanley's legal rights were jeopardised by having his original charge dropped. Losing the right to be heard by jury, he claimed, 'was entirely unacceptable'. He wanted importuning back on the charge sheet.

'When I heard this, I thought he had gone out of his tiny fuckin' mind. Here was my lawyer asking for the original charges to be reintroduced. I began to wonder if this was about showboating and Jacobs simply wanted his day in court.'

The case was again adjourned, but meantime the lawyer went to work behind the scenes.

'A week later, Jacobs called me. As I held the phone my hand shook. There was so much at stake.

'I've taken the Chief London Magistrate to lunch, on the QT of course, Stanley.'

'Well, that's very nice, David. I hope the food was delicious.'

'We had lobster, and a very nice pink champagne, as it happens. But that wasn't best part of it.'

'No?'

'No, I told him you had been the victim of police harassment.'

'Christ, that's a bold approach.'

'I argued the whole thing was a set-up, the victimisation of a celebrity much loved by the public, and the public would indeed see this to be the case. And I maintained the public would condemn the police for taking such action, hounding an entirely innocent man.'

'And what reaction did you get...?'

'I also argued that since the charges were reduced from importuning to indecency, this surely indicated the police were themselves not convinced?'

Stanley listened to Jacobs tell him this and thought, 'This man is either brilliant, or he's madder than the fucking March Hare.'

It turned out Jacobs wasn't in Wonderland at all. The Chief Magistrate deliberated on the lawyer's argument – for a considerable length of time – and then came to his decision. He offered to have the case dropped. No charges. Not importuning, not indecency.

Nothing. Clearly Jacobs' strategy of demanding his day in court to defend the importuning rap had worked. The Chief Magistrate had found the very idea of going up against Jacobs much harder to swallow than his lobster.

But the charges would be dropped with one proviso: that Stanley did not sue the police for wrongful arrest and that he *never* reveal the details of this arrangement to the press.

'Jacobs managed to keep a wry smile from his face when he answered, "Oh, I think I can guarantee that."'

Regardless, the whole horrendous episode still had to be concluded in court. And Stanley was still terrified it would go awry, that the police and the Crown office had something up their sleeve.

When the case came to court on 31 March it proved to be something of a farce. The Metropolitan Police, unaware that their attempts to lock up another pervert poofter had failed, still looked smug in court, despite having no hard evidence. And why shouldn't they be smug? They'd achieved countless prosecutions on their own word. But when the Prosecutor revealed that the Crown (thanks to the Chief Magistrate's intervention) did not wish to pursue charges, their faces dropped lower than the bottom step of the Madras Place toilets.

And that should have meant the curtain closing on this worst episode of Stanley's life. However, Jacobs, almost as great a showman as Liberace himself, wanted a grand finale. Now in his court room theatre he became the full Atticus Finch. The second he heard 'Charges dropped' Jacobs leapt up from his bench and demanded in a full-blown voice: 'Does this mean that Mr Baxter leaves this court without a smirch on his character?'

The local magistrate took a moment and through gritted teeth and a forced smile, said: 'Yes, indeed.'

With total victory in sight, Jacobs pushed on. 'And this means that Stanley Baxter leaves court entirely vindicated and retaining the high character and unsullied reputation he has always possessed?'

'Well, yes... indeed.'

Jacobs knew exactly what he was doing. He knew that every paper in the land would have to print the line Jacobs had demanded.

'David Jacobs was my hero. He found a way to get me off and not go for the cops, which would have been bad.'

Outside the court, the assembled British press asked for a comment from the free man. Stanley's reply was perfect.

'I would hope you give as much space to my acquittal as you did the news of my arrest.'

Back in Glasgow, Alice recalls that Bessie was elated to hear her Sonny Boy had been shown to be innocent.

'She told me that local ladies were waiting in the paper shop as she went in and pointing to the headlines they declared, "There you are, Mrs Baxter! He's innocent! We all knew there was nothing funny about Stanley!"'

But while the London papers all carried articles revealing the acquittal, the headline (with reduced point size) 'STANLEY INNOCENT OF SEX CHARGES' had far less news impact. One journalist Mamie Crichton, even wrote in the *Scottish Daily Express*: 'Well, no smoke without fire', astonishingly, as she was leaving her own newspaper open to libel charges.

Stanley may have escaped jail, or any kind of legal punishment but that's not to say he wasn't penalised. The naturally fearful worrier had spent three months in a state of sheer anxiety, terrified that one mad moment had ruined his life.

Today, he finds it hard to talk about the episode. And when he does, he describes it as *le scandale*. Perhaps by giving it a French farce-like title he's trying to make it all sound distant, more abstract and less serious than it actually was. There is little doubt that if the actor *had* been found guilty his career would have been over. What would he have done? Suicide thoughts apart, he believes it unlikely he could have survived in the business. Yes, Gielgud had carried on after his arrest, but that was in times when the media scrutiny was less fearsome. And he had spent much of his career in the theatre, not in the harsher spotlight of television. Stanley wasn't being melodramatic. Years after his own legal battle, Liberace spoke of the impact on his professional life.

'The court case has cost me many years of my professional career by implying that I am a homosexual… It has caused untold agonies and embarrassment and has made me the subject of ridicule.

'In 1956, people were destroyed by that accusation. It hurt me. People stayed away from my shows in droves. I went from the top to the bottom in a very short time, and I had to fight for my life.'

What Stanley does feel is pretty stupid in that he was not more cognoscente of what the police were capable of.

Interestingly, despite being found not guilty the actor suffered an immediate backlash. Not from the police, as you may expect, who had been thwarted, but from other gay men, not of the showbiz world.

'When walking along the street they would literally take fright when I came into view. They feared guilt by association.'

Yet, the actor had to move on. Ronnie Barker once said the most difficult thing to find in anyone's home was yesterday's newspaper. Stanley simply had to believe that.

23
Spanked Bottoms

PETER SELLERS OFFERED an insight into the mindset of an actor searching for his own identity when filming Billy Wilder's 1964 comedy, *Kiss Me, Stupid*.

'The trouble is you find yourself trying all the time for satisfaction,' he explained, 'and then never really being satisfied with yourself. I suppose that's good for an actor, but sometimes it is awful, like a battle you can never win.'

After filming *Crooks* in the spring of 1962, Stanley found himself playing out his own version of this battle in his own head.

'Having performed those eight characters in *Crooks* my worry was what would happen next? Would my roles be as big? Would I get the chance to shine like Sellers? And would the film companies – and the British public take the view I was toxic, in spite of being found not guilty?

'The added problem was in knowing I was in fact guilty, of being a homosexual.'

At least he had the chance to make an impression, even if the second film in his three-part contract, *The Fast Lady* certainly didn't offer a comedy palette. Anally-retentive civil servant Murdoch Troon (Stanley) falls in love with a car, The Fast Lady, and lovely Claire Chingford, played by Julie Christie. Murdoch, a motoring virgin, has to learn to drive the car in order to convince Claire's frighteningly protective father Charles (James Robertson Justice) he is a worthy suitor. The real star of the film, says Stanley, was the classic 1927 Bentley. (It would later sell for £550,000 to a private collector.)

'Murdoch Troon was just a daft laddie in a kilt. In fact, James Robertson Justice on the first day of filming said to me, "What do you think of this rubbish?" And I said, "It is rubbish, but I think it will be successful rubbish worldwide, whatever you or I think of the script." This was a film about learning to drive and at the time it was an experience everyone was talking about. People could empathise with the beginnings of what has become road rage.'

Stanley didn't reveal his true thoughts on the script to Gordon Hislop of the *Sunday Express*.

'It's the best film part I've had,' he lied through shiny teeth.

Speaking about the love scenes with Julie Christie, Stanley was asked if he would 'become a heartthrob to the mums'.

'Not me! It's not the great lover part, more the dour one. Really, it's a comedy role, such as I played dozens of times at the Citizens,' he replied.

Julie Christie, he says, was less than keen to ride in *The Fast Lady*.

'During filming I noticed she was reading the script for *This Sporting Life*, one of the current so-called kitchen sink dramas, starring Richard Harris, which was being made on another sound stage. Julie announced, "This is the kind of film I really wanted to do." Which was a little snobby considering *Fast Lady* was only her second movie. But we got on fine and she really was incredibly beautiful. You knew she would go on to become very famous indeed.'

To play the daft laddie, producers insisted Stanley look more Caledonian and had his hair coloured with an awful ginger tint to take advantage of the Eastman Colour film.

'It came out an awful shade of orange,' he recalls, with a shudder. 'I had to walk around with a tangerine head for weeks.'

Thankfully, the 95-minute piece was played and directed with such charming innocence that it didn't really matter if Stanley looked like a walking satsuma, or there were a few storyline potholes along the way. The following year would prove Stanley's box office predictions to be correct.

Meantime, after filming the actor enjoyed a real confidence booster when he worked with Peter Sellers for the first – and only – time. Sellers agreed to film an ad for Guinness, to be screened in film theatres by Pearl and Dean.

'It was made by an Indian director and involved the daft story of a man selling a pyramid to his friend. But the director couldn't decide the accents of the two men so Peter and I went through a range of options.'

Stanley would go first with a Welsh or whatever and then Sellers would follow suit or offer Irish. Stanley would then chip in with Home Counties and Sellers would match it. The scene became like two weightlifters in a contest, each lifting a little more than the other.

'It was fun but I remember at one point the director actually suggested we try an Indian accent. Can you imagine that happening nowadays? Anyway, I got out of it saying I couldn't possibly do that because I'd end up doing an impersonation of Peter Sellers doing an Indian accent. Peter glowed at the compliment.'

In the end, the director called a draw on the accent battle and settled for North Country.

'We got on well,' says Stanley of the day's filming with Sellers. 'I'd heard he could be difficult but I didn't find that at all.'

Filming over, in September Stanley and Moira found themselves driving back to Glasgow where he would return to work – in variety at the Alhambra. Why? After all, this was the theatre he couldn't wait to leave behind?

'The timing of the Glasgow offer filled a slot before I filmed the next film. And Dick Hurran gave me all the spiel about how he had built this wonderful new stage setting, and there was only one person they could put on that would appeal in the way that Max Bygraves did. And that was me.

'It was all about ego, I guess, going back home again as the returning hero. But as I drove north, I worried more and more about *le scandale* and worrying if people in my home town would take the Mamie Crichton view. And knowing in my heart of hearts that I was gay, and in the eyes of the law a criminal, didn't help.'

How could he forget? Wilfred Brambell had barely time to pull on Albert Steptoe's fingerless gloves in the classic TV sitcom when he was arrested in a public lavatory in Shepherd's Bush, West London as part of the police entrapment strategy. Brambell wasn't lucky enough to have David Jacobs fighting his corner. In

November 1962, the sitcom star was given a conditional discharge and ordered to pay 25 guineas costs. But the stain of the conviction remained immovable for the rest of his life. The purge on gay men was relentless.

Stanley had to focus on the work ahead. Yet, when he walked out onto the Alhambra stage for rehearsals in what was now labelled The Starlight Room, he stopped in horror. The black velvet, star-studded walls were surrounded by more lights than a Broadway theatre ever used. There was chrome and glitter everywhere. If MGM had designed theatres this is what they would have looked like. Stanley was cast entirely in the wrong movie.

'I thought, "Christ, this is just a great big empty stage. You can't do mini plays with a front cloth, there is no way I can do my old act, there was no way to create a set."

'When I wanted a sketch what they had to do was black out the starry backdrop, run on with furniture and run off.

'Dick Hurran basically fucked the whole *Five Past Eight* comedy idea.'

Hurran was getting full houses – but he was paying stars like Max Bygraves £8,000 a week. It made no business sense.

'Hurran argued we were playing to capacity. But we always used to play to capacity anyway. And now these seats cost so much more. Plus, there was a limit to what Glaswegians could afford.'

Stanley was also faced with difficult choices to make about his act. Drag guaranteed laughs but in the wake of the accusations of homosexuality, could he risk it?

'I thought about cutting drag out but reckoned that would be a confirmation that I was scared.'

Despite the set difficulties, the audience reaction was great and the crits, overall, were good. Except for one. Stanley subscribes to the Orson Welles' view on crits: 'Every actor in his heart believes everything bad that's printed about him.'

And to this day the wound made by that single bad review hasn't healed. Jack House of the *Evening Times* wrote: 'Dickie Henderson has left us and his place has been taken by the prodigal son.[15] He is very funny in his own mind.' The critic noted: 'Stanley did a couple of female impressions too many.'

Stanley believes, like Billy Connolly, that Scots critics prefer their performers to flop in London and come back with their tail between their legs.

Regardless, the Glasgow variety reprise proved to be eight weeks of sheer stress. Yes, he got to touch base with a few friends and see Bessie, but what if a former lover had come out of the woodwork and spoken to the newspapers? He felt he'd been tempting fate. The stint over, Stanley was relieved to get back to London and lose himself once again in a corner of Beaconsfield.

The next film in the contracted deal was *Father Came Too*, which charted the adventures of a pair of newlyweds doing up an old house. James Robertson Justice starred (again) as the father-in-law from Hell, Sir Beverley Grant, who shatters the bliss of newlyweds of Dexter Munro (Stanley) and his bride Juliet, played by Sally Smith.

'It was supposed to be Julie Christie in the female lead but we lost her to superstardom.' (Julie had been 'stolen' by old pal John Schlesinger and whisked off to make the deliciously dark comedy-drama, *Billy Liar,* released in 1963.)

Stanley enjoyed working with pals Ronnie Barker, who played work-shy workman Josh, and Leslie Phillips, as sneaky estate agent, Roddy Chipfield. And Stanley made a new chum in Cardew Robinson, as the fireman. But the script proved to be as robust as the house's fake exteriors.

'The subject wasn't as universal as *The Fast Lady.* [Not quite zeitgeist then, perhaps]. But it had its moments, thanks to a wonderful performance by Ronnie.'

Stanley regrets not getting to know Ronnie Barker better.

'I think the gay/straight thing sort of came between us. I was married but hadn't come out and that meant you couldn't become intimate with someone who was straight and not a close pal. But we got on very well.'

Stanley's antennae had picked up correctly his chum wasn't entirely comfortable with the notion of same-sex relationships. In Barker's authorised biography, writer Bob McCabe quotes Ronnie, who is talking about a friendship with actor Glenn Melvyn as saying:

> With Glenn it was a very strong friendship. Without a hint or a whiff of any sort of homosexuality! That frightens me, homosexuality. I'm appalled. I would be disgusted at it. I'm quite happy for it to go on around me, but if someone said something to me, I would be appalled.

So there.

Ronnie may well have been 'appalled' at a running gag in the *Father Came Too* storyline. It called for the ebullient James Robertson Justice's character to pull back the bedclothes and spank Stanley's striped-pyjamaed bottom, by way of an early morning alarm call. JRJ hated the storyline. 'This is too much like homoeroticism for me,' he bellowed. For the record, Stanley wasn't keen on that part of the script either. And overall the film was a dud. Still, at the end of 1962 the actor could at least wallow in the great notices he picked up for *Crooks*. Then the December release of *The Fast Lady* added to the Christmas glitter.

'Stanley is spot on with his gormless comic style', said the *Radio Times*.

The Great British Public clearly had not let *le scandale* stop them queuing up at the movies to see the funny Scot. And this success certainly bolstered Stanley's fragile state. Although, as events would prove, not nearly enough.

24
Dick Swap

STANLEY'S WRONG MOVE in returning to Glasgow was one of a series of career howlers he'd make over the years. In April 1963, he accepted the lead role in theatre show *Luv,* the story of two old pals who meet on a glistening bridge, listen to each other's woes about their lives and partners – and determine who will jump off first. *Luv,* running at the Arts Theatre, was just what Stanley didn't need. Not only was it a stark reminder of his incompatibility with Moira, he would be playing an angst-ridden soul who's miserable on stage for two hours every night. Plus matinees.

To compound his problems, eye-fluttering, raven-haired Fenella Fielding (later dubbed the 'mistress of double entendre') was cast as his girlfriend. A secretary in a London theatrical agency just a few years earlier, Stanley wished she'd stayed with the typing pool. The future *Carry On* star, as Kenneth Williams had discovered during *Pieces of Eight*, would stay under the spotlight 'till she suffered radiation burns'. Stanley didn't like the idea of being upstaged at all. And he had no idea Fielding's talent was such she would one day be praised for the eponymous role in Ibsen's *Hedda Gabler*. The seductively-voiced, outrageously camp Fielding, he felt, was 'just too big' on stage.

So why choose *Luv* in the first place? The trade papers revealed Beaconsfield was to close, with Independent Artists Productions running out of backing. And its umbrella organisation Rank Films didn't beat a path to Stanley's door to extend his contract. A residual effect of *le scandale*? Very likely.

But there was also a shift in public preference. Light comedy/ farces had lost their appeal. (*Luv* was a dark comedy.) And earthier dramas were now in vogue: the British kitchen-sinkers such as

Billy Liar, directed by John Schlesinger, and a new wave of writers, novelists and playwrights had emerged in the '50s who came to be labelled 'Angry Young Men'. The likes of John Osborne (*Look Back in Anger*) and Alan Sillitoe (*Saturday Night and Sunday Morning*) reflected both a post-war sense of resentment of austerity, a real feeling of abandonment and a belief that change had to come about. The heroes of these novels, plays and films demanded far more from life than a mind-numbing factory job and a Saturday night beer session. The protagonists wanted rock 'n' roll music, a car and a decent life.

The new wave of films was also informed by the political backdrop: the Cold War induced threat and fear caused by the prospect of nuclear war, as evidenced by the Cuban Missile Crises and John F Kennedy's assassination. And the purge on homosexuals.

This new film genre was about as far removed from Stanley's talents as it was possible to go. Julie Christie had seen the writing on the wall. Now, Stanley simply had to make the most of the *Luv* he hated.

'The play itself was complicated but to compound matters, Fielding would speak total shite about the so-called "method". What she wanted was to be centre stage. "Up with this I'm not about to put," I thought.'

He didn't. Despite having nothing else to go to, Stanley decided the Arts Theatre stage wasn't big enough for both of them and was out of there faster than Nathan Detroit could sing 'Sue me!' But the newspapers were fed a different line.

'STANLEY BAXTER SUFFERS NERVOUS BREAKDOWN' ran the next day's headlines.

'Later, Fielding suspected my reasoning and called me up, saying [affected voice]: "Darling, it wasn't because of me, was it?" And I said, "No, of course not," because I didn't want *that* getting into the press.'

Stanley hadn't had a breakdown, but he was certainly troubled, still worn and torn by *le scandale,* and he resorted to anti-depressants.

'They made me pee a lot. And I got off them as soon as I could. I had seen what could happen to people who took drink and drugs.'

A worried Kenneth Williams believed Stanley had been damaged considerably by the demands of Ms Fielding. He rang Moira and was told Stanley was on 'special pills' and 'under doctor's orders, and seeing no one.

Stanley had taken himself off to the Surrey countryside to convalesce, to find calm. But one afternoon he agreed to see Jimmy Gilbert. Jimmy had been working on a new TV series with his current golden boy, Dick Emery, but Dick had taken the huff and walked out.

'I'd heard Stanley had a bit of a breakdown but took the chance and called to see if he was interested in taking over from Dick,' recalls Jimmy.

'He seemed well enough and wasn't at all keen on all that "boring green grass" of Surrey. He was clearly fit to come to work.'

In a bizarre role swap, Stanley took over Emery's part in the Jimmy Gilbert production while Dick teamed up with Fenella Fielding in *Luv*.

'I suppose it was all a bit weird when Stanley and Dick swapped with each other,' said Jimmy. 'But then *Luv* flopped and Dick came back to work in television.'

Stanley's return to work with Jimmy resulted in the fortnightly three-parter, *The Stanley Baxter Show*. Transmitting in May and June 1963 it was a huge success, although such was the star's troubled spirit and 'bad nerves' he never fully appreciated his return to the television spotlight.

'I can't remember too much about it, except that it featured a series of topical gags and I would get to voice a range of characters, such as newsreaders or ordinary people in the street. And it gave me the chance to perform different regional accents.'

He did however enjoy the chance to work with old Citz colleague, 'the lovely' Joan Sims.

'Kenny liked her as well. You couldn't not like Joan.'

Joan would come to lunch with Stanley and Moira at Bewdley Street. However, one comment she made to Stanley later in private caught his attention. Joan thought Moira was 'a bit funny', that there was 'something odd about her behaviour' she couldn't quite put her finger on.

Kenneth Williams meanwhile finished his run as Private

Detective Christoforou in Peter Shaffer's *The Private Ear and the Public Eye* at the Globe Theatre. The one-act comedy dramas were a major success and Williams considered it to be his best performance on stage. Maggie Smith sang the praises of her co-star: 'Kenneth taught me how to recognise the one word in a sentence which would turn it from a commonplace statement into something wildly funny.'

The play made stars of them both. And not surprisingly, the producers announced plans to take the show to New York.

Williams refused to go: 'I feel like Dr Johnson. I suppose it may be worth seeing, but not worth going to see.'

As fate would have it, Stanley was offered the Williams part. It was a fantastic opportunity for the Scot, at the age of 37 (and underemployed) to star on Broadway, to make his mark in New York theatre history. The music of *Gypsy* almost began to play in his head. Almost. He turned it down because his pal had already turned down the Manhattan transfer. Ego?

'I was a fool not to go. It was a major mistake.'

Still, new work offers did come in. Stanley leapt back in time to play Boswell to Roger Livesey's Dr Johnson in an episode of an American television spy anthology series, *Espionage*. The fee helped pay for a house move.

In the New Year of 1964, Stanley and Moira sold up in Islington and switched to a new, larger home in London's Highgate, at 18 Shepherd's Hill. The house was set over three storeys and had a lovely big garden. But it also had four sitting tenants in the top floor bedsits – who had to bypass Stanley and Moira's living room. Stanley relented to their pleas not to be evicted – and had to endure the trail of visitors who would come through his front door.

'We should have thrown them out and said, "Tough tittie!" The £4 a week they were paying hardly made a difference. But we didn't.'

He had other things on his mind. Bessie Baxter wasn't slow to point out that Gordon Jackson was currently starring in Hollywood film *The Great Escape*. (Stanley didn't watch John Sturges' prison camp classic until 2004 – a little peeved he hadn't been offered a Scots role, which Gordon had, and little Angus Lennie landed the part of Jock 'The Tunneller' Ives. But when Stanley did watch it, he declared it 'fantastic'.) And such was the success of the television three-parter, the BBC offered Stanley another showcase series, *Baxter On ...*, a six-parter going out fortnightly in which he took a look at a different subject each week: travel, television, law, theatre, class and films. The offer certainly helped to push *le scandale* a little further to the back of his mind. But there was another worry to contend with.

During filming at Ealing, Stanley realised Moira's behaviour was becoming increasingly odd. He had come to appreciate she would never rival Katie Oxo (the matriarch of the TV stock cube ad family) for homemaker of the year but almost all efforts to keep domestic life together had gone down the pan.

'I would come home at night from rehearsals, all wound up from the day, and I'd find I'd have to put my hand in a basin of dirty water to get a cup just to make some tea.

'I would say to her, "Darling, I'm not asking a lot. But could you just sort out some stuff for me when I come home?" And she would smile and look at me in agreement but not registering the importance of any of it.

'The problem of course had been building up for years. But now I simply couldn't cope any longer. It was then I thought I'd have to find a place of my own to live.'

Alice recalls that at 37, Moira's mind was not on chores at all, it was on having a baby.

'She never mentioned that to Stanley, though. She reckoned Stanley's needs came first.' (Not his domestic needs, perhaps.)

Stanley didn't pick up on the maternal signals. Why would he? And while sex between the couple was extremely rare, Moira still used birth control pills.

'I look around today and think it would be nice to have had children and grandchildren. But at the time I was so self-absorbed. And of course, what sort of parents would Moira and I have made?'

Total absorption in the highly impressive series of *Baxter On...* paid off and Stanley's creative input flow was aided by vibrant new writers such as Marty Feldman and classy co-star June Whitfield.

The critics loved this clever contemporary take on the world, which illustrated wonderfully that Stanley had the wit and talent to become a television luminary for years to come.

But the BBC sacked him. Management simply deemed the series had been too costly to make.

'We used lots of feature film inserts and split screens which cost a fortune and the process was actually more expensive than making feature films. And then there was the issue of outdated work practices.

'For example, the actors would sit there in make-up waiting while the sparks and cameramen all trotted off to the canny for a three quarters of an hour tea break. As a result we didn't get the hours in and it was all too bloody dear.'

This was the first of several firings in Stanley's life due to the high production costs of his shows. And on each occasion, he felt drained and abandoned.

As a spirit-lifter, he took off to Amsterdam with Kenneth Williams for a July break. It proved to be a disaster.

'It was pissing down with rain for a start as we went around Arnhem looking at the sights. But I had made the mistake of booking us into a gay hotel, thinking that would please him. Well, it didn't, for there were people coming in screaming at night and he hated the noise and all of it.

'I wasn't mad about the place either so when I woke up on the Monday morning – with the sun now shining – I went round to the Rembrandt Hotel and booked us into two rooms. And when I got back, I rang him up, feeling all pleased. "Right, shall we go for coffee?" And we did.

'And I said to Kenny, "Look, I've got good news. We're out of that nasty, faggotty hotel and we're into a respectable place."'

'Well, yes, and I hope you'll enjoy it. I'm leaving! I've booked my ticket home. I'm not staying here a moment longer!'

'I felt like drowning him in one of the canals. And I spent the rest of my time on my own.'

Once the Williams portcullis came down there was no lifting it.

'Kenny was becoming harder to deal with. And with incidents like this, friends simply stopped seeing him, which probably didn't help his mental health.'

An entry in Williams' *Diaries* the previous year highlights his singular way of thinking: 'Of those people who want sincerity and trust! How perfectly dreary they all are. And how untalented.'

Stanley and Kenneth were clearly very special friends, but such was their own demands of people – and of course each other – it was inevitable they'd fall out almost as soon as they'd meet. And while Williams' mind was fragile, Stanley's was hardly A1.

The Joe Meek story was a reminder the Sword of Damocles was still hanging over Stanley's head. Meek, the producer of 'Telstar' (the worldwide guitar tune hit), was caught by the Met police while cottaging in the same Madras Place toilet that had nearly been the downfall of Stanley. With a couple of co-sinners, they had had to walk half a mile in single file to Caledonian Road police station where they were registered as homosexual persons. Worse was to come. The subsequent newspaper stories led to extortion demands from those claiming to have 'known' Meek. Ironically, as heterosexuals enjoyed a liberalisation of sexual attitudes, gay men were ever more fearful. Stanley didn't give up adventuring, he found it impossible, but determined he would now seek occasional gay company in private saunas.

His main focus however was on work. But where? The BBC had let him go. At this time Independent Television was not an option; it had neither the production values nor the kudos. The Scot was becoming despondent. A couple of hours at the cinema to see *Mary Poppins* lifted his spirits for just about that length of time. However, just as Stanley was getting over Dick Van Dyke's dodgy accent, his agent called with some great news. It was an offer to star in what was hoped would become a classic British film, playing alongside a top cast plucked from television, including Reg Varney and *Steptoe* star Harry H Corbett. The movie, *Joey Boy*, said Ronnie Waters, could be the platform on which Stanley could rebuild his film career. Stanley prayed Ronnie Waters was as clever at reading film scripts as he was in choosing legal representation.

25
Loving Sydney

THE FILM OF THE YEAR in 1965 was John Schlesinger's *Darling*, a daring, sexy send-up by Stanley's chum of Swinging London, starring Julie Christie. Right behind it in terms of thought-provoking screenplays was plane crash classic *Flight of the Phoenix*, starring another colleague and friend, Oscar-nominated Ian Bannen.

Joey Boy, sadly, was a long way away from either. Set in wartime Britain, the screenplay featured Joey Boy Thompson (Harry H Corbett) in a daft tale about spivs who set up an army social club – which turns out to be a knicker elastic's width away from being a brothel. Stanley starred as Benny 'The Kid' Lindowski.

'The combined talents of TV comics Harry H Corbett, Reg Varney and Stanley Baxter are sadly wasted in this fitful film,' said the *Radio Times*.

Stanley agreed with the crit.

'I knew as soon as I began filming that it would be pretty disastrous but I really had to be busy at that time. I even tried desperately to have the film rewritten but failed.'

The consolation prize was the all-male cast got on well together.

'Harry was a nice man. Very easy to work with, and he took acting very seriously.'

The British public in the mid-'60s were now in the mood for racier, sharper comedy, highlighted by the success of Williams' new radio revue show, *Round the Horne*. Stanley's pal was fast gaining infamy – to paraphrase a line from *Cleo* – thanks to a series that featured two camp characters Julian and Sandy (Williams and Hugh Paddick), who spoke in double entendres and polari.

'I couldn't believe my ears when I heard it. They were speaking the language of the queens in Singapore – and getting away with it.'

What the hip, cool British public weren't ready for however was Joe Orton. In February, Kenneth Williams appeared in Orton's play *Loot* at the Arts Theatre alongside Ian McShane, Geraldine McEwan and Stanley's one-time stage partner Duncan Macrae. (Williams waspishly described the latter as 'startling'.)

However, the pre-West End tour show closed after six weeks with critics complaining about its outrageous content and poor construction. Orton would improve the play, and public sensibilities would change. Years later however, Stanley would still regret not paying attention to Williams' woes about appearing in an Orton production.

Meantime, Stanley's spirits lifted when offered the lead role in *The Confidence Course*, Dennis Potter's first television play, appearing alongside Dennis Price and Yootha Joyce.

'I got to meet Dennis Potter beforehand and he struck me as being frighteningly intelligent. He was nice enough, but a very serious type and not overly friendly.'

Stanley played a strange, oddball character called William Hazlitt who attacks the claims of the confidence tricksters.

'I loved doing that play,' he says purring with delight at the recall.

'When I had to play absolute straight characters in plays, such as commanders on submarines and stuff I was pretty rotten; I guess I was standing outside of myself laughing at me. But *The Confidence Course* called for me to play a neurotic and strange creature. This I could really get to grips with.'

But the dramatic role was a false dawn. Casting directors never asked to see Stanley's neurotic or strange again. Indeed, in the summer of 1965, he seemed to be cast in the role of Forgotten Man. Perhaps some casting directors were still affected by *le scandale*. Perhaps they simply didn't know what to do with Stanley. He wasn't a natural leading man in the Alan Bates or Albert Finney mould, nor was he a natural clown like Ronnie Barker. Peter Sellers and Alec Guinness had captured the chameleon roles and Stanley wouldn't do sitcom.

'I seemed out of synch with the time, where the Beatles and the cheeky *Carry Ons* were in vogue. I didn't have long hair and a silly grin on my face. My favourite films were in the '40s.'

He adds, 'You know, maybe the '60s swung for the likes of Julie Christie and Twiggy and Terence Stamp, but not for me.'

Stanley's sexuality continued to haunt him. And while the current television play *Horror of Darkness* was an indicator society was moving, to a certain extent, in the right direction, Nicol Williamson's character tells another man (who is straight) he is in love with him. The play ends however when the gay man slits his own throat.

Just when Stanley was reaching the point of despair, his agent called.

'I got an offer from Brian Rix to take over from him at the Whitehall in a farce called *Chase Me Comrade,* and then to tour the show in Australia in the autumn.'

Stanley hated farce ('the silliness of it all') but it was work, a chance to see Australia and, he admits, a chance to live something of a gay life again. Moira, as always, accepted his decision.

'Anybody else would have gotten rid of me but she was devoted. Fixated.'

He says Moira was becoming more neurotic at the time. But it's only now he realises going off to Australia most likely made her worse.

Stanley, however, was thinking of escape, and fun. When he arrived in Adelaide, where the show opened, his eyes opened wide.

'I thought, "This is bizarre! What are these cosy people doing in this vast island, where it all looked like 1930s Britain." It was more old-fashioned than Glasgow when I was growing up.'

The crowds were half decent, then on to Melbourne to a poor reception. 'Before setting off I was asked if I wanted to direct the show and I should have said yes, because the bloke who did was a complete cunt.

'But the Aussie cast were great, so chip-on-shoulder in some ways, but so nice in others, and we had some great laughs. And although I was depressed about the poor houses, I thought, "Never mind. At least I'm away from all these bloody journalists and reference to the court case." I was anonymous, although still the star of the show.'

Opening night in Sydney however was a resounding success.

Suddenly, Stanley's decision to break from life and feel the sunshine on his face looked to be the right one.

'I loved Sydney Harbour, the beaches. And I stayed right at Bondi Beach, in the front half of a wee villa where I could see right out across the bay. And I hired a little car to drive up to the Theatre Royal on Castlereagh Street.

'I just loved the city to the point I thought of buying a house at King's Cross, so it must have made a real imprint, a real sunshine dream.'

And then the thunder clouds rained down. After the Sydney opener, which, it transpired, was full of exiles, nobody turned up. The Aussies hated farce as much as the Scots.

'To add to the pain of empty houses, I came to learn Australia just wasn't a place for an actor to be. The money was rotten – I couldn't believe how bad, and the management was so anti-Equity. I felt it was a great pity because if it had been a bit more like Hollywood I would have been tempted to move there.'

A grace note was that Australian culture wasn't half as butch as he'd expected. In a letter to Kenneth Williams, Stanley wrote, 'The gays and norms mix easily enough. And when they are punching each other with exuberant mateyness it's often difficult to tell which is which.'

However, another letter to Williams in October – where he attempts to comfort his depressed pal – indicates Stanley's own soul was not in good shape. Living a constant lie was a heavy weight he was struggling to carry:

> Well I've been along the road you are travelling now and nobody knows better than I how awful and nightmarish it is imagining a sort of total destruction of one's whole personality.
>
> You have awful sick thoughts or at least I did, of becoming a thing instead of a human being. Be of good cheer.
>
> Love, Stanley.

Williams had been appearing in a poor play *The Platinum Cat* and needed a break badly. He called Moira for Stanley's number and Stanley agreed to break his return journey and meet his friend in Beirut. Williams was joyful at the prospect of seeing Stanley.

'Cable from Stanley. He arrives Xmas morning, 9.35. I must meet the plane. He is wonderful.'

The holiday was less than wonderful. The pair 'didn't meet any interesting people' and felt they were being ripped off. 'Kenny complained the whole time,' says Stanley.

Williams was filming *Carry On Screaming* at the beginning of 1966, which was entirely appropriate because his *Diaries* for 12 January reveal a drama queen at his best:

> It is with brutal acceptance that I acknowledge Stanley Baxter's ignoring of me since the return from Beirut. I have telephoned etc but nothing. Now that I look back on it I can see no intellectual justification for thinking Stanley was the *one friend* who could help me in that last crisis.

Oh, the ingratitude. Stanley had been prepared to break his journey to cheer up his chum in Beirut, but that meant little as far as Kenneth was concerned. Again.

Yet, travelling back to London, Stanley was in a happier state than he'd been in the summer. Yes, the show had been a failure but he'd had the chance to see and enjoy Australia and felt he had gone some way to taking his friend out of his malaise.

But on arriving at 18 Shepherd's Hill, Stanley was met by Moira – and something of a shock.

'I supposed she'd gotten used to me being away because I'd done the three-month tour with *The White Heather Club*. But when I came home, I discovered Moira had kept all of my correspondence. Every single word. I thought, "Oh my God. Does this woman have a real problem?"'

Stanley could see the signs of a depressed woman.

He was right to panic. Moira's problems would become much worse.

26
Arse Banditry

STANLEY WAS ABLE to push the Williams ingratitude behind him (a little) because just before leaving Australia, Scottish Television producer Francis Essex had called with the offer of a one-off TV special.

'Going back to Scotland seemed like failure after what I had done in London but I reckoned I'd do my best.'

The return meant Moira could be with family again for a few months. Stanley hoped that would improve her mood. And, of course, Bessie rejoiced to see Sonny Boy back home, especially with Alice having emigrated to Africa. Now 76 and living opposite cousin Alma in Melrose Gardens, Bessie had been showing signs of ill-health. Years of defiant smoking had resulted in emphysema. Stanley was rather taken aback when he arrived back in Glasgow to see how his mother had aged.

But his focus was on work. *The World of Stanley Baxter* was to be a platform; he'd let London know what it was missing out on. He even surrendered to drag (having realised his female characters were a gags guarantee) and produced a new creation, the pushy and aspirational lower middle-class lady Rosemary Gusher, clearly a creature from Bessie's afternoon tea brigade. But the TV special was to produce more than a clutch of funny characters. Stanley began a 'wonderful' friendship that was to spill over into a massively successful TV partnership.

The floor manager on the STV show was David Bell, a 29-year-old with dark, film star looks, clear ambition and a great eye for television. Bell had grown up in the Borders in a mill family but when Scottish Television opened in 1957 he banged on the doors desperate for a job as a trainee cameraman. David Bell was a popular, likeable man who disappointed only the legions of women who fancied him rotten. David was the boyfriend of Stanley's old dance pal, Bruce McClure.

'David and Bruce became a couple one day when Bruce worked on a show at STV. David was up on stage talking to one of the cameramen who nudged him and looking in the direction of Bruce said, "See that fella down in the stalls?"

'Yes.'

'Well, just watch yourself.'

'Why?'

''Cos' he's an arse bandit.'

'Well! I had no idea!'

Now he did.

'The warning actually served to switch on the light of possibility in David's eyes and within a couple of days he and Bruce were a couple.' (Perhaps the cameraman hadn't noticed that David would suffix most of his sentences with the word 'dear'.)

Bruce introduced Stanley to David and the pair hit it off immediately. David Bell was exactly what Stanley needed in Scotland at that time: an intellect, a real talent with a special grasp of entertainment and a great friend. The producer also had a wicked sense of humour and was hugely ambitious. It was no surprise to anyone when he soon moved a couple of miles west along the road to the BBC to work as a director. This was fortuitous for Stanley.

Soon after his station switch, David called Stanley to inform his pal he was putting together a TV showcase *Six of the Best*, featuring the top Scots comedians. Would Stanley be interested in making a show to be screened alongside the efforts of the likes of his old pal, Jimmy Logan?

'I said I'd like to do one of them *if* I could do what I did with the BBC in London and had film facilities, so I could film myself playing different parts. Of course, it was very difficult back then on camera taking two separate shots and joining them together because you never knew until the next morning whether you had a line down the middle or not.'

The challenge was to make film-standard television without cinema-high budgets.

'I've got a brilliant idea, dearie!' said David. 'The BBC's old Black Cat studios are empty now Auntie [Kathleen] has moved along the road, but the former cinema still contains the original gantry, lighting and other vital TV equipment.

'We'll re-open it!'

And with the boundless enthusiasm of a young Cliff Richard in coffee house 'let's-put-on-a show!' 1959 musical *Expresso Bongo*, Glasgow's own Bongo Herbert added, 'This will be our very own Culver City![16]

Without the union tea breaks Stanley had experienced at Ealing, and with David and Stanley carrying out most of the camera/directing work – and the fact the building rates were next to nothing – production costs were kept to a minimum. The pair worked sublimely together, although their relationship never became overly personal.

'We were good mates,' says Stanley. 'Anything more would have spoiled that.'

Not surprisingly, their effort was chosen by BBC Scotland management to be the best of the *Six of the Best* showcases. And the prize – unknown to the entrants – was to make a full six-part series the following year.

Meantime, a rather tight-for-cash Stanley returned to theatre in Scotland in May with Jimmy Logan in a farce, *One for the Pot*, at the Empress in Glasgow, with stints in Edinburgh and Aberdeen. But apparently selective memory had kicked in; he'd forgotten he didn't like farce, and indeed Scots, as a nation, didn't take to it.

'It went down like a fart in a spacesuit,' he says of the show. We played to V-shaped audiences (the seating shape taken up when box office is sparse).'

One for the Pot did however produce a success story. Leeds-born, 19-year-old John Kaye Cooper would later become one of Stanley's few trusted television directors. (He became Controller of Entertainment at LWT, putting the likes of *Blind Date* and *Gladiators* on air, going on to become controller of ITV in 2007.)

Meantime, the stage show production coincided with Stanley's 40th birthday, but as ever he didn't celebrate the occasion.

'I got a telegram from Kenny saying, "Congratulations on a

very significant date." But I thought, "It's not significant to me."'

At least the pair were communicating again. Williams was in better spirits, lifted by his success in television revue *International Cabaret* and the delight of an upcoming holiday in Tangier with new best pal Joe Orton and his partner, Kenneth Halliwell. Stanley's circle of gay friends was also growing, thanks to David and Bruce and they'd all get together for drinks and dinner parties at each other's houses.

But work on the new BBC Scotland series was a year away and Stanley couldn't continue to rent in Glasgow and not earn money. By July, with he and Moira back at 18 Shepherd's Hill, the unemployed performer was starting to panic. However, a welcome break from over-worrying arrived one afternoon in the form of Kenneth Williams who came around to lunch – and then matter-of-factly (and not unusually) announced he was bored rigid with the Baxters' company.

'Let's go round and see Joe,' said Kenneth.

'Joe who?' said Stanley.

'Joe Orton, of course,' said Kenneth, and the pair took off to visit the immensely talented young writer whose work would enter the pantheon of theatre greats.

Stanley was extremely interested to be meeting the provocative playwright. Although Orton never publicly acknowledged his long-term partner Kenneth Halliwell as such, he led as openly a gay life as he dared. And he was very daring. The meeting began well, as Joe Orton laughed hard at Stanley's rendition of Edna Welthorpe, the Orton-created model of Home Counties respectability.

'This was a great chance to meet a wonderful playwright, an incredible talent. And as we sat down, we were served tea by a cosy queen who turned out to be Kenneth Halliwell, Joe's partner. But as usual Kenny never stopped talking. You couldn't really get a chance to chat to Orton because Kenny would turn the conversation back around to himself. Still, at least I got a chance to meet Joe. Although thanks to The Bastard [Halliwell] I never got another opportunity.'

But what to do about work? By the autumn, Stanley was so worried he agreed to another tour of duty with *The White Heather Club*, this time under the aegis of Scots entertainer, Andy Stewart.

Stanley's skin shrivelled at the notion of digging into the tartan-lined trenches once again and dodging flak from kilted whisky-drinking ex-pats. But this time he was absolutely guaranteed a percentage of the box office and although he says he was reluctant to leave Moira behind – again – at the same time he admits he truly welcomed, and needed, the three-month break from the marriage. In September 1966, Stanley and the rest of the tartan army, including the Alexander Brothers and Kenneth McKellar, set off to conquer North America with a 'hugely demanding' 21-city tour.

'You'd arrive at a hotel, look for pegs to hang up your clothes, do the show, and then having socialised with the second-generation Scots ladies, go back to the hotel and rinse out your Bri-Nylon shirt and hang it over the radiator.

'In the morning, you'd repack the shirt and smalls and repeat – month after month.'

One of the (few) golden moments in the tartan tour was the chance to play Carnegie Hall in Manhattan, New York. And he had a great night too one evening in Detroit when he went along to see Norman Wisdom who was appearing in town.

'He was charming,' says Stanley of their post-show dinner. 'And full of energy. I wasn't surprised to learn that little Sir Norman was something of a world-class swordsman. [The showbiz term for the priapic performers of the day, a nod to the parts played by the lustful Errol Flynn.]

'I think any comedian worth their salt is highly sexually charged, whether homo or heterosexual. Sexual and creative energy is tied up. Of course they are going to be at it with more than one partner! It's in the nature of the animal. And there is the greater opportunity. That's why artists are such easy pickings for the tabloid press.'

Stanley's sexual energy was high, particularly given the anonymity offered by new cities. With the help of an international gay guidebook, *Spartacus*, he located the appropriate steam baths. The Alexander Brothers, two very good-looking young Scots who performed traditional music in their kilts and thick hose, also introduced Stanley to some of the most interesting brothels in North America. And these interludes helped make the trip just about bearable. Just.

But Stanley never received his promised percentage of the box office.

'The house looked to be doing good business and the list of dates was as long as Elton John's tour itinerary. But when it came to being paid, we were always told by the agents at the North American end the bookings weren't as great as they'd seemed, and a lot of the tickets given out were freebies to make the halls look busier. And my manager could do nothing about it. He didn't have access to the box office. I felt I was robbed.'

Moira, as expected, was overjoyed to see her love return at Christmas time but Stanley would have been far happier if she had been angry at his selfish sojourn and announced she was divorcing him.

That's why he was glad to escape again, this time to Glasgow to star in *Cinderella* at the Alhambra as an Ugly Sister. Buttons was played by Scots skiffle king, Lonnie Donegan, but casting of Stanley's fellow Ugly Sister – the Sophie to his Natalie – was more interesting.[17]

Some months earlier, Stanley and Freddie Carpenter had gone to Danny La Rue's club in Soho for a night out and both were highly impressed by a young comic feed. The little man on stage made a big impression and both Stanley and Freddie reckoned he'd be ideal for the second Ugly. There was only one problem. Stanley pointed out he wasn't Scots. (Howard & Wyndham theatre bosses in Scotland at the time were insisting on using home-grown performers, a reaction to the cost of imported stars such as Max Bygraves.)

'Freddie protested, "He doesn't *sound* it, but he is Scots!" And when I heard that I knew that Ronnie Corbett could be perfect for the panto.'

And he was.

'I guess I got on even better with Ronnie Corbett than I had done with Ronnie Barker. Perhaps that was because Corbett was more camp. And he certainly didn't mind doing drag, while Ronnie Barker always felt uncomfortable, as indeed I did. During the two-season panto run we became very friendly.'

Ronnie Corbett, although a panto virgin, didn't adopt a less-than-equal position to Stanley.

'He didn't like me to prompt him when to speak or anything like that, although I was the senior comic. Like all small men he was tough. But he was easy to get on with and a very good singer – and dancer, with those neat little steps of his.'

The return to the Alhambra wasn't the talent showcase Stanley would have hoped for. But at least it was a wage, and he was back with friends – Bruce, David, and to a certain extent Freddie Carpenter, who directed the lavish spectacle. Stanley also managed to bring John Kaye Cooper into the production, suggesting to Freddie that John would make a very good ASM.

'Freddie wasn't keen on the idea. "You fancy him, don't you!" he threw at me when I made the suggestion. But I simply knew John would be very good. And he wasn't even gay.'

Freddie Carpenter was a wicked witch of a boss to John Kaye Cooper and Stanley himself wasn't averse to putting the young man in his place from time to time.

'He [Stanley] would come into the wings and give me a telling off,' says John. 'Interestingly, he'd do it in character, as Natalie the Ugly Sister. Later, when working with Barry Humphries his Dame Edna would do the same.'

The ticking-offs were fair and John came to like, and very much admire, Stanley.

'I could see that Stanley was a man riddled with insecurities but someone who comes to life when he puts on a costume. I also noticed he didn't want to do too much rehearsing with Ronnie Corbett because he wanted to be on top of his own game before he'd share a stage. Stanley worked out much of his moves on his own. I was also a bit surprised when he told me he hated his own voice, which at the time I thought odd. Over the 13-week stint, I came to appreciate he's a terrific guy. But put him around two or three people and he withdraws.'

The panto was a massive success and in the New Year of 1967, Stanley and David took off to Torremolinos for a gay holiday. The resort was then little more than a fishing village but an idyllic place where gay men could relax without being demonised.

'Holidays by this time were an excuse for sex. But David and me never became an item.'

The next few months would later come to be described as the 'Summer of Love', a time which, looking back, evokes memories of psychedelia and free love.

The Rolling Stones may have been singing 'Let's Spend the Night Together' but gay men didn't share in this sense of hedonism. Britain was still not a place where homosexuals could meet other men in public and feel safe. Perhaps it wasn't entirely a coincidence that 'Telstar' man Joe Meek killed his landlady – and then himself. Coincidentally, in 1966 Cassandra columnist William Connor, who had 'outed' Liberace, was knighted but would die after a fall the following year, aged 57.

Stanley didn't factor Moira into the equation when he set off for Spain. He says his relationship with his wife had now become even more distant. And when he chose not to bring her back to Scotland while he filmed the new TV series with David Bell he made this a physical and emotional reality.

'I told her I'd be working so hard she'd be better at home in London.'

It was a decision he would come to regret.

27
The Wee Culver City Collapse

BEFORE FILMING BEGAN on the BBC Scotland series, Stanley was shocked to learn of the death of Duncan Macrae. Later when he discovered his stage partner had died of a brain tumour, which often produces symptoms of extremely irrational behaviour, he was able to understand his erstwhile chum's more outrageous moments.

For now, Stanley worked hard on the ideas for the new series, fleshed out to precision by Alex Mitchell. He came up with the likes of a very clever take-off of intrepid Australian travel reporter Alan Whicker in *Whicker's World*, in which Whicker investigates the world of ballroom dancing. It gave Stanley the chance to play dancers (male and female) and the sour-faced Glasgow seamstress faced with sewing on a million sequins. But the highlight has to be Whicker interviewing posh Scottish Country Dancing star Marjorie Ferguson.

> WHICKER: 'Is it fair to say you are the Queen of Exhibition dancing?'
> MARJORIE [laughs]: 'Well, it's fair to say I've been making an exhibition of myself for years. For a Sassenach such as myself, Scottish Country Dancing conjures up images of Hogmanay, *The White Heather Club* being televised live from Scotland with artists such as Andy Stewart and Moira Anderson.'

Cue tartan music, and a bedroom in which a couple make a bed, shower and get dressed all in time with tunes such as 'Step We Gaily'.

Little Angus Lennie looked to be having great fun as the husband. And there were good quickies in the series such as the new mum with baby in pram sketch: 'He looks just like his father – a red-faced, toothless, baldy wee man.'

There was also fun to be had filming. One day, Stanley, David and the crew took off to film a quickie on Edinburgh's Calton Hill, where Stanley would become Cleo Lane. While Stanley was being made up in the wig, dress and make-up, David Bell chatted with the local policeman, on the beat to make sure the film crew weren't pestered.

'This policeman, by way of making conversation, said to David, "Aye, this Calton Hill is fairly notorious. This is where the poofs come at night for a bit of a carry-on. You know, there's even some wear women's clothes..." And just at that moment my car drew up and I stepped out in full Cleo kit. The cop's face was a picture.'

There was more delight when Stanley's CSE pal Peter Nichols turned up in Glasgow with his celebrated play *A Day in the Death of Joe Egg*, being performed at the Citizens. The play was groundbreaking, a comedy which told of a young couple's caring for their physically disabled 10-year-old girl, who used black humour as a coping mechanism. Peter Nichols had drawn upon personal experience to write the play; he and wife Thelma had a disabled daughter. Peter had taken Stanley's advice to give up on acting and concentrate on writing – and *Egg* was to set him on the road to becoming a playwright of international standing. The mood of the play, the theme of survival, trying to make the best of things while smiling, underlined the feeling the world wasn't all chasing hedonism and listening to the Beatles' *Sgt. Pepper's Lonely Hearts Club Band*; there were race riots in the United States, protests against the Vietnam War, and the Six Day War between Israel and Egypt.

'I thought it brilliant.'

Peter Nichols noted some disappointment in Stanley's voice during their chat: 'He wanted, he said, to play legit theatre in the West End. But no one had asked him.'

During filming, Stanley also met a young man who was to become a lifelong pal. John Reid was an extremely bright, good-looking young man from Paisley with a dynamic personality matched by his will to succeed. At the time the teenager was working in a gents' tailors but had performed as an amateur actor and as a singer with a showband.

'John had become close with David Bell and David introduced

us. John was a bit star-struck and he loved everything to do with the business. I remember once after we became chums, he turned up to visit me at my digs and was horrified to see me washing my socks. He didn't think that was what 'stars' did. It was a reality check for him.'

It's unlikely John ever saw a star wash his own socks again, certainly none of the acts he would look after during his time as an A&R (Artists and Repertoire) man with Tamla Motown in London, nor the acts he would go on to manage such as Elton John – who became his first long-term partner – Billy Connolly or Freddie Mercury and Queen.

At first, Stanley wasn't sure John would go on to develop a career in showbiz.

'He was a wee bit pushy and I think I was a bit dismissive of him. But he was good-looking, not exactly a Cary Grant, yet always perfectly dressed. And at the same time, he did have a fantastic drive to succeed.

'I guess energy and sheer talent sealed it for him. John became a millionaire in his early 20s and it wasn't down to luck. He was a great example of if you want something thing badly – and you're talented – you get it.'

In July, the 1967 Sexual Offences Act came into force, decriminalising sex in private between gay men. However, Britain's gay men such as Stanley weren't waving pink flags in celebration. The Act didn't apply to Scotland (Scotland wouldn't legalise homosexuality for another 13 years, after huge public pressure) and gay men couldn't appear to be homosexual outdoors. (Gay rights activist Peter Tatchell in his 1992 book *Europe in the Pink* claims that the legislation facilitated an increase in prosecutions against homosexual men.) There were more arrests of gays in 1967 than the previous year because of a police – and public – homophobic backlash.

Filming over in August, Stanley drove back to London and was stopped in his tracks by the newspaper billboards. Joe Orton had been murdered by his jealous partner, Kenneth Halliwell. The story was headlined across the nation's evening newspapers. The following day, *Guardian* theatre critic Philip Hope-Wallace wrote:

> Joe Orton had an irreverent eye and a splendid ear for comic dialogue. It was ruthless, mordant, epigrammatic, and formal in a way which caused people to make comparisons to Oscar Wilde.

Stanley says Orton could have gone on to become a TV or a film great, if he had time to get over his sexual madness period. 'It was incredibly sad. And Kenny had great affection for him.' He adds, 'But I still can't think about Joe Orton without recalling Kenny cutting in on the conversation.'

Shortly afterwards in September, Stanley took a call that would make an incredible impact upon his career. Network schedulers had watched previews of his BBC Scotland show and considered it to be so good it was to have a national screening. But Stanley wasn't overjoyed to hear this.

'The show was made for a Scottish audience and full of Scotticisms. Thankfully, I had insisted to BBC Scotland I have approval of any shows that made it to the national audience.'

Auntie in London was apoplectic with rage.

'I said I was prepared to give them four of the less Scottish episodes and there was a reluctant acceptance.'

Both the six-parter in Scotland and the shorter network series were extremely well received, which led the network to come up with an interesting vehicle for Stanley. The idea was to team him up with Kenneth Williams in a new comedy series. Williams was certainly excited at the idea of the two CSE chums back together, the old Rangoon magic being recreated onscreen. But not his Scottish pal.

'I felt that we couldn't work together as actors. He was simply too difficult. But as a compromise I said I would direct the show. I could have coped with that.'

The truth was Stanley wouldn't have wanted to share a spotlight with his chum. Regardless, Williams couldn't see any altruism in the Baxter offer to direct. The next night, at a prearranged dinner, Williams nibbled on pasta while his pal swallowed large lumps of cold shoulder. Stanley slips into Williams whine as he recalls his erstwhile friend's argument.

'Yes, yes, you want to build up the great Baxter career at the

Beeb! On my back! Well, you're not doing it!'

Williams also recalls the dinner debate:

> The atmosphere was awful. Within five minutes Stanley was on about it again saying 'Your career is at a crossroads you know. You can't go on with *International Cabaret* for ever and it's only realising a fraction of your talent. I am willing to work on this show for you and then we could take the best of the stuff and present the whole thing on Broadway.'
>
> 'I said I wasn't interested in Broadway, unless he meant Hammersmith.'

After the dinner date, Williams wasted no time in blackening his friend's name at every opportunity. This abuse continued for a couple of weeks until word got back to Stanley. He confronted Kenneth in their favourite cafe and, as was often the case when caught out, Williams was suitably contrite. In his *Letters* (to friend Noel William) he concedes:

> Well of course you are quite right about Baxter. He is a very good person fundamentally – and his friendship matters to me. I go right off people now and again and I'm capable of utter treachery.

Stanley accepted the Williams' apology. But it left a little scab.

'You didn't know whether or not you'd have dinner with the bubbly Ken or the suicidal Ken. And it wasn't as if I could really talk to him, chat about my own personal problems, with Moira or whatever. He didn't want to hear about any of that. Oh no. You were there to entertain him and cheer him up. Or listen.'

Frankie Howerd cheered Stanley up when he wrote to him, saying he'd loved *The Stanley Baxter Show*, broadcast on BBC2 in the autumn, in colour. A short time later, Frankie asked Stanley to appear on his own show – as Hitler. Stanley turned down the offer, never keen to appear as a guest artist and make do with the less bright spotlight and certainly not alongside a comedy giant like Howerd. To compound the problem, Frankie had tried to ask Stanley directly, calling his agent to get Stanley's home number. But the secretary wouldn't give it out.

'However, you give us your number, Mr Howerd, we'll pass it on to Mr Baxter.'

'Oh, listen, dear! I don't think so! My number is routed to all and sundry while his is a state secret?'

A short time later Stanley walked into the BBC for a meeting and Frankie was sitting around on a leather couch.

'He gave me the bum's rush. He turned and looked away. He clearly took my refusal personally.'

Still, Stanley's star was in the ascendancy again, and it was a happy actor who returned to Scotland to star in a panto. Again, he was starring in *Cinderella* with Ronnie Corbett, but this time in Edinburgh. But Howard & Wyndham boss Peter Donald took great exception to one part of Stanley's performance, the *Parliamo Glasgow* sketch, which, ironically, was on its way to becoming a classic. He wrote to his star on 4 December:

> Dear Stanley,
>
> I would be grateful if you will try to ensure that when you put on your local accent it is not in such broad 'Glasgow' that your Edinburgh fans cannot understand it!

Peter Donald was missing the point of course; the idea was that some of the Glasgow dialect was so dense the audience had to listen for the translation which Stanley provided.

Stanley won his *Parliamo* battle, and then delighted in an early Christmas present when former *On the Bright Side* director Michael Mills arrived in town. Mills had, by this time, become the BBC's Head of Light Entertainment and was determined to lure Stanley back to London with the offer of a new series, having salivated over his latest offerings. It was a perfect opportunity to leave the smallness of Scotland behind, to forget about the little feuds with Freddie, the snobbery of the H&W bosses and to resurrect his UK career back in London. It was a wonderful offer the actor couldn't possibly refuse.

Yet, Stanley told Santa he could stick his series back in his sack. Why? He had come to love the control he enjoyed at his Little Culver City – and the fun he was enjoying with David Bell, John Reid, Bruce McClure and Co.

'Michael looked confused so I explained to him, "Look, I know what will happen if I come back to London to film. The whole thing will get too expensive. And I know what the unions are like. The sums will become stratospheric. Instead, I can make the series here and get away with fucking murder. They will let me do just about anything I want and I can deliver the programmes so much more cheaply."'

All fair enough points.

Stanley won the argument and in the spring of 1968 he was back in his Little Culver City, making a network series. Once again, he fed off television for ideas but one was to cause great consternation. Stanley did a take-off of Kenneth Williams' *International Cabaret*. Williams, currently playing the Khazi of Kalabar in *Carry On Up the Khyber,* didn't like the impersonation at all.

'He flushed the friendship down the toilet. Again.'

Stanley had better fortune with a take-off of *Dr Finlay's Casebook*, the series based on the adventures of two Highland doctors. The premise was that the maidservant Janet (played by Barbara Mullen in the drama) had a medical affliction whereby she would begin and end each sentence with a Highland-accented 'Ho ho ho.' Both doctors noticed her condition and debated how it could be treated. Barbara Mullen loved the spoof.

'That one's a devil,' she said of Stanley in an interview with the *Sunday Mail.*

The series was fun to make but sad news arrived during filming. Tony Hancock died in June, his career in a slump and having sacked the major talent around him including writers Galton and Simpson and Kenneth Williams.

'I felt sorry for him,' says Stanley of Hancock. 'He had huge problems. We all have problems with depression but he seemed to have the world on his shoulders.'

In September Stanley received news his mother was seriously ill and had been admitted to Glasgow Western Infirmary. Bessie Baxter was fading by the minute. But she wouldn't let that prevent Stanley's light shining for a second.

'One day during a visit I mentioned that I felt bad about having to leave quickly. I had to kick off a football match for charity or something and I suggested I would cancel. My mother would hear none of it. She sat up straight as a board and ordered, "Certainly not, Stanley! Your public comes first!"'

On 29 September, at 8.45pm, Bessie Baxter, star-creator, mother, performer, piano player, mahjong expert, home entertainer and housewife, the single most powerful force in Stanley's life, passed away. She hadn't quite reached her 79th birthday.

'I was sad to see my mother pass on. She had spent her life trying to make me a successful entertainer and she succeeded. But part of me was glad to see her go. She had imbued in me a permanent anxiety, a chronic fear of under-performing to the point that professional life was almost always filled with worry.

'I think she was proud of me, although she always played it down. She would come backstage, where you would be greedy for praise from your mother, and you'd ask if she enjoyed the show. She'd say, "Oh, yes," with a slight acknowledgement. But when you asked her about *Francie & Josie* she'd say, "Now that *was* good."

'And while she was my mother, we weren't *completely* close. And in a way I never really forgave her for creating this barrier between me and my father, although she would be amazed to hear me say that, and probably very hurt.'

Stanley's eyes look upwards in reflection. 'It's a story that has been repeated throughout showbiz history, from Shirley Temple backwards and forwards. Bessie was a theatrical mum in that respect, with all the faults of a theatrical mum.'

The funeral however wasn't a sombre affair.

'It was like a huge cocktail party,' recalls Alice. 'Everyone told funny stories and all Mum's friends, many of them spiritualists, said Bessie was right there with them in spirit.'

There was another loss to negotiate at the time. David Bell, now freelance, had been headhunted to work on the likes of *Juke Box Jury* for the BBC and current hit chat show, *Dee Time,* for London Weekend Television.[18, 19]

'I was gutted. We had had a magical time together and I thought, "Oh shit." It was like losing my right arm. He was a close friend, a mate. And a protector.

'People would complain about me when I got on my high horse about how things should be done and he would always back me up saying, "He knows what he's doing, dear, do it!" Other directors would have fought me but he trusted me not to hang myself.'

Stanley lost another pal thanks to the career move. John Reid also announced plans to move to London, to live with David Bell and try and break into the music business.

'I had to leave,' says John. 'Paisley wasn't the place to be gay. And my dad couldn't come to terms with my sexuality. I really had to leave for London.'

David called and asked Stanley's advice on the idea of John coming to London.

'John keeps phoning me, Stanley. He wants to come south.'

'Well, you're on your own. He's a nice guy, David. Why not?'

'Do you think I should?'

'Yes, get him a job somewhere. Maybe a record company or something.'

'And he did introduce John to a pal, and in no time at all his determination and talent saw John become Head of Tamla Motown for the UK.'

The Wee Culver City dream had died. What to do next? Remarkably, Stanley agreed to go back to London, to star in a Joe Orton play, *What the Butler Saw*. Set in a psychiatrist's office, the madness begins when Dr Prentice interviews young Geraldine for a secretary's job, but insists on her being nude. His wife then enters, dressed in her underwear, whom we learn is being blackmailed by a hotel porter who has her clothes, and pics of Mrs P in the nude. To add the delicious chaos, Dr Rance, a crazed psychiatrist, arrives to carry out an inspection and diagnoses madness all around.

'When I read the play I thought it was a brilliant piece of writing, a work of genius. And I really wanted to be involved when offered the part of Dr Prentice. I know it has been described as farce, but it was so much cleverer.'

Indeed, Orton's work was gut-wrenching, hard-hitting, twisted, deviant, perverse... and wonderful. Yes, Kenneth Williams had had very troubled times when performing *Loot*. But that was four years ago. Society was now much more aware, more liberal. Orton's work was no longer seen as being quite so subversive. (*Loot* went on to pick up the *Evening Standard* drama award for Best Play in 1966.) *What the Butler Saw* would be a fantastic play to appear in. Or at least that's what Stanley hoped.

But before rehearsals began, December brought with it an intensely sad moment for Stanley. David Jacobs, the solicitor whom the actor believed had saved his life, was found hanging from the roof beams of his garage by a silk scarf. The inquest determined the death was a suicide. Others close to Jacobs however suggested he may have been the victim of a blackmail plot. There were also claims he had been killed by the Krays because he refused to represent them. (It was later revealed David Jacobs had sought police protection prior to his death.) Close friends of Jacobs argued he was not in the state of mind to take his own life. They revealed the lawyer had sent Christmas cards just two days before his death, expressing good wishes for the New Year. British actress Suzanna Leigh, who appeared alongside Elvis in the 1966 film *Paradise, Hawaiian Style*, revealed he'd sent her a lunch invite to take place two days after the day he died.

'I was really taken aback to learn of David's death,' says Stanley. 'If not for him my career would have been over. And very possibly my life. I owed him so much.'

28
Nymphromania

CORAL BROWNE WAS a tough-talking Aussie with a mouth as dirty as a dingo with fleas. The actress had arrived in London aged 21, picked up her luggage and almost as quickly, an upper-class English accent, which she would produce wonderfully on stage. The lady from Melbourne was also known to be very much into conversions; not in a religious or even a domestic habitat sense – she simply loved to seduce homosexual men.

To add to her semi-notoriety, while touring Russia in a Royal Shakespeare Company production of *Hamlet* in 1958, Browne became close with the expatriate British spy, Guy Burgess. And when she came back, she promptly told the story of the actress and the spy to playwright Alan Bennett. (This later became the basis of the 1983 television film *An Englishman Abroad*, in which Coral Browne starred and was directed, coincidentally, by John Schlesinger, with Glasgow used for some of the Moscow scenes.)

Stanley certainly looked forward to appearing in the West End run of *What the Butler Saw* alongside this ballsy lady, with the show scheduled to run at the Queen's Theatre in March 1969. If anyone could help sell Orton's high comedy and incredibly vulgar jokes, Coral could.

He was also delighted to be sharing a stage with the great Ralph Richardson, star of *The Four Feathers* in 1939 and more recently the 1965 release of the epic *Dr Zhivago*, although he was rather concerned during rehearsals when Ralph – who played Dr Rance – couldn't appreciate he was saying 'nymphromania'. But the slight speech impediment wasn't the major problem impacting upon the performance. Ralph was having trouble remembering his lines. Coral Browne also had reservations about Richardson's casting.

She later revealed to Orton's biographer John Lahr:

> Sometimes it was difficult for him to learn because he had no idea of what the words meant. Ralph got terribly depressed, terribly down, thinking he'd made a mistake. Taking a part in a 'dirty' play.

Still, with such great writing, a great cast and a top London producer in Binkie Beaumont behind it, this show simply couldn't fail – could it?[20]

On the first night in Cambridge however the prognosis for Stanley's Dr Prentice and the rest of the Orton cast looked bad. The theatre was almost empty.

'Ralph, now 67, managed to get words out, mostly in the same order they were written, and the play picked up. Word then went around of this incredibly clever and funny play. By the Saturday night the auditorium was packed. You couldn't get a ticket. And at this point the cast were loving the performances. It looked like we had a hit on our hands.'

Then came Brighton.

'Brighton, for all its raffish reputation, is not a place for radical theatre and the people who go to the Theatre Royal are very middle-class and reactionary. In fact, they hated it. As every possible sexual deviation was spewed out, the audience looked more and more horrified. They had not paid to see these three artists produce *that* sort of material. And we paid a price for it.'

Argus reporter Adam Trimingham wrote:

> This was pretty strong stuff for the delicate regulars of the Royal Circle. One by one they took their leave with the creaking of seats and muffled whispers of outrage almost providing more amusement than Orton's black comedy.

Stanley's stay in Brighton however was demanding for another reason. When the troupe booked into their hotel, the determined Coral decided she would go mountain climbing. And Stanley was to be her personal Ben Nevis.

'I was the next gay man on her wish list,' he says, grinning. 'In fact, she married two gays, her agent Philip Peerman, and later, in 1975, Vincent Price.'

After the first show the rapacious lady made her intentions evident.

'She said, "Now, darling, I've booked some rooms for us," and she had. They were adjacent rooms and I was allocated this tiny, tiny room with a connecting door.

'I said, "Darling I can't stay here. I've no wardrobe space." She simply smiled and said, "Darling, I've got plenty of wardrobe space. Just come in here."

'I thought, "I know what this is all about. I'm not going to have this sort of thing going on in the middle of the night!" So I moved up to an awful wee attic room. Although I liked her – she was great fun – I wasn't at all interested. She was older than me for a start.' (Coral was 55 at the time to Stanley's 43.)

Coral Browne (eventually) came to terms with the rejection and the cast moved on to Oxford. Again, word of mouth lured the students in and they loved it.

But then came the all-important test – the West End. The first night at the Queen's Theatre on Shaftesbury Avenue was to be a showcase for the Gallery First Nighters Club, a charitable organisation made up for the most part of very nice mink-wearing, middle-aged, upper middle-class ladies. These mink-wearers had paid good money to see those very nice performers, that gentle Ralph Richardson, the ever-so-slightly wicked Stanley Baxter and the actress who played society ladies so well, Coral Browne.

'The first half of the actual first night went very well,' Stanley recalls. 'Binkie Beaumont came backstage at the interval and said to me [takes on pukka General Montgomery voice]: 'Gone very well. Better than I could have hoped."'

The cast agreed. 'Think we're home and dry', was the declaration.

But the production was far from shore. As soon as the curtain went up in the second half the barracking started and audience fights broke out.

'Big Sophie, whom we knew to be the leader of the gang, began yelling, "Take it off, it's rubbish." Over and over again. "Filth! It's rubbish!"

'I said to Binkie's PR lady, "I hope you've got photos of all this going on outside because we can use it for publicity." But she said very softly – and snootily – "HM Tennants (The Management) don't do that kind of thing." And I said, "Well, the First Nighters are going to empty the place." And they certainly did.'

The second half had been torture for the actors.

'The sound of seats going up was like machine guns. And the more the audience hated it the more the performance would go down.

'I actually thought I'd done okay though until I bumped into Warren Mitchell [who played Alf Garnett in the hit BBC television series *Till Death Us Do Part* which had premiered in 1965], who lived around the corner. He'd been at the show and said the only person who'd sailed through the performance with great *sang froid* was Coral Browne. All I could say was, "Well, she is a very strong Aussie broad."'

Performing night after night to 'V-shaped' audiences was purgatory.

'Orton, at this point, should have been staged for college audiences, not a Binkie Beaumont production in the West End.'

Alec Guinness seemed to be in agreement.

One day just before a show, Stanley was coming down the stairs and Richardson was coming up. 'I believe Sir Alec was in last night. Did he come backstage to see you?' Stanley queried.

'Yes, yes he did.'

'Well, did he like it, Ralph?'

'No. No. In fact, he, he, he, said he hated it. He didn't care for it at all.'

'Well, did he give any reason? Was it too farcical, or not farcical enough? Or too erudite? Or too much a mixture of farce and erudition? Or what?'

'Oh, it's difficult to say because everybody that comes backstage has a different reason to hate it.'

Perhaps surprisingly, initially at least, Stanley was not defeated by this news.

'In fact, it cheered me up. Ralph Richardson was such a distinguished actor, so many years older than me and far more famous in the legitimate theatre and he too was suffering like the rest of us.'

But Stanley later told the *Sunday Mail*: 'I won't do that again. It was important for me to be loved by these anonymous people out there. It was why I went into the business.'

During the run, Stanley began to suffer from depression. The continued barrage of criticism took its toll and he resorted to pills.

'Only Coral Browne's bravado and backstage gossip kept me going. Twenty minutes before curtain every night she would give me all the gossip and dirt from the previous night's performance.

[Stanley slips into Aussie accent]: 'Well, I've got an old fuck of mine in front tonight.'

'Who's that then?'

'Another of my lovers, Anthony Holland [the stage actor].'

'Anthony Holland? But Coral, I thought his sexual preferences lay elsewhere?'

'Rubbish! When I was with him at the Old Vic, they used to hear the change clattering out of his pockets as he got up Maggie Courtney over the dressing room sink.'

'Well, that sort of thing did make you laugh and get you relaxed, which was why she was doing it.'

The three-month theatre sentence over, Stanley took a much-needed holiday in Torremolinos, again with David Bell, although this time it wasn't so gay-friendly. Franco's Government had cracked down on the growth of the gay tourist trade.

'To go into a bar you had to be accompanied by a female,' says Stanley, shaking his head in disbelief.

The trip abroad was again as much about a break away from Moira, whose behaviour had become even more unpredictable. An arts course at Hornsey College captured some of her attention but now she cared even less about work around the house. Stanley decided he needed domestic help. Although he had once berated Bessie for employing a live-in maid, principles were pushed aside for the sake of a sharp crease in his shirt sleeves. He didn't however hire a maid. On the suggestion of a pal, Stanley found a Japanese man-servant.

'His name was Oki and he was a part-time student. It was very successful and it worked very well, although you couldn't get a close relationship with people who had an imperfect knowledge of English.'

By late summer, Stanley felt re-energised enough to work again and in August 1969 accepted the lead role in the musical *Phil the Fluter* at the Palace Theatre.

'David Bell said to me, "Are you mad? Have you not had enough?" But my answer was that I felt the recent theatre experience was like coming down in a plane – you have to go back up or you will never do it again.'

Brave thought, and to defend Stanley's decision, on paper the venture looked sound. Here was a chance – Stanley's first – to star in a glorious West End musical, with fabulous production values, elaborate scenery and costumes.

Harold Fielding had spared no expense on this musical written by the highly talented David Heneker – who'd already had huge West End successes with the likes of *Half a Sixpence* and *Espresso Bongo* – and *Phil* had been adapted by the highly talented Beverley Cross. *Phil* didn't have much of a storyline, more a collection of songs – but it also co-starred Stanley's old pal Evelyn Laye of *The Amorous Prawn* days and former pop idol Mark Wynter, who had a big hit in 1963 with 'Venus in Blue Jeans'. The role also appealed to Stanley's ego, requiring him to sing and play an incredible 12 characters, proving to the world how wonderfully versatile he was.

But could he sing? As a boy when he'd tried to sing at Baptist church in Glasgow, Bessie would give him a great dig in the ribs. And of course, the last time he had sung onstage – in *On the Brighter Side* – he had developed serious throat problems. Stanley had a semi-breakdown during rehearsals

'I got the shakes. I panicked. I had a little quease and took to my bed for a day.'

There was another problem to deal with. Ten years hadn't improved Boo Laye's memory.

'I needed her to be spot-on. But Boo missed lot of lines in rehearsals. Even towards the end, she'd be shouting, "Give me the book, give me the book!"'

Stanley says Boo was also working the management quietly behind the scenes – again – to make sure she had the best chance to upstage everyone else.

'This show seemed to be everyone else's baby. It was Evelyn's, it was the director's or the musical director's, who thought he was God. It wasn't mine, I was powerless and I couldn't handle that.'

As the rehearsals continued through October, Stanley's depression worsened. His troubled personal life was also a major factor. His marriage, after 17 years, existed only on paper and he reckoned there was no chance of ever finding a long-term gay partner. Encounters were brief and often fearful. And despite the 1967 legislation, homophobic witch-hunts were still taking place by police.

Censorship was also rife. For example, when Sheridan Morley's biography of Noel Coward, *A Talent to Amuse,* was published there was no mention of Coward's homosexuality 'because of fear of losing royalties' – despite Coward writing songs such as 'Mad About the Boy'. And film director Billy Wilder had to cancel plans to reveal his Sherlock Holmes to be gay in the upcoming *The Private Life of Sherlock Holmes*. Studio bosses would have none of it and Wilder had to blur the lines, suggesting young Sherlock was sexually confused, as a result of an adventure with a sex worker.

Stanley wished deeply that he was not gay. But what to do? In desperation, he sought out psychiatric help. He had heard of men who'd had treatment for their homosexuality (Frankie Howerd, it was claimed, took LSD to attempt to alter his sexual preference). Sadly, Stanley's psychiatrist found his patient's angst to be as dull as an am-dram production of an Ibsen play performed entirely by accountants.

'He seemed nice enough to begin with but during talks I said to him, "I think one of the problems may be my homosexuality." And I added he ought to know the whole truth for the sake of the diagnosis, that it was part of my emotional problems.

'But he looked at me quizzically and said, "You're married, aren't you?"

'I said, "Yes, but it hasn't been totally successful." He said dismissively, "Oh, rubbish! Never mind that. Go back to your wife."

'And I replied, "I don't really think that's the answer, do you?"

'All the time we chatted he looked out of the window at his new Rolls-Royce in case a sparrow had shat on it.

'Can you imagine a psychiatrist giving you the bum's rush after you open your heart to him?'

And with that the doc wrote out a prescription for drugs that Stanley became hooked on for a number of years.

'I think the Mogadon affected my memory, which has suffered ever since. I only got off them when I read an article by the actor Peter Barkworth, who explained how he was addicted to Mogadon and finally broke away.'[21]

At this time – a case of very bad timing in fact – Kenneth Williams was pouring his heart out to Stanley and talking of suicide. In his *Diaries* he notes:

> At one point when I said to S, 'I sometimes feel I'm so useless I just want to die,' he said, 'Oh well, if you did, I should just follow you. I don't think I could go on. I really don't.' And I was so utterly overwhelmed.

The friends, united by their loathing of their sexual preference and sense of being trapped, were worried about each other. On 13 November, the opening night of *Phil the Fluter*, Williams hoped desperately that his friend would find success. He said in his *Diaries*: 'Otherwise I fear he will be splintered forever.'

Williams' concerns were assuaged. The audiences loved the show. The crowds loved Boo.

'Her walking on stage was like watching a million-watt light bulb being switched on,' says Stanley.

'The audience had a love affair with her every night.'

And they loved Stanley. Too much, in fact.

'Although I had top billing in the show, I thought it would be nice if I came on second last for the bows, because of her distinguished career.'

Stanley's professional generosity backfired. When he took his bow, after having performed his 12 characters, the theatre erupted and he got a huge ovation. When Boo came on the decibel level dropped – just a little – but she found that unacceptable. So a new rehearsal for a different finale was called, giving Boo more time to make a grander entrance. And then another finale, where Stanley would come down the stairs last. But again Stanley got the biggest ovation.

'Eventually, the chorus kids mocked up a Suggestion Box marked "New Finales".'

In the end Boo herself solved the problem. Stanley, in his little hat and Evelyn, in her gorgeous vast satin dress, came down the stairs at the same time.

Whoosh!

As a result, Boo was the sweetest woman in all the world. Stanley even began to enjoy the performances during those first few days.

Yet, *Phil* failed to amuse the critics. Their feelings were summed up by the *Radio Times*, who described it as 'Confection' while *The Guardian* said the show was 'Less than inspiring'. After all, this was the time of psychedelia, of going to San Francisco and sticking flowers in your hair or watching the surreal *Monty Python* on television.

The bad crits affected audiences and the show was pulled after three and a half months, with Danny La Rue brought in to fill the space.

Back at 18 Shepherd's Hill, Oki had returned to Japan to complete his studies but he recommended a friend as his replacement, Kazu.

'He worried about his recommendation in case we were disappointed, such was the Japanese sense of responsibility. But the new boy was fine.'

It wasn't just his work Kazu was passionate about.

'He fell madly in love with Moira. He saw that we were sleeping in separate rooms and that sort of encouraged him. And I suppose the infatuation developed over a period of months. I discovered later he actually wanted her to go back to Japan with him.'

Stanley isn't sure if Moira and Kazu had an affair, although he assumes they did, and certainly wouldn't have blamed her if she had.

'We awoke one morning and he had gone. He left a note on the pillow which read, "Sorry. No excuse."'

But the incident – and his lack of jealousy – highlighted how far apart he and Moira had become. Stanley decided he had to escape the marriage for good and moved out, into a little flat off Judd Street in Central London. It was a chance to lead his own life, to play the role of Single Gay Man. Discreetly. Moira of course was distraught, but Stanley believed he had no choice. Kenneth Williams moved into a flat in the same building, which at least proved to be a welcome distraction because in the New Year of 1970 Stanley certainly had problems to contend with.

In one year, he had appeared in two West End failures. Yes, theatre work was still being offered but nothing grand, and he would sooner die than take on a cosy role in some safe middle-class revival playing an 'anyone for tennis' oaf.

Stanley made the vow never to play the West End again. And he never did. But he seemed to be running out of options fast. Going back to the Alhambra in Glasgow wasn't one. Stanley's prediction about its sybaritic descent into financial madness had proved to be correct and the theatre closed its doors. It was time to worry. Again.

29
The Suicidal Zapata

THE START OF the '70s was an incredibly theatrical time, of glam rock, of Bowie and Elton and Rod all attempting to out-do each other. But Stanley, now almost 44, still preferred to look as butch as possible. He did however make some concession to the more flamboyant times, as Kenneth Williams later remarked, telling friends that Baxter had 'gone for all this Carnaby Street gear.'

Stanley's new outfits however were not part of a bright new beginning in his personal life. Despite the fun he'd had in the Judd Street flat, with a variety of men coming and going, the move had lasted just a few months. Guilt – and Moira's constant calling on the phone – saw him return home.

Stanley's life as a gay man, he reckoned would be intermittent at best. But at least his career was moving in the right direction again. BBC Scotland offered a series, to be shown on the network.

'I had to think much more about network ideas and one I came up with was taking off George Formby, who meets Marlene Dietrich on the train.'

Shot in rich, grainy black and white, Stanley plays Dietrich playing a spy, Nola Alexandrov. Set to board a train, she meets a mysterious Russian spy, Boris (complete with a very heavy Russian accent).

NOLA: Do you have a secret message for me?
BORIS: I trust you know how to deal with a code?
NOLA: Of course. I go straight to bed and take two beach boys.
BORIS: You mean Beecham's?
NOLA: I know what I mean.

She is told to meet her contact on the train. Nola enters a

compartment where a gentleman is hidden behind a newspaper.

> NOLA: This compartment is so dirty. Where does all this smut come from?

The man drops the newspaper and we see it's George Formby.

> FORMBY: Eeh, I work it into all me pictures, luv. Stuff like 'Camay Knickers' and 'Me Grandma's Flannelette Nightie.'

He then pulls out a ukulele and sings the 'Chinese Laundry Blues'.

It was a funny, clever juxtaposition. Another creation was a wonderful pastiche of Robert Donat's 1941 film, *Goodbye Mr Chips!* Stanley's version *Goodbye Mr Crisp!* sees Mr Crisp turn out to be a pupil, grey moustache and all.

In November, Stanley was back in pantoland, having agreed a two-year deal earner to star in *Mother Goose*, first at the King's, Edinburgh, and the following year in Glasgow alongside stunning Patricia Michael as Principal Boy, who enjoyed a 'special friendship' with the star.[22]

'There's something about the whole Principal Boy thing that can appeal to a certain (gay) man,' he says with a glint in his eye.

Stanley had sex with half a dozen women during his lifetime. There were always Coral Browne-like actresses (with partners at home) keen to prove to the Scot what he had been missing out on all these years.

'It usually happened when I was a bit drunk,' he says, smiling. 'There were some women so intent on having sex that this need in itself created desire. And I suppose the 10 per cent of me that is heterosexual would kick in.'

Ironically, Stanley's congress with females had to be kept very quiet indeed, and not just because the ladies invariably had partners. There was no way Moira would have accepted a female threat. And she would have been devastated. But his fun with girls dressed as boys apart, Stanley loved his panto stints.

'Television was always a struggle in terms of coming up with ideas. But the comedy in panto was easier in the sense that writers such as Russell Lane and Gary Dennis were feeding me great gags and Bruce McClure helped me dream up slapstick.'

And panto time meant power. Stanley was virtually the director. Yet, the performer's need to be in control – and be the centre of attention – extended beyond the professional arena, says Russell Lane.

'Here's an example. If you go into a restaurant with Stanley, he'll sit facing outwards. And he'll joke, "It's so the waiter doesn't stab me in the back." But the actor/director in him always wants to see the potential audience in front of him.'

The panto audiences loved *Mother Goose* and the TV critics gobbled up *The Stanley Baxter Show*, which went out on Friday nights on BBC1 in January. He was also delighted to play a monkey. Not just any monkey, but a PG Tips monkey in the cult(ish) series of TV tea ads.

Meanwhile, although Stanley had given up on the West End, London producers had not given up on him. In the spring of 1971 he was offered the part of bank clerk Brian Runnicles in new comedy, *No Sex Please, We're British* at The Strand – but he turned it down flat – a show that would run for an incredible 16 years and 6,761 performances. This was the theatrical equivalent of Ronald Reagan turning down *Casablanca* or Montgomery Clift passing on *Sunset Boulevard*. Yet he doesn't regret it.

'I thought the basic premise, that people got unsolicited pornography through their letterbox and became hysterical about it, was pretty poor.' (Kenneth Williams also passed, claiming performing the script would have been 'Chinese water torture'.)

There was another reason for turning *No Sex Please* down, the show Michael Crawford would have so much success with.

'It meant working with Evelyn Laye again. And while we were good friends off-stage, she was essentially a *star* player. The idea of helping others to get laughs was totally foreign to her.'

While Stanley could (for the moment) afford to be choosy(ish) with his career, life at home was far from carefree. Returning after a panto stint in Scotland simply polarised his feelings towards Moira. Now, he says, he was worn thin by the fact he never knew what he would come home to, the physical or emotional chaos. And so again Stanley moved out of 18 Shepherd's Hill, leaving Moira behind.

'Money wasn't tight at the time, but I wasn't entirely flush, so I reckoned I would rent out the ground-floor and move Moira up to the top, into a self-contained unit. In retrospect, that was really unkind of me. The whole house had once been hers, and now she had a small part of it. She felt this was a demotion and rightly so. But I also reckoned I just couldn't live with her any longer. And at least if I got a cry for help, I could be down the hill in five minutes.'

Stanley moved into the top floor flat of a converted 1930s art deco-style house in a quaint quarter of Highgate Village, just along the road from Sir Yehudi Menuhin; future neighbours in N6 would include George Michael and Sting.

He met Moira every day for lunch.

'I knew she was vulnerable. Christ, sometimes she would even talk of killing herself now that we were apart. But I knew this was a cry for help, that she simply needed to be reassured by me.'

For the very first time in his life, apart from the short stay in Judd Street, Stanley was living alone. He came to relish his independence. The house was organised perfectly; he knew where everything was and he hired a housekeeper to come in and clean a couple of days a week. Independence was such bliss he never again surrendered it.

Perhaps it was down to this more relaxed frame of mind he broke one his own golden rules and agreed to appear as a TV guest star. His appearance in anarchic and infantile comedy *The Goodies* showed that he could (although very rarely indeed) change his mind.

'I quite liked the script, the idea of playing a daft Scotsman chasing the Loch Ness Monster,' he argues, unconvincingly.

He could share *The Goodies* spotlight knowing he'd be off to Glasgow soon to film a one-off special, *Time for Baxter*, scheduled to go out on Hogmanay.

This time around, he was reunited with David Bell, working as a freelance. Yet, the show didn't leave either Bell or Baxter brimming with delight.

'It didn't have the really good ideas the previous series had. It all felt a bit flat.'

What also lacked buoyancy was a lunch with CSE pal John

Schlesinger in Glasgow. John's new film *Sunday Bloody Sunday,* in which divorced Glenda Jackson shares bisexual Murray Head with gay Peter Finch, had just been released.

'John asked me what I thought of *Sunday Bloody Sunday* and I said, "It's very good, although not as good as your previous film, *Midnight Cowboy*." But I really should have known better. People in showbiz don't want to hear the negatives about their product.'

Yet, there was delight in knowing the Rangoon Four had all built successful careers. Kenneth Williams, as well as enjoying *Carry On* success, had a hit radio series with *Just a Minute*. Peter Nichols's play, *Forget Me Not Lane*, was running at the Apollo Theatre in the West End. As indeed other friends of Stanley had. John Reid was now manager of rising star Elton John. And the two Ronnies teamed up for a BBC sketch show that would run for the next 16 years.

It certainly wasn't professional jealousy which saw Stanley put his head in the oven and turn on the gas. Or at least, that was how Kenneth Williams –'The little bastard that he was' – reported the story. The truth was a little more mundane. Back in London at the end of the panto run, at the time of electric power cuts, Stanley had turned on the gas oven for heat.

'But I let the gas run for too long before I tried to light it – with a lit candle.'

The blast blew him back across the kitchen, removing some of the hair from his head and a top layer of skin in the process. But that wasn't the worst part of it. On the day of the accident, Stanley was scheduled to go to dinner with Kenneth Williams and Gordon Jackson. He explained to Williams over pasta how the accident came about but his chum's *Letters*' version revealed his gift for lily-gilding had not diminished.

> Stanley ran into the hospital in a panic, screaming, 'Will I be blind? Will I be able to see again?' And the nurse said to him, 'Oh, just go home and take an aspirin!'
>
> It has burned all the front of the hair and he is combing it forward to compensate and painting in the eyebrows. This, plus the fact he is growing one of those Zapata moustaches has combined to produce the

> most macabre effect. 'You look AWFUL,' I cried and he said, 'You are a hell of a morale booster, you are!' And I retorted, 'Oh, I could never lie! [Which is about the most ludicrous statement ever made.]'

Williams had made up the moustache tale. Stanley never had real facial hair in his life.

Meanwhile, fortunately for the scorched Zapata, the actual missing hair grew in quickly enough because Stanley had a new TV series to film. But it wasn't with the BBC. (A very lethargic Auntie hadn't bothered to ring again, not even thanking their star for his three hit series and a Hogmanay special.) In April 1972, David Bell, now working full time with London Weekend Television, rang with some exciting news. David had talked LWT's Head of Entertainment Cyril Bennett into developing Stanley's show.

'I think you'd like to work at LWT, dear,' David said excitedly to Stanley.

It was great news. LWT, with current hit sit-coms such as *Doctor in Charge* and *Please Sir!* was the place to be. It was an amazing chance to bring The Wee Culver City team back together again and Cyril Bennett assured budgets wouldn't be a problem.

The problem was in Stanley coming up with enough ideas for the requested four-parter. And again he wouldn't trust others to pitch in. They had to be his. He was afraid others' conceits simply wouldn't be good enough. He was afraid they'd produce failure – for which he'd carry the can.

'Someone like Russ Abbott would be given a bundle of scripts and he would pick what he liked and tape it. I *had* to come up with the ideas. They had to be mine.'

And he knew he had to have two or three absolutely terrific ideas for each one. In the summer of 1972, Stanley once again fed Ken Hoare with the outlines and the pair came up with some of their best-ever sketches. Filmed at Elton John's house in Virginia Water in Surrey (John Reid and Elton had recently moved in together and David and John had remained close friends), the idea was that Stanley took off the current Oxo ad which featured a housewife called Katie.

In Stanley's spoof, the second assistant director on the Oxo ad hears a call going out, 'We need Katie for the next shooting,' and not being too clever, phones Katie Hepburn. In the kitchen sequence, Stanley then plays Hepburn doing 'all that emotional stuff' with the stock cubes, as she would have done had she been in the ad.

Filming went well. And a couple of days later, Stanley had a relaxing lunch at Elton's house. However, as the group were enjoying the gentle sunshine, the calm was broken by the creaking of a rusty old bicycle. Stanley turned around and on top of the bike was film legend Katherine Hepburn, wearing a blue sailor's hat. It later transpired Hepburn had been visiting the Forbes' residence next door. Stanley still doesn't know if the Forbes let their guest know a television actor had been taking her off and she popped over out of curiosity, or she was simply out riding her bike. Either way, he was terrified to meet her.

'I was practically speechless,' he recalls, grinning. 'It was all so bizarre her turning up. And besides that, I was a huge fan. I wouldn't have impersonated her had I not liked her. But she wasn't to know that.'

Stanley and Elton however didn't hit it off quite so well.

'I'm not sure why but I think it may have been to do with Kenneth Williams. I know John Reid and Elton went to his dressing room once after a show to say hello and Kenny threw them out. He was in one of his moods. And maybe Elton thought I was as difficult as my pal. But I'm just guessing.'

Filming the series, he says, was 'ball-breaking', however he took a holiday in Greece with Moira and Stanley's testicles had almost returned to their original spherical condition when he arrived back Scotland to appear in a variety show, *The Stanley Baxter Show*. Stanley didn't want to travel north, but he'd agreed as a favour to Bruce McClure who was producing and Moira certainly wasn't happy to see him go. Each night after the show at His Majesty's Theatre in Aberdeen Stanley would ring his wife but one night there was no reply, and he was a little worried. Stanley asked John Maynard, a friend who lived close by, to pop in and see if everything was as it should be.

It wasn't. John found Moira in the bath, the water red with her blood.

When the return call came to his hotel in Aberdeen, Stanley was distraught. But he wasn't convinced Moira had intended to take her own life.

'The depression had really taken hold and she attempted suicide. Or rather, it looked like an attempted suicide. But I think it was self-harming, a cry for attention. She was trying to get me back for leaving her behind in London and I'm sure that's why she slashed her wrists.

'Since I'd left Shepherd's Hill there were several times when I would ring her, and when I couldn't get her on the phone I would of course go down and see that she was alright. And that would be the routine. One night, when all was quiet, I was desperately worried and I got a mate to come with me to check for the worst – and we discovered she was fine. But Moira came to expect that attention and reacted accordingly.'

Stanley didn't leave Aberdeen and make his way back to London to see Moira recover in hospital. He felt he was damned if he did – and damned if he didn't. Despite knowing the bath water was crimson.

'This would tell Moira I could be pulled back on elastic. Yet, I knew she was very ill. And when I did see her I reassured her I would always be her friend.'

A few days later, Moira sent Stanley a letter of apology.

'I feel so much love,' she wrote. 'I need to pass it on. I'll never do something so foolish again.'

The letter had an impact. The following month, the successful *Mother Goose* moved on to Newcastle, this time with close pal Mark Wynter and *Carry On* star Bernard Bresslaw ('a nice man with an incredible intellect'). Stanley invited Moira to stay with him at his digs in Whitley Bay.

But why repeat *Goose*, one of the most demanding pantos with 18 costume changes a show after having worked hard all summer on the LWT series?

'The television series took three months to film but I was paid for only two hours of television. With *Goose* I was on a percentage of the business and because of the television profile I was packing them in. The panto rate allowed me the luxury of doing such TV.'

Cyril Bennett meanwhile wanted more TV from Stanley, a new six-part series for LWT, working alongside David. But the actor – and creator – was horrified at the very idea.

'No, David, I had trouble enough dreaming up the ideas for the four!'

'But Stanley, Cyril will give you as much back-up as you ask for.'

'David, I can't do it.'

'Well, what about another four-parter? The last was so successful and the audiences loved it.'

'No. And that's my final answer! I don't have the ideas in me. I'm too drained.'

David was disappointed to say the least. But he had a final card to play.

'What if we did just ONE hour? And it was only you and dancers. Could you dream up enough ideas for an hour?'

'That's a wonderful idea! Yes, yes, I could do that.'

The hour special allowed Stanley time to breathe and feeling relaxed and even excited, he came up some great ideas for movie pastiches. But he had no idea this newfound joy was to be replicated in his personal life.

30
Love in Leeds

WHEN NEW SITCOM *Are You Being Served* exploded onto television screens in 1973 it created serious concerns at the BBC. One of the massive strengths of the series, according to the early viewer surveys, was John Inman's effete character, Mr Humphries. But the saucy salesman had in fact arrived surreptitiously.

Writer David Croft in his biography *You Have Been Watching* revealed he didn't write Mr Humphries as a gay character because 'we wanted the audience'. Mr Humphries' onscreen mincing was entirely an Inman invention. Croft added, 'The BBC [ironically, given the number of gay employees] said we should 'drop the poof'.

Regardless, the public appreciation of Mr Humphries was hardly cause for a victory celebration amongst Britain's gay population. Inman's character, Stanley felt, was a 'nelly on the telly' who would define gay men – and fuel homophobia. If anything, Humphries was an added reason to stay deep in the closet. But that didn't mean Stanley had given up on occasional encounters. If sex was food, life was one of grabbing quick, often unedifying snacks. Until one day in the spring of 1973.

Stanley was introduced by mutual friends to a 28-year-old German accountant called Marcus. The pair had a two-day fling. At first, the brief encounter was exactly that.

'My sex life at the time had gone back to how it had been during Glasgow theatre times. When I'd be having sex with blokes, I'd say to them, "Oh, I'll tell you who you must meet! They are wonderful in bed." And they'd say, "What? You're passing me on?" But I thought that was what you did. They wanted to be emotionally involved. I didn't. I'd say, "For God's sake, this is just sex."'

Marcus was 'just sex'. Or so he thought.

'Marcus took me completely by surprise. Something was happening between us but I didn't wish to acknowledge the fact. And so I tried to shut him out of my life altogether. But he kept phoning up all the time. He began telling me there was something special between us. But I didn't want to know.'

In May, Stanley took himself off to Rhodes (alone) for a holiday, and to think. He really liked Marcus but all of this relationship business had to be contained. He couldn't let a lover into his life. Think of the complications. Think of the risks if they were seen on a regular basis. On his return, Stanley was focused and secure in the knowledge work was the top-of-the-bill feature in his life. But Marcus had other ideas.

'He would ring up and I'd say, "Look, I'm rehearsing [the one-hour LWT special]. I can't see you!" But he would persist. He'd argue, "Ah, but you *can* see me and you're not going to get away."

'Gradually, I found I was falling in love.'

Stanley and Marcus had lots of common ground. They both loved MGM musicals and the Hollywood greats. Marcus also had a very dry sense of humour. And he too didn't suffer fools gladly. Just as importantly, while he adored Stanley, he had the strength of character to impose his own will. For the first time since the Bill Henry adventure, Stanley was caught up in an emotional whirlwind.

'I loved Moira of course, but that was totally different.'

In the months ahead, Stanley introduced Marcus to friends such as Julia Mackenzie, Russell Lane, John Reid and Bruce McClure and they all quickly became chums. David Bell however was harder to be convinced.

'Marcus told me that David thought he was freeloader, trying to hang on to my coat tails.'

David eventually came around. And as remarkable as it may sound, so too did Moira. In fact, Moira and Marcus became very good friends. They would have lunch together, without Stanley. Marcus lived close by and he would pop in every day and see that she was all right. Moira, at this time, didn't at all fear losing Stanley to another man; she feared not having him in her life.

It was rather ironic that Marcus would be seen out more often with Moira than Stanley, but that was the way of things. What

Stanley did appreciate at the time however was how much energy the new relationship brought to his work. As a result, the autumn filming at LWT for his one-hour special was an incredibly productive time. He appeared for the first time as the Queen, in the form of the Duchess of Brendagh, a deliciously subversive piece which was to become an immense talking point. He produced classic sketches, such as a take-off of the hit drama *Upstairs, Downstairs*, even though he says the producers and some of the cast of the original were incensed when they heard about Stanley's homage.

'Cyril Bennett told me that Jean Marsh, who had devised the series and played Rose the maid, was so angry when she heard we'd received permission to use the actual set.'

Somewhat incredibly, Cyril Bennett's LWT let Stanley send up its own material.

'Thankfully, when Jean saw the final result, she told me it was brilliant and loved it.'

On 21 December, *The Stanley Baxter Big Picture Show* went out on Sunday night to universal applause. Almost.

'There were, of course, the letters from outraged colonels from Brighton saying that if they knew my address they would come round and horsewhip me, thanks to the Brendagh sketch.'

The Duchess of Brendagh (the Queen) gives an address in the form of an appeal for racial harmony:

> It is easy to dismiss and dismiss the customs of other races. But can we ignore the simple Indian family who still beat their clothes on the rocks of the water's edge – even though Kilburn is rich in launderettes.

Stanley then moved from the edges of racist condescension to mocking the Queen Mum.

> Since I last spoke to you, many have written saying you admire many of the lovely old pieces you've noticed in my home. My mother, sadly cannot appear today in person.

This single hour of TV had taken five months to make, but Stanley was in his glory. Except for the times Moira came to lunch at the LWT building. Her behaviour was strange – even by Moira's standards – and on one occasion she began dancing around outside the studio, then tried to enter when the red light was on.

'David Bell called out anxiously, "Keep her in the lobby. Don't for God's sake, let her in!"'

The troubled spirit with the sad eyes was now becoming trapped in her own mind. And it had nothing to do with Stanley having a new partner.

'No, she told me she was hearing voices. She would think the television was talking to her.'

Several doctors were consulted but could offer little hope because Moira refused to take prescribed drugs. Stanley arranged for his wife to see a psychiatrist, who agreed she was suffering from schizophrenia but didn't feel her behaviour was bad enough to warrant being sectioned.

What could Stanley do? He was clueless but opted to go off to work. The actor was contracted to appear in *Mother Goose* at The Grand Theatre Opera House Leeds with *Father Came Too* friend Cardew Robinson and close pal Mark Wynter, who was this time playing Principal Boy ('The only male I've ever seen play a good Principal Boy.')

But during the run, Stanley had another problem to contend with. Marcus insisted on making trips to Leeds to see his new love.

'I was shitting myself the whole time. Even when we'd do something entirely innocent like having lunch in a cafe I'd be twitching. The whole gay thing was murderous.'

Still, Stanley felt like an excited schoolboy when Marcus appeared. His lightness of spirit contrasted sharply with the bleak winter. Up and down the country the miners' strikes were biting.

'I felt the miners were holding the country to ransom,' says the former Bevan Boy insurrectionist.

At least the panto was fun to work on, helped considerably by the antics of Cardew 'The Cad' Robinson, the music hall comedian who played a range of larger-than-life bit parts in films, who lived up to his nickname.

'He would pull women regularly from the stage, making assignations across the footlights. It was all very unprofessional, but I really liked him. And it was fun watching all aspects of his performance.'

During the run, Stanley met a rather manic young man who had also been signed up by LWT. Freddie Starr liked Stanley from the start.

'He seemed a nice bloke,' says Freddie. 'Very posh for a Scot. And you wouldn't get his sort of shows on TV now, considering the crap that's produced using two cameras and a monkey directing them.'

One night after the panto however Stanley answered a knock on his dressing room door and was stunned to see an old friend. It was his first army fumble, Reggie Short, still with the same splayed feet but no longer painfully thin. Reggie had become a trade union activist and the pair enjoyed a nice chat about their best times in Burma. But selective memory kicked it when it came to recalling their most intimate moment. And of course, Stanley certainly couldn't tell Reggie about his personal life. How could Reggie cope with hearing his army pal had a permanent man in his life – and a wife with a serious mental illness? Stanley wasn't even sure if *he* could cope with either.

31
The Morally Inhibited

STANLEY HAD A wry smile on his face in February 1974 when he read of John Reid's adventures in Australia. Now travelling the world with Elton, his career had soared into the stratosphere. John had been hitting journalists, and subsequently the headlines, all in defence of his partner.

'I saw less and less of him,' says Stanley of the pop manager. 'It was a shame but John was always busy.'

Stanley was busy too with the demands of the next one-hour special, *The Stanley Baxter Moving Picture Show,* which included another *Upstairs, Downstairs* pastiche. He came up with the idea that some well-known actors would appear in the Bellamy household, giving him the chance to play the likes of Sir John Gielgud and Sir Ralph Richardson. The scene opens with Mrs Bridges chatting to Rose.

> 'We've seen some comings and goings to be sure, Rose. First, Lady Marjorie goes down with the *Titanic*. Then Sir Richard goes down with Ann Thrax.'
>
> 'I thought anthrax was an infectious disease of sheep?'
>
> 'Sir Richard was no snob!'

Hints of cunnilingus and bestiality in the opening paragraph – Stanley wasn't playing safe at all. But then he took the greatest risk of all, letting the audience in on the act. Rose whines:

> 'It's been a winter of terrible shocks, Mrs Bridges. The heads of the house both met untimely ends and then young Mr Lawrence was wiped out under a brewer's dray.'

'And us not knowing about it until we read the new cast in the *TV Times*! Bringing in a special guest! If you please! National Theatre or not, we're as good as they are, my girl.'

'Thank gawd Miss Elizabeth was spared the chop.'

'Only just. They says she's hanging on by a thread. Mind you, she's got one of the finest men in Harley Street fighting to save her.'

'Her doctor?'

'Her agent. He says unless she recovers the power off speech by next week he's taking it up with Equity.'

[She continues]: 'Oh, I wish things didn't have to change, Rose. The house has got such memories. Remember the night I rushed in and told you the Old Queen had gone?'

'Yes, and I told you not to speak so disrespectfully of Mr Hudson!'

'I never heard what Gordon Jackson thought about my impression of him, though I think he would have winced a wee bit and then laughed. However, nobody likes being impersonated. They feel vulnerable.'

The show also featured Maurice Chevalier as an angel singing from heaven of all that's wrong in the earthly world.[23] The tag line revealed Maurice up in heaven singing, 'I pray that Bob Monkhouse lives for ever more...' Sadly, Bob, says Stanley, took the huff.

Stanley's imagination had again swelled to provide the right material for a massive spectacular, but programme costs soared exponentially. The accountants chewed their nails to the quick, as you would expect, but Cyril Bennett reassured Stanley the sack wasn't being woven as they spoke.

'Cyril would say to them, "Economise somewhere else; he's our flagship."'

The flagship, on this occasion however, reckoned he needed a little more money – for himself. Working on one show for five months – for one fee – was not a business practice Fred Baxter would have endorsed. He asked for 'an extra grand' and got it.

Filming went smoothly (Moira wasn't invited along), except on one day when Freddie Starr, while working nearby on *Ready Freddie* with David Bell, caused Stanley's heart to flutter. And not in a good way.

'I was doing one Busby Berkeley-type scene and Freddie said he wanted to run right through it and pull his pants down. Bizarre.

'I'm sure it was working with Freddie that led to David Bell developing shingles.'

John Reid meanwhile created a major disruption in the Stanley camp. He had expanded his empire and was now looking to make movies, with David Bell his Hollywood producer. In the late summer of '74, David and John set off on a recce to the States. Shortly afterwards, with filming over, Stanley and Bruce joined the two of them in Los Angeles.

'It was all quite exciting and good fun having the four of us together. And, of course, I loved the idea of spending time in LA.'

The trip began with a bang.

'As we checked into the hotel in Los Angeles, Bruce was asked by the receptionist how to spell his name. "Big M small C etc – just the same way as Doug McClure, the actor." And the receptionist said, "Oh, we've got Doug McClure staying with us." Sure enough he was and I met up with him in the hotel sauna a while later.'

The former star of *The Virginian* wasn't gay, as such. But the TV cowboy Trampas certainly wasn't averse to having intimate fun with gay men.

Back home, Stanley let panto offers slide that year; the demands of the special (broadcast on 22 August) had taken their toll. However, all the effort was rewarded in February 1975 when *The Stanley Baxter Moving Picture Show (Part 2)* won an incredible three BAFTAS. Stanley managed to beat off such British comedy luminaries as Ronnie Barker for *Porridge*, Arthur Lowe in *Dad's Army* and Michael Crawford for *Some Mother's Do 'Ave 'Em* to pick up the best Light Entertainment Performance. David Bell won the Light Entertainment Programme award, coming out ahead of *The Benny Hill Show, Monty Python* and *The Two Ronnies* while Bill McPherson won the Design award.

The actor was again at the top of the television world, fast reaching iconic status. But any sense of satisfaction lasted for as long as it took to make his thank-you speech. Bessie's mantra 'must do better' were the loudest words in his head.

'After I picked up the BAFTAS I suffered a continual nightmare, asking myself, "How the hell do I follow that?" But I think this is the case for many showbiz people. It's the subtext of success.'

He could have taken an easier route, of course. At this time, *Fawlty Towers* was running away with the ratings, Frankie Howerd returned with the phenomenal *Up Pompeii!* and old pals Ronnie Barker and Fulton Mackay were feeding *Porridge* to the watching masses for the first time. But sitcom was a taxi Stanley didn't need to share with other people. After all, he was making shows that had become national events. And it was his name alone on the titles.

In the spring of 1975, Cyril Bennett looked to his flagship to continue the success with the third in the trilogy of specials. But Stanley wasn't keen. How could he keep up the standard with David Bell still in La La Land, trying to become the next Robert Evans? Stanley, after some heaving and pushing, came to the party, but he didn't take to replacement director John Schofield at all.

'He wouldn't let me near the edit suite at all, because he reckoned I would be interfering, which of course I would. And on the set he was horrid to underlings, which I hate. I have a great respect for the people who put the plugs in.'

Stanley's reluctance to make the special didn't however limit his coming up with great ideas. In *The Stanley Baxter Moving Picture Show (Part 3)* the star sends up Noel Coward and Celia Johnson with the very clever crackly black and white spoof, *In Which We Starve*. Coward sings a woeful song at the piano and the camera cuts to:

> Johnson: 'Oh, that was awfully nice. And sometimes I think the war, our war, is... awfully nice.'
> Coward: 'Well, here in peace haven the sheer ghastliness seems so terribly far away. We've been lucky here. Dammed lucky. I often think those German airplanes show an enormous respect for the British Navy. They wouldn't dare drop one of their horrid little bombs on this house.'
> Johnson: 'Especially since you painted that enormous swastika on the roof.'
> Coward: 'It will be unspeakably exquisite when it's all over. No more ration books. No more sirens. Nothing to fear except the occasional post-war revival of *Bitter Sweet*. And thankfully little Jimmy will be able to

> sleep in his own bed again.'
> Johnson: 'Yes, it's absolutely frightful the way he keeps leaping into Nanny's bed when he hears the siren.'
> Coward: 'Yes, and he's nearly 27.'

He also produced one of his most talked about TV sketches ever, the *Towering Inferno* (1974) take-off, *Towering Quake*, in which he appeared as Hollywood actress Carol Tobin caught atop the burning building. As usual, Stanley's production values were epic (and ruinously expensive), his scenes of devastation, giant flames burning buildings and crashing scenery made the sketch look almost as authentic as the film.

'Disaster movies are nothing new,' proclaims New Yorker, Carol. 'Britain has been making them for years.'

Ken Hoare also had fun with short gags such as: 'Daisy, Daisy. The bisexual made for two.'

Again, it seemed Stanley and his principal writer were on the same radical wavelength. Billy Connolly believes Stanley and Ken were subversive.

'It's a privilege when gay guys bring you into their world by using risqué material that hints at gayness. Don't forget these guys have had to live in a Masonic darkness, but what Stanley and Kenneth Williams would do is share the joy, and the daftness, of it.

'I loved it when Stanley was in frocks because he was annoying little journalists all the time. And he would parody film in a really camp way, which I loved. Really, there was no other way to see material like this. This was revue material on television. And I thought it was brilliant.'

Ken Hoare wrote of his working relationship with the star and offered real insight:

> Stanley dreams up a high percentage of the basic subjects for the show. Some of his notions are devastating and I can't wait to slave over a hot typewriter. Others are borderline or dud and we soon lay them to rest by mutual consent.
>
> Our second meeting is always the tricky one. Stanley's perfectionism is well known. There I sit in rigid expectation as Stanley reads the first

> of my sketches. I test the silence by dropping pins. The decibel level is enough to make him look up, put the script down and sigh. 'It's beautifully written,' he admits.
>
> But beautifully written is good news only if you happened to be Jane Austen. Laughter so fierce and prolonged that Stanley requires mouth-to-mouth resuscitation was what I was hoping for.

Meanwhile, Stanley still had to resolve the situation with Marcus, who was now almost a constant in his life. The more he saw his lover, the more he worried about being outed. Newspapers had become, if that were possible, even more homophobic. Yes, the BBC TV film of the time *The Naked Civil Servant*, John Hurt's fascinating portrayal of Quentin Crisp, picked up fantastic reviews, but pancake-wearing Crisp was seen as a national oddity, and hardly a role model for gay men who were still living in terror. TV's Jason King was the current case in point. Peter Wyngarde, once voted 'the man most UK women would love to lose their virginity to', was arrested in a gentlemen's toilet in London along with a truck driver and charged with committing 'a lewd act'. The actor later denied being a homosexual, just as Stanley had done. Regardless, ITV dumped him. At the same time Larry Grayson was refusing to admit in interviews that he was gay. He was 'just pretending'.

Yes, Elton John, David Bowie and Freddie Mercury could parade like peacocks on stage and offer the possibility they *might* be gay – but not tweed-wearing actors like Stanley who had worn the overcoat of heterosexuality, from the outset, as a cover. The public, and the newspapers, he reckoned, still wouldn't stand for it. That's why it was Stanley and Moira – certainly not Stanley and Marcus – who attended the Royal Gala premiere of Barbra Streisand's movie *Funny Lady*, the follow up to *Funny Girl*.

Stanley agreed to be presented to royalty because it was a chance to meet his idol Streisand, but he admits he was anxious about meeting the Queen, given he'd shown the world his Brendagh. And his fears were heightened by Fleet Street who asked: 'Will the Queen snub the cheeky Scot?' At the Gala, the Queen stopped and spoke to Stanley. And after she passed down the line she returned for another chat. Of course, the theatre audience could see this on the big screen.

'When she came back, I thought, "Oh dear!" but she said to me, "I think you've met my daughter, recently." And very sycophantically I said, "Yes, and how very lovely she looked!"

'How arsehole-creeping can you get?

'And then she went over to Barbra, who looked at the Queen in a bemused way and asked, "Why do you have to wear those big long white gloves?" As I heard this I thought, "Oh, fucking no!"'

In November, Stanley returned to panto at the King's, Edinburgh, with *Jack and the Beanstalk* and his life appeared to be relatively calm. The audiences were great and Marcus was kept hidden in the background. But turbulence arrived in January 1976 when David Bell returned to the UK, the tinsel dream having faded. But not to London. David moved to Glasgow, to become Head of Entertainment at Scottish Television. Stanley's heart sank at the news. Who would help stop him worrying – and know instinctively how to transform his ideas into television? After a holiday in Greece with Moira, Stanley put his concerns aside and determined to make his next TV special even better than the last.

'Bruce Gowers came in and luckily he was a fantastic director and we set to make *Stanley Baxter's Christmas Box*.[24]

'Bruce had great ideas for direction and he would let me go into the edit room. But he was so good I never had to interfere.'

The director had great material to work with such as the idea of spoofing Jacques Cousteau's terribly serious series, which studied the creatures of the deep. Instead of looking at sea life, Stanley's Frenchman studied the human life-forms who played around on a summer beach.

'We had the fat, Channel-swimming girl in the water – I got to play the girl, using a balloon suit – wearing a bathing costume and cap who gets captured in the net and examined like a specimen by Cousteau.'

Stanley was prepared to suffer for his art.

'We weren't sure if the balloon suit would survive the open sea. The night before filming I put it on and climbed into a bath for half an hour.'

One three-minute Cousteau scene involved hiring a launch and taking it to Margate for several days. (Amazingly, Cyril Bennett approved the enormous budget.)

Stanley also came up with a take-off of the 1944 movie *Cover Girl*, but instead of playing a Rita Hayworth-type, his central character was a very big lady who is then transformed.

> PRODUCER [in loud American accent]: 'We'll shoot the works. Cosmetic surgery. Diet sheets. Hairstyling, panel-beating, respray, the lot! Operation Cover Girl here we come.'

When the big woman is transformed into a screen beauty, Stanley had the idea she then appears in a snow scene in which she sings…

> Snow balls I know give a lift when you're low
> There are no balls like snow balls for me
> Nothing's as nice as the tingle of ice
> Though some screwballs might never agree
>
> I love to lay with some guy on a sleigh
> Or ride about slewed on a sled
> I've always found when there's snow on the ground
> Can't get balls out of my head.

Outside of work, the very hot summer months of 1976 were spent with Kenneth Williams. Kenneth, currently appearing in a flop play *Signed and Sealed*, was even more depressed than usual and talking (again) of suicide. Supportive Stanley suggested his pal go to America and relaunch his career with a review show.

'But paranoia was the order of the day and he questioned every motive. It was very hard to stay friends with him.'

Moira too was continuing to battle against the dark forces in her mind. She'd finally agreed to take drugs but the positive, stabilising effect didn't last long. Stanley came up with an idea. He bought her a nice little penthouse flat just a couple of streets away in Highgate Village. And for a couple of months a calm entered his life.

However in November disaster struck. At the end of a special conference in Croydon to consider the future of LWT, Stanley's boss (and huge fan) Cyril Bennett fell from his apartment window. Later, the coroner said he found no grounds for suicide. He was 'looking for his car'. Stanley was devastated by the news and thought differently.

'He was a very troubled man. His marriage had broken up and he even came to live with me for a short time. There's no doubt in my mind that Cyril's death was suicide.'

It would take Stanley some time to recover from the loss of his 'wonderful' father-figure. And while there was some relief in the fact Michael Grade had since joined LWT (he was also a great fan of Stanley's work) the actor was extremely suspicious of the rising power of John Birt.

Meantime, Stanley had to return to Glasgow for panto rehearsals, reprising *Jack and the Beanstalk*. The opening night saw the audience in raptures but the *Daily Record* again attacked the Scots star. 'Pantomime should not be so sophisticated that gags shoot over the heads of kids. Panto is for kids and the performance should be judged by their opinions.'

Stanley's response in the *Glasgow Herald*? 'Interesting,' he said. 'Get the kids to write the reviews then.'

There was further flak to contend with on Christmas Day when his LWT special was aired. One of the sketches attracted complaints from the nation's 'moral guardian', Mrs Mary Whitehouse. Mrs Whitehouse, having polished up her brass neck for the event, said to a press conference: 'I didn't see the show myself but I hear it was pretty bad. I'll be making a complaint to the IBA [Independent Broadcasting Authority] nonetheless.'

Perhaps Stanley (via Ken Hoare) was being a *little* bad with one of his sketch characters, a lady-who-lunches type called Faith Douche. Faith makes a television charity appeal 'on behalf of the morally inhibited':

> The nation's inhibited will never know the freedom the rest of us enjoy when we stroll into a back-street bookshop and eagerly thumb through Red Hot Ruby, the Young Nympho – or whoever happens to be behind the counter.

Not stopping at the red traffic lights of self-censure, Faith drove right down Transsexuality Road all the way up to Homosexuality Lane (apologies to the late Ken Hoare):

> Will Shakespeare, though no prude was a man flawed by inhibitions. Much as we admire his magnificent plays and poetry would we not admire him more if he had openly avowed 'I'm a poofter and the dark lady of the sonnets is really a bit of rough trade from Southwark?'
>
> Alas, poor Will did not have the NCMI behind him – only the lad from Southwark.

The nation was outraged. Or at the least the editor of the *Daily Record* was. The Leader Column of 29 December announced: 'Stanley Baxter, that accomplished comedian, is in trouble. His Christmas Show, says quite a few critics, was downright dirty. Did Stan and Ollie ever have to crack a dirty joke?'

No, but they never had to walk the tightrope of clever satire and earthy humour either. Stanley however took the criticism on board.

'I was so sharp I almost cut myself. And I decided not to go down that route again.'

But Santa did bring some very good news. David Bell had had enough of regional television and quit STV to return to LWT as Executive Producer. Stanley was ecstatic. And with David at the helm Stanley managed to park his usual anxieties to declare he felt 'wonderfully confident' about his next television show. He was speaking far too soon.

32

Death by Porridge

IN FEBRUARY 1977, David Bell was LWT's Controller of Entertainment with a big office, two big leather chesterfields and a big, welcoming smile on his face. Meanwhile, Michael Grade, whom Stanley liked enormously, had raced through the ranks to become Director of Programmes. The actor couldn't have asked for a more personable boss to step into Cyril Bennett's shoes. It was, in short, the Dream Team in operation.

However, Stanley became unsure at all if he wanted to play. Signs of stress emerged when it came to choosing his director for the next special (with David Bell promoted above the position and Bruce Gowers on his way to the US to work on *The Golden Girls*). Stanley reckoned no one else seemed quite right. But his fussiness wasn't about the content.

'I worried about being able to produce another great show. And the fact I had David and Michael supporting me totally, in a strange way, added to the pressure.'

The pressure stopped Stanley in his tracks. He didn't work with LWT for an entire year, yet he didn't spend all the time staring out the window. In August 1977, he agreed to film an ATV (Associated Television) Christmas special, *Bing Crosby's Merry Olde English Christmas* over at Elstree. Other names on the rather incongruous line-up included David Bowie, Twiggy and Ron Moody. And for the first time that year Stanley actually became excited at the prospect of standing in front of a camera.

'I loved the idea of working with Bing. And in fact, it all came about because one of Bing's sons who was studying at RADA at the time, had seen my shows including the *Upstairs, Downstairs* sketches and recommended me. But there was a certain serendipity about it all because for ages I had been saying to David I'd love to do a take-off of the *Road* movies.'

The idea was that Stanley play Bob Hope, alongside the real thing. 'The sketch involved Bing turning up at this big manor house and discovering it has Bob Hope as a ghost – with me of course playing the spectre.'

Stanley remembers being so worried about Bing's reaction he reckons he didn't do a great job on 'Bob'. He needn't have been so afraid. Bing not only laughed, he laughed loudly, and for quite some time.

'Bing yelled, "Wait 'till I phone Bob and tell him how wonderful this is!" And that's a measure of how nice a man he was.'

Bing's people were very keen that Stanley do his *Upstairs, Downstairs* characters, in particular Hudson, Rose and Mrs Bridges.

'They wanted me to play Mrs Bridges alongside his new wife Cathy, who, incidentally, was somewhat lacking in thespian talent.

'So I got Ken Hoare to write up a sketch for Cathy and me, where I play the three characters welcoming Mrs Crosby, with a highly deferential Rose of course curtseying before Mrs Crosby at the door.

'Then, for the big finale I had to sing "Side By Side" alongside Ron Moody and Bing but the sound man called out, "Bing, we can hear Ron and Stanley but we can't hear you." And Bing called out, "These guys are worse than Hope." And we all laughed.

'There was no temperament with him.'

Stanley got on really well with the 'lovely' Twiggy and they chatted away together lots of times.

'But I didn't like Ron Moody at all. He was a miserable bastard, in fact, who loved to upstage people. The director actually had to pull him up about it.'

He adds with a little laugh: 'Fagin was a jolly man compared to Ron Moody.'

Bob Hope (probably) got to hear the finished result.

'Bing said he'd called him and let him hear a tape. And he said Bob loved it. But perhaps he was just being nice.'

Stanley had no real contact during filming with rock chameleon David Bowie. The pop star remained aloof.

'I can remember him giggling away one day with one of the

make-up girls and he often stood in the corner of the room, silent. But to be fair, perhaps he was a bit shy too.'

Filming over, on 11 September, Stanley received a letter from Bing Crosby, now in Spain, who said how sorry he was not to have had the chance to say goodbye in person.

'I want to get one of the still pictures to show Bob,' he wrote. 'And hope your future efforts are rewarded with the success you deserve.'

It was one of the last letters the legend ever wrote. Bing died of a heart attack during that holiday.

A few days later Stanley set off on a holiday – of sorts – this time going back to Los Angeles with David Bell and Bruce McClure. Earlier, David had shown tapes of Stanley's shows to a major TV producer who was interested in the Scot. He reckoned a few months in Los Angeles was just the thing to re-energise his friend – and set them both on the road to international success.

'I met this man who looked like Santa Claus and of course, being very American he was way over the top; you know the types who shake hands and won't let go until the blood supply to your elbow has been cut off.'

'Stanley, I want to say that not only are you the greatest light entertainment artist in Britain, but in the world.'

'Well, thank you.'

'You know, I really think we could do a fabulous 15 episodes together.'

'Fifteen? No. Sorry, that's not the way I work. You don't realise, I'm five months writing, doing post-production, all for one hour's television.'

'Stanley, you've just got to work harder!'

'Harder? No, I don't think so!'

'No? Well, look, Stanley, what about 12 episodes? And, of course, I can get you Lily Tomlin as a guest star.'

'Perhaps. She is wonderful. And she could certainly be a guest star in a show of mine. But I couldn't even do *six* episodes. And it's nothing to do with working harder. It's the way I work. I come up with ideas, play all the parts, I have to agonise over each script, then there are the costumes...'

'Yes, yes, and I love your pastiches and the dancing girls sketches, although we couldn't have you doing things like that sketch where she sings "Summer Time". They wouldn't go for that out here.'

Santa Claus was a couple of presents short of a full information sack. He hadn't done his homework, or he'd have understood Stanley's modus operandi in that he demanded/needed to control every aspect of the performance.

'We drove back to the hotel in David's hired Mercedes and his silence was confirmation he knew Santa's TV series just wasn't going to happen.'

Stanley realises it's preposterous he didn't hire a team of the very best American writers. But then his walking away from the LA opportunity wasn't just about programme content.

'I didn't want to flop in the States. The *Daily Record* would have loved it.'

There were also personal reasons. He didn't want to leave Moira alone, and there was Marcus to consider. And while he feared failure, he also feared major success. International celebrity could bring with it a searching spotlight.

'If you become an international star you lose your anonymity,' he said to magazine *Scottish Field* at the time. 'You can't avoid being asked by journalists about who you are currently shacked up.'

Curiously, that year Elton spilled the beans in *Rolling Stone*, acknowledging his bisexuality, adding 'we all are to various degrees'. Yet, the British press desisted from the expected homophobic rant. *The Sun* didn't even mention the story and the *News of the World* treatment was downbeat. 'Elton: My Love Life Isn't So Strange.'

Meanwhile, one of the major comedy hits of the year was ITV's *Man about the House* spin-off *Robin's Nest*, in which Richard O'Sullivan and Tessa Wyatt lived in sin above their little bistro, the first 'common law marriage in a sitcom'. Was the moral climate changing for the better? Stanley wasn't going to take the chance.

Meantime, the show – his only real working stint of the year – had to go on. Edinburgh City Council, who had backed *Jack and the Beanstalk* in Glasgow and Edinburgh, had decided to complete the trilogy in Manchester. The councillors fancied themselves as producers but the experience suggested they were clueless. The

Manchester Opera House production of December 1977 collapsed like a broken beanstalk. Stanley and the cast (Christopher Beeny of *Upstairs, Downstairs* fame played Jack) emptied the place.

'The owners of the rival Palace Theatre wanted to finish off the Opera House so they put on their own panto with Ken Dodd starring, opening the same night.

'That really fucked us but I wasn't blameless. I made the mistake of playing Dame in English. But as she is essentially a working-class figure I should have stuck with Scots. It was a huge critical mistake on my part and I paid for it.'

In the same month, LWT kept the flame burning with a compilation show, *Stanley Baxter's Greatest Hits* and some extra Christmas tinsel came with the news that Peter Nichols' tale of Nee Soon life, *Privates on Parade*, was voted Comedy of the Year in London, starring Denis Quilley and Nigel Hawthorne.

But would his friend's success encourage Stanley to pull his professional socks up and get back to making television? A little more income would certainly have been useful too. In early 1978, the flat below in Highgate Village became available for a song and Stanley grabbed at it. He took the dividing entrance away to give him a large house with identical upstairs and downstairs living rooms, sitting rooms and bedrooms. Two of everything. Perfect for a Gemini who'd been living a double life for so long.

Meanwhile, David Bell kept pushing his pal to make another hour-long special, but Stanley kept delaying, citing the problem of finding the right director as a reason. Blah blah. Finally, a name was suggested that rang Stanley's bell. Not loudly. But just enough to resonate.

The name was John Kaye Cooper, Stanley's former panto assistant in Glasgow who had moved up the ladder from STV to Thames to Yorkshire Television, where he became a drama director.

'David Bell rang me out of the blue in 1978,' John Kaye Cooper recalls. 'He said, "Now, dear, what are you doing wasting your time with all those drama queens in Leeds! Why don't you come down and work with us light entertainment queens here in London! Come down and have a wee interview, dear." I was simply elated. *The Stanley Baxter Show* was *the* top show on television.'

Stanley wasn't entirely convinced David Bell had made the right choice.

'My nerves were shot to bits at the idea of coming up with ideas and wondering if John was up to the job at this time.'

John admits the pressure was intense.

'Stanley had a say in everything, from wigs to orchestrations to costumes to lighting. He could be quite difficult and testy and we had a few rows. But David taught me to stand my ground – if I thought I was right. Looking back, I had to deal with a lot worse later with Michael Barrymore. Stanley was a joy to work for in comparison.'

But a perfectionist nevertheless. Who loved his genius to be recognised. John recalled:

'I'd be summoned up to the house in Highgate in the morning and we'd plot a whole scene out, just the two of us, and work out where I'd do the split screens and close-ups.'

John had learned the same living room-planning technique David had used with Stanley in Glasgow.

'The next day I'd have to act all innocent as Stanley went through the process of "originating" the ideas we'd agreed the day before. It was a game for us, going on in front of the other actors who all thought we were really clever.

'If another actor made a suggestion Stanley would look interested but say, "Mmm. I don't know. What does John think?" And John knew his place; which was that he would "agree" with Stanley.'

Stanley's working world had to be as it was in Millport, or at Aunt Alice's. He had to be in control of the cousins.

And who could argue with success? *Stanley Baxter on Television* contained some great moments such as a rather daring George Formby sketch 'They Get Away with Murder on the Telly', with 'George' bemoaning the fact he never got away with as much smut as they do nowadays. He sings, while playing the ukulele of course:

> They can get away with murder on the telly
> There's no limit to the license on the box
> Some narrow-minded viewers
> Really made the switchboard hum
> They complained about a blonde who lay naked on her tum

While someone sprinkled Johnson's Baby Powder on her back...
They can get away with murder on the telly

Stanley, daringly, and somewhat astonishingly, included a verse making fun of the gay rights movement via football:

They can get away with murder on the telly
There's no limit to the license on the box
They say gay lib is gaining ground and bound to take its toll
I don't mind those all-male love scenes
But I'd rather on the whole
That men just shook hands
When they scored the winning goal
They can get away with murder on the telly.

But then he really took a chance with...

They can get away with murder on the telly
There's no limit to the license on the box
When asked his job a quiz contestant answered fair and square
'I'm a master baker,' he replied and didn't turn a hair
But Nick Parsons he just looked aghast and said,
'That's neither here nor there'
They can get away with murder on the telly.

And he came up with a *Ben Hur* classic pastiche, 'The Semi Final', featuring Stanley performing a brilliant Robert Morley. The spoof involved using a *Match of the Day* commentary to describe the Biblical battleground: 'And over on the far side we have King Herod, one of the great names of genocide, played brilliantly by Robert Morley.' Herod approaches the Slave Girl, Esther, who asks him in a strong Italian accent:

'My master has grown a cold (sniffs). You promised me love. Why cannot I a have it?'

'Away with you!'

'Yes, why cannot I have it away with you?'

'Silence! Another word and I can have your tongue ripped out and your voice dubbed into English by Joan Collins.'

Stanley also had the very clever idea of a *Generation Game* spoof with Sir John Gielgud (with a false-nose fitted Stanley looked remarkably like the acting legend) fronting the show. But filming on 28 August almost killed him. The sketch copied the *Generation Game* format where a giant two hundredweight vat of sludge was poured slowly over the heads of contestants, except on this occasion it would be 'Gielgud' underneath. Except when it came to it, it wasn't poured gradually at all. John Kaye Cooper recalls the horror which unfolded.

'We did two or three rehearsals and went for a take. Then I watched in sheer fright as this massive, brim-full plastic dustbin wobbled. The supports began to collapse and this quarter ton of sludge started to plummet – right down on top of Stanley.

'I thought straight away he would be killed, or at the very least disabled. It was terrifying.'

After hitting Stanley hard and knocking him to the floor, the giant vat should have crushed the life out of his body but two benches either side of him, which were props for the sketch, miraculously got in the way. Seconds later the near-tragedy turned into a pantomime.

'Floors at that time all had a shiny covering to make them look mirror-like,' says John. 'Now, with this porridge on top it all became lethal. As four or five of us rushed to Stanley's rescue we hit the sludge, became covered in it and skated across the floor on our backsides.'

Stanley, meantime was laying in agony.

'After the whole lot crashed down upon me I immediately called out, "Don't try and lift me up!" And that was fortunate because I knew straight away something serious had happened.

'I was fully conscious through it all and aware that it was too serious to be painful. Both legs had gone numb and the thought going through my mind was "Am I paralysed?"

'You didn't need to be a hypochondriac to be that worried.

'Somehow, I called for a stretcher of some sort, however improvised. And they had one lying around, some gunny sacking between two poles.

'And then just as they were about to carry me out of the studio an astonishing showbiz moment occurred. As I was lying there, still all covered in sludge and in agony with what turned out to be a fractured pelvis [in two places], the make-up girl came towards me and said, "I'll just have that nose back, thank you. They cost a lot of money you know." And so it was yanked off.'

He adds, 'The whole episode was filmed so it is on record. But I doubt if it will ever make Denis Norden's *It'll Be All Right on the Night*.'

The proboscis-free but still fully made up Stanley was taken to St Thomas's Hospital in London for intense examination.

Amazingly, the sludge had set hard around him in the improvised stretcher. The doctors could scarcely believe the sight before their eyes.

'A surgeon looked at the mess and said, "What's this?" And I said, "Porridge" as if to suggest it was perfectly normal to be covered in it.'

Later, a worried Kenneth Williams went over to visit his injured friend. But his self-obsession somehow got in the way of his concern. Williams was denied entry, and walked off in a hissy fit, only to discover later that Stanley had been having a tube removed from his bladder.

At least Stanley didn't need surgery, with the doctors recommending considerable bed rest over the next few months. Ian Bannen was one of the many friends who called while the actor recovered in a Hampshire nursing home. (Judi Dench wrote a lovely supportive letter.) Stanley however didn't seek compensation for his accident.

'John Reid thought I was mad not to. But I didn't want to be an ambulance chaser. I thought it would sour relationships with LWT and of course I liked the bosses so much. Yet, that's not to say I was happy at all about the men who hadn't fixed the equipment properly.'

Meanwhile, Stanley had lots of time on his hands to do nothing but think.

'My main thought was about how soon it would be until I could retire. Part of me was saying, "The stress of it all is too much."'

Pain and career anxiety were not the only problems the actor had to contend with.

'David picked Moira up from home one day and brought her to the hospital to visit me. But no sooner had she arrived when she skipped out into the corridor and began dancing around.

'I didn't know what to do about her condition at all. I suggested she go back to the doctors and she promised she would.'

It wasn't until March 1979, his pelvis healed, that Stanley was able to complete the TV special. It was screened the following month.

'Unfortunately, I had done the easy shooting first, the sitting on seats and so on. The action filming had been left to the end.'

Stanley gritted his teeth and completed the shoot. And most critics reckoned he produced some of his best work ever.

Yet, there was a slight drop in the audience figures. Whatever the reason, the dip affected Stanley very deeply. He hadn't been brought up to do less well. Such was his mental state he took to tranquilisers again.

'I didn't even want to do panto that year,' he says of the stint at the King's Theatre, Edinburgh. Kenneth Williams, as expected, was no help in times of real crises.

'I remember sitting with him in Osteria Lariana and telling him that I was very, very low. And I explained a great part of the problem was Moira. I told him of how she was slipping into little overdoses and I would be going round to see her and reviving her. And suddenly Kenny cut in, "Yes, yes! You're not much fun anymore! A bit boring. Very boring."

'Anything more serious than an eye infection he didn't want to know.'

Stanley dragged himself back to panto, the only positive being Marcus would come up and stay for weekends.

'We'd stay in digs, always booking two bedrooms. One or two people knew he was my partner and by this time I felt I had to take the chance. I'd never had anyone I could really cuddle in life, until Marcus. Not even Bill Henry.'

Cinderella was well received but Stanley's state of mind was precarious. The need for continuous affirmation had never been so pronounced. That's why Stanley faced the '80s with a trembling heart.

33
Santa's Sack

IN EARLY 1980, the dark, depressive impact of Thatcherism and the nihilistic punk music of the period matched Stanley's state of mind perfectly. He simply didn't have the energy to create new television. In February, LWT kept the Baxter profile – and the bank balance – up with a repeat of *Stanley Baxter on Television*. But the actor's abeyant state continued right through to the end of the year when he returned to Glasgow and the less mentally demanding world of panto with *Cinderella*, at the King's, again with Angus Lennie and the Bruce McClure Dancers.

In November 1980, *The Glasgow Herald* revealed: 'Stanley Baxter has broken all existing box office records, with more than £250,000 already taken.' The show ran at an incredible 92 per cent capacity, a real confidence lifter. But not enough to think about a return to television, and certainly not as a chat show guest. The actor admitted to the *Sunday Mail* he would run for his life if *This Is Your Life* came calling and revealed he'd turned down *Parkinson* eight times and *Russell Harty* three times.

'The only television chat show I've done was *An Afternoon with Mavis Nicholson* and even then I was on pills beforehand. I agreed only because Mavis is such a sympathetic character and I had seen her interview my friend Kenneth Williams.' That wasn't quite true. Stanley had to be bullied into talking to LWT-based Mavis by David Bell.

'I was a fan of her work,' he admits, 'but I knew the drag question would come up. And sure enough the first question was "What does your wife think of you playing women so much, Stanley?"'

The gay issue, he felt, was implicit in the question; it painted a picture of someone who loved to dress up as a girlie. 'Fuck chat shows,' he says, reflecting his feelings as the 54-year-old who wanted to pull a duvet over his head and hide from the world.

Meanwhile, LWT kept the Baxter flame burning – and the ad revenue coming in – with a Christmas repeat of his last series. What LWT were also doing was buying time in the hope that their flagship would come out of dry dock. The patience was rewarded. In the New Year of 1981 David Bell managed to convince Stanley the way forward was to go back to the six half hour format. One major factor in Stanley's agreeing to return was the arrival at LWT of Bruce McClure (he argued Bruce would help with ideas but the truth was he wanted another friend around).

John Kaye Cooper, who directed the series, recalls David wasn't too happy with the idea of hiring Bruce, initially. 'He felt it looked as though he were hiring an old boyfriend.' Stanley however felt he had been 'bullied' into making the series and attached another condition. He suggested they rob some of the material used in the last series filmed at BBC Scotland. David agreed and so he, Stanley and Bruce would meet at David Bell's house in West Hampstead (now owned by Emma Thompson) to thrash ideas around.

'Bruce suggested we add some *Good Old Days* material featuring vaudevillian characters,' says Stanley, 'and we did, and that was successful. But now and then he would suggest films to pastiche but with no twist, no hook. Of course, you can't do pastiches without a hook. That's why much comedy these days is disappointing, because the writers don't bother with a pay-off.'

John Kaye Cooper reveals Stanley and David would fight.

'It wasn't about the series, it was more a chemical thing. They were great pals but sometimes over cocktails or dinner they'd have great screaming rows about some old MGM film or whatever. And then they'd laugh and be the best of friends. An outsider may have reckoned there was a real sexual tension in the air, but the pair weren't an item.

'And they did have real fun together. Unlike lots of people in the television business Stanley and David didn't need drugs to get a high. They'd simply put on a record of Broadway musicals and dance around the room, to *Chorus Line* or whatever and do the routines.'

But the fun and music didn't help Stanley fill the ideas vacuum. He was always anxious. And working on the series was tough, even with the recycled Scottish material.

'I reused the Ethel Merman *Everything's Coming Up Roses* gag, which was all about her voice blasting buildings, chimney stacks crashing down, all that sort of thing, was used. But now copyright laws had kicked in and I had to sing it. That was hard to do.'

Some of the new ideas were at least radical, such as the take-off of the *Holiday '81* travel show, which featured a holiday in Iran, with Stanley playing the Ayatollah. (Try that nowadays.)

He lampooned marital knowledge quiz show *Mr and Mrs* and he came up with a Tarzan sketch in which he plays Tarzan *and* Jane; Tarzan plays cards all day and keeps girlie magazines – and eats Jane's mum. Tarzan arrives back at the hut and presents Jane with magazines. Jane is delighted:

> 'How did you get these magazines, Tarzan?'
>
> 'Tarzan lord of jungle. He take anything he wants. I take them from white man.'
>
> 'Their camp?'
>
> [He thinks for a moment...]
>
> 'Some of them.'

As well as coming up with the ideas for the series (which transmitted in October and November 1981) Stanley, as always, needed to be in control of almost every aspect of production.

'I wasn't going to have people double as me for dress fittings, as Ronnie Barker did. I wanted to do all the characters because I wanted everything exactly right.'

It was madness, considering there were 12 to 15 costumes in each half hour.

'You can see I was making a rod for my own back.'

The size of a tree.

To promote the series, Stanley agreed to an interview with *The Guardian*'s Polly Toynbee. The journalist realised she was talking to a complex character.

> He insists on being chaperoned by Rita Boorman, the LWT PR. For a man who cavorts so unflatteringly in so many guises he displays surprising vanity about being photographed.
>
> Then he talks about playing more men than women, and women have no reason to feel insulted. 'What do you want? Gallantry? I don't believe in any of that. Nor would feminists. I'm not a female impersonator. I'm a people impersonator. I watch people all the time. It's what I like doing best, how they sit, move and talk, hold their knives and forks, pick their nose.'
>
> Stanley goes on to concede impersonating others is escape. 'I hate playing myself,' he says. 'I like to retreat into playing other people. I'm not entirely sure who I am.'

Toynbee adds:

> Throughout the interview I had the feeling that Mr Baxter was switching from character to character as we changed subjects. Which was the real one? Was there a real one? Did he know he was doing it?
>
> I asked him if he was acting being interviewed by *The Guardian*. He looked a bit put out and asked Rita. 'Am I?' Rita put her head to one side and thought for a moment before answering 'Well, yes, I think you are acting.'

The writer liked the actor, 'acting' or not.

> He is so plastic, malleable, so mercurial you come away with an impression of a charming, endearing vulnerable man. But also of a host of shadowy characters, not all of them benevolent, like spirit guides who seize upon him at unpredictable moments. He is the medium for all these ghosts and it isn't always clear exactly who is in control.

His chemist prescription was proof all was not well in Stanley's head at the time. But at the same time, LWT bosses were delighted with the series and newspapers claimed there was talk of selling it on to the States. Of course, it was never going to happen; it was at times too subversive. At other, too old-fashioned for the market. Kenneth Williams wrote in his *Diaries*:

> I was struck by Stanley's obsession with the past. It was all about old

> films, film directors, film stories rejigged, film personalities (Jimmy Durante etc) and so was fine for the middle-aged but it had nothing for the young.

After filming, in November a very jaded Stanley took off with Marcus for a five-star holiday in Barbados (Moira, he says, accepted the arrangement).

'I hated it,' he recalls of the break. 'There was rampant homophobia on the island and when the locals saw two men together, we really got some abuse.'

He didn't go back to panto that year; the holiday hadn't helped with his nervous state. And in the spring of 1982, Stanley was further depressed when the BAFTAS were announced, with *The Stanley Baxter Series* a winner. Why the disappointment? Stanley didn't get one. David Bell and John Kaye shared the BAFTA for the best Light Entertainment Programme. It was rather like Adam and Eve being credited with creating the world. Nigel Hawthorne took home the Best Comedy Actor award.

'Stanley was really hurt,' says John. 'He felt he had been ignored. And he had.'

'I had a right to be ever-so-slightly miffed,' says Stanley, with some understatement. 'But I didn't for a second resent Nigel getting the gong for his *Yes, Minister* work.'

The disappointment didn't push him in the direction of another six-parter. After lengthy debate he chose to do another hour-long special, the easier option. *The Stanley Baxter Hour* contained a spoof on *Brideshead Revisited*, based on the sort of song Noel Coward would have written today. The show also saw a reappearance of his BBC Scotland Rosemary Gusher sketch, where the old bitter and jealous school chum visits a successful actress backstage, who has just played Medea – and destroys her by reminding her of her mistakes.

> ROSEMARY [in posh Glasgow accent]: 'Oh, Anita, I had to come and tell you how much I loved your wee show.'
> ANITA [beams]: 'You liked it?'
> ROSEMARY: 'I loved it. I've never laughed so much in all my life.'

ANITA: 'That's not exactly the reaction we look for in a Greek tragedy.'
ROSEMARY: 'Still, I loved the young man on stage with the golden curls.'
ANITA: 'He's my lover.'
ROSEMARY: 'You're quite right dear, at your age, to have a last wee fling.'
[The actress is set to burst into tears and the despair continues when Rosemary asks]: 'Oh, Anita, did you forget your line at one point?'

'Hannah Gordon wrote to me after the show went out and said, "Stanley, if only you knew how true that is."'

Filming over in late July, Stanley set to work on the panto script (he liked to be prepared). But it was hard to think of fun sketches when Moira's neighbours told Stanley his wife's behaviour had again become confused. One night, she was seen running down the corridors of the flats naked. More appointments were made with more psychiatrists.

There was also concern over Bruce's health. He and David had taken off to Los Angeles on holiday, but this time around David reported that sun worshipper Bruce hadn't been sun bathing. Bruce simply wasn't himself.

Stanley also had the critics to worry about. Would they like the special? Thankfully, *The Stanley Baxter Hour* went out in October to great reviews and the following month it was time to start the *Goose* panto stint alongside Angus Lennie. (The Edinburgh date was the first of a trilogy – which included Glasgow and for the first time, Sunderland.)

But while the panto experience was enjoyable, and Stanley had fun working with little Angus, Moira turned up in Glasgow, confused and rather lost. Stanley tried to send her home and she agreed to go, but at the airport decided to fly to Belfast 'to commune with the spirit of theatre director Tyrone Guthrie'. Stanley took a call from the Irish hotel manager who revealed Moira had checked in with no money.

'He took her back to the airport where I had her picked up,' he recalls. 'I was at my wits end. I had no idea what she would do next.'

Not surprisingly, David Bell couldn't even begin to convince his friend to return to LWT in the spring of 1983. Stanley needed to relax, to allow the ideas to flow back into the brain. And the weeks turned into months as he took Marcus on mini-breaks, took Moira to lunch every day and took in movies such as Tom Courtenay's brilliant stage insight, *The Dresser*.

In November, however, just as Stanley was beginning to get his act together – both literally and figuratively – and think about his next television show, Santa Claus delivered an early Christmas present. The sack. LWT's 24 December repeat of *The Stanley Baxter Hour* would be his last ever appearance on the television station.

'John Birt (now Director of Programmes) called me in to his office to tell me.[25] He said, "It's not that we don't like the shows. It's just that we can't afford to make them anymore."

'I felt bitterness. I felt I had been deserted. David was still there but he couldn't overrule John Birt.'

Stanley's shows had been enormously expensive. It took three days to build a *Ben Hur* set. One day's shooting produced only three minutes of television. And filming was slow because Stanley played most of the characters.

But what to do now? 'Wonderful' Cyril Bennet was gone, David Bell had been neutered. And Stanley's friend and staunch supporter Michael Grade had since gone off to seek his fortune in a Hollywood sitcom production house. As a result, the isolated and defenceless flagship who had brought 14 awards to LWT, was sunk.

34
Benny from *Crossroads*

STANLEY'S EGGSHELL CONFIDENCE was smashed into even smaller pieces. Sacked. Again. Without warning. No one had ever come to him in the preceding months and said, 'Make the ideas a little smaller, Stanley'. No one had ever said they didn't want a *Ben Hur* spoof. At 58, he had lost control and felt his career was dead. All David Bell could do was offer sympathy. All Stanley could do was hang around the house and read the newspapers.

The headlines on 14 February 1984 brought a wry smile to his face. Elton John married German sound engineer Renate Blauel in Australia. Another example of a gay man trying not to be? Thirty-two years after his own attempts at conformity, Stanley could at least understand Elton's motivations. But *The Sun*'s headline didn't indicate the world had become less homophobic; 'GOOD ON YER, POOFTER!' Later, John Reid, who was joint best man with lyricist Bernie Taupin, caught up with *The Sun's* man in Sydney and smacked him on the mouth. *That* story brought a genuine smile to Stanley's face.

In March, work, of sorts, appeared when Stanley was asked to appear on the David Bell produced *Children's Royal Variety Show* at Her Majesty's Theatre, with Bruce McClure co-producing. Stanley teamed up with Angus Lennie to do a routine that he first did with Alex Finlay back in the '50s. But rehearsals threw up one worrying moment. Bruce couldn't get his sketch timings right (he wasn't even close) and David knew instantly there was something wrong and said, 'Get him to a doctor, quickly!' David was right to be alarmed. X-rays revealed Bruce had a brain tumour.

'That explained why this sun worshipper could no longer take the heat. And perhaps a lot of other things. Perhaps even the stutter had been down to living with this tumour for years.'

Stanley, David, John and Russell were stunned. Bruce had a matter of months to live.

Sadly, Stanley couldn't tell Kenneth Williams of his friend's condition during their frequent summer lunches, or even complain about being abandoned by television. (Why see his woes fall on deaf, self-obsessed ears?) All he could do was act happy for the sake of keeping Williams entertained – and their relationship intact. The Scot's performances must have been good.

'His capacity for enjoyment and his relish for the ludicrous is infectious', says Williams of his chum in his *Diaries*. 'Nowadays, I feel like a languid moon to his ebullient sun. Even when he does mention depression it is funny.'

Yet, Stanley did share concerns with Kenneth about their mutual friend Gordon Jackson; Williams had noted Gordon had a little squint at one side of his mouth.

Another friend came up in conversation during the Osteria Lariana lunches. Peter Nichols had published his autobiography, *Feeling You're Behind,* and Williams was upset about being portrayed as overly camp during the Singapore years. He'd clearly forgotten the little floral-printed socks he wore on parade. Williams wrote of Nichols: 'I hope I don't paint such a shabby picture of my friends', displaying a complete absence of irony, given he'd rubbished most of his pals at some point in their lives.

Those summer months however saw Stanley pick up a little work and an awful lot of money. He voiced a British Telecom TV ad, the 'It's For Yoo-oo' series in which he became the likes of Quasimodo and Custer (the characters getting a phone call at the pivotal moment). The actor Stanley was paid more for three days work than he had ever been paid for an LWT show.

But in spite of no regular TV work emerging, Stanley wasn't for leaping back into theatre, turning down the chance to star in his favourite play, *Harvey*, in the West End.

'The producers at first reckoned I was too old. And then they thought, "No, he can do it." But I couldn't. I was too afraid.'

For now, time was spent visiting Bruce in hospital and looking after Moira. In recent months her erratic, unpredictable behaviour had descended into fits of rage, sudden outbursts of temper or even naked dancing in the garden.

'She would sit on the bench across the road from my house and stare up. And then she would come and knock at the door. I'd say, "What do you want, Moira?" And she'd say nothing and go off and dance around the garden.

'At other times, she thought people were listening to her through the intercom so she pulled all the wires out. The neighbours were incensed and took her to court and the magistrate said, "I'll give Mrs Baxter three months to sort things out and leave."

'The tenants then wrote to me saying, "Three months is too long! If you don't take her out of here immediately, we are going to phone *The Sun* newspaper."'

Fortunately, the tenants were basically decent people, but what to do now? Stanley wouldn't divorce or disown his wife, due to guilt and genuine feelings for her. Yet, he feared if he invited her to live with him she'd become a wrecking ball and demolish the walls of his own life.

'I said to her, in a moment of calm, "Look, you've got to leave the flat," and she agreed to go up north and see her sister, Nell, who lived in the Borders. But when I picked her up to take her to the station all she was carrying was a wicker basket that looked like a fisherman's creel containing a few sticks of make-up and the bouzouki she'd been learning to play. I couldn't even reason with her. It was pointless.

'And so she boarded the train, met Nell, and then panicked on the realisation she had left the bouzouki on the train.

'So Nell, a lot older than Moira, drove all the way to Glasgow, picked up the bouzouki from the left luggage and they drove back.'

Moira's nephews were summoned, and they persuaded their aunt she should 'go into a nice little hospital at Dingleton, in Melrose'.

'A few days later, Nell wrote me a nice letter saying that if ever she'd thought that I'd been neglecting Moira or exaggerating her condition to suit my own ends, that notion was dispelled.'

The hospital called and told Stanley Moira would have to be sectioned.

'I said, "Don't apologise! She needs help badly."'

A few days later, he travelled north.

'It was heart-breaking. She was kept in this little cell-like room. "This is imprisonment!" she yelled. And I felt so, so, sorry for her. I said, "Look, I'll get you out, Moira. But you mustn't keep on throwing fits."'

Moira's sectioning meant she was forced to take a lithium treatment. She had previously refused it, and of course couldn't be pressured. With this treatment programme in place, Stanley returned to London, all the time keeping in constant touch with medical staff.

In November, it was time to return to panto, completing the *Goose* trilogy at the Sunderland Empire. There was never a thought Stanley would cancel. After all, it would have made no difference to Moira. And he needed to work again, effectively for the first time that year. But this time around, panto wasn't a cosy comfort blanket.

'They were the most stupid audience I've ever played to. Looking out at them from the stage was like a scene from *Deliverance* (the 1972 Burt Reynolds mad, murdering hillbilly movie). It was like looking out at a load of in-breds.

'It's not that they barracked the cast – they just didn't do anything. And they certainly didn't laugh, even though it was a terrific, tested production.'

From the moment of his arrival at the stage door, Stanley knew he would have a taxing time.

'I asked the theatre manager if I could have a phone installed in my dressing room. Of course, I needed it to check up on Moira.

'But he looked at me is if I had asked him for a Rolls-Royce.

'Later on, the stage door man took me aside and said, "You know Mr Baxter, no one has ever had a phone in their dressing room except Benny from *Crossroads*."'

It says a great deal that Paul Henry's screen character who had learning difficulties carried far more weight than the man whose TV shows cleared streets. Eventually, however, Stanley was given a phone.

But each night on stage was 'torture'. No matter how hard he worked, this audience simply refused to laugh.

'You know, Sid James died on stage in Sunderland,' Stanley deadpans. 'And I don't blame him.'

The Sunderland experience stretched Stanley's resolve to the limit. He had a dying friend in hospital, a wife in a mental institution and no TV career to look forward to. And a panto audience who looked like they would rather have been listening to banjo music. He was *that* close to the edge.

But then one afternoon, pre-matinee, the 'Benny' phone rang in Stanley's dressing room. It was Michael Grade. Bill Cotton had persuaded Michael to return to Britain to become BBC Controller. And one of Michael's first signings, he determined, would be Stanley Baxter.

'He called and said, "Would you like to come back to the BBC?"'

Would he!

Almost as importantly, the offer allowed Stanley the chance to stick two fingers up at John Birt, over at LWT.

'I was anxious about the offer, of course. I knew there would be more new ideas to come up with. But at the same time, I was excited and overjoyed at the idea of being back at work on television.'

And the good news kept coming. In the New Year of 1985, Dingleton Hospital's Head Nurse rang to say that Moira was feeling a lot better. 'And she'd like to speak to you, Stanley.'

'You could tell straight away sanity had returned. It was her old self. She said, "Hello, darling. Listen, I'm awfully sorry about all this nonsense. Anyway, they've given me pills to take – and I *will* take them. Can I come back? Will you meet me?"

'And I said, "Of course you can. And I will." By this time, I knew I would be earning again, and I had the panto money so I said to her, "Moira, listen, I've had Marcus find a wee house for you quite close by. It has a garden," she loved gardening, "and it hasn't got neighbours or anything."

'She said, "It sounds divine!" But I added a cautionary note. I said, "Look Moira, it's at number 13 Cherry Tree Road, you're not going to get superstitious or anything."'

A few days later in February, Stanley met his wife at Euston Station. 'I picked her up and we went along to the new house. Of course, all the time I was wondering if she would wreck this one the way she had the last. But when she walked in through the door, she surveyed the scene and announced, "I not only like it, I love it!"'

From that point, Moira's troubles, if not over, were certainly chemically contained and she came to enjoy her life at 13 Cherry Tree Road. And Stanley resumed the routine of meeting her every day for lunch. Moira was again a joy to be with. The warmth they had once shared flooded back; so much so, in fact, that if he hadn't met Marcus, he says, he would have asked her to move back in.

'In my own way, I loved her.'

Yet, at the same time, living with Marcus was never an option. Britain was still so anti-gay that when new TV soap *EastEnders* ran a storyline featuring a kiss between two gay men questions were asked in Parliament.

It's not surprising so many gay men tried very hard not to be, including John Reid. Now long split from Elton, John announced he was to marry Sarah Forbes, daughter of neighbours Bryan Forbes and Nanette Newman. Stanley took his pal aside and warned he was making the biggest mistake of his life. John took his advice and called the wedding off. And he would thank him for that many times in years to come.

Stanley's spirits meanwhile took another upward turn with the arrival of an unusual job offer, a voice-over for Arabian Nights animation adventure, *The Thief and the Cobbler.* He would be playing a cartoon thief alongside Kenneth Williams.

The pair (called, respectively, Gofer and Goblet) laughed about the fact they were to be reunited in toil (of sorts) for the first time in almost 40 years. (The star of the film was Vincent Price, who played the Grand Vizier. Interestingly, The *Hammer Horror* favourite was married to Stanley's old chum, Coral Browne. Price was gay, but the predatory Ms Brown saw the star as another irresistible challenge.) The film sat on the shelf for years before being released in 1993.

In May 1984, Stanley's mood dropped drastically. He had been upset the previous month by news of the death of Tommy Cooper, who had collapsed during a live TV show being produced by David Bell. But he was simply devastated when Bruce McClure died. Stanley, David and Russell knew how much they would miss Bruce's incredibly dry, dark, Glaswegian sense of humour, this ability to take the grey in life and turn it into coal-black comedy. Bruce was the master of the cutting one-liner.

Thankfully, Stanley had the distraction of his upcoming TV show to work on. He offered the newspapers a nice line: 'After a trial separation of 14 years, Stanley Baxter is pleased to announce a reconciliation with the BBC. He has exercised his conjugal rights very quietly with Auntie at their home in Shepherd's Bush and anticipates a happy event later this year.'

Stanley and Auntie indicated to the press pack they would soon be going at like rabbits because the agreement was to make 'two specials and two series during that time'.

The press wondered, understandably, if the BBC could afford the Rolls-Royce of comedy vehicles that was Stanley Baxter?

'Whatever it costs,' replied a resolute James Moir, BBC's Head of Variety, showing how keen the BBC was to capture the weekend entertainment market.

BBC bosses tried to ease the burden on Stanley by offering him six writers to work with. That was pointless as Stanley would trust no one but Ken Hoare.

'Ken ended up writing everything. His stuff was by far the best.'

It's madness to think the six new writers couldn't have come up with clever ideas. This was as much about control as content. But this mild megalomania was always Stanley's undoing.

'I would wake at 4.00am and walk around the room, worrying about the scripts. I can't help it, that's the way I seem to do things.'

There's little doubt however the fear of failure fuelled the performer because he managed to produce a fabulous Christmas hamper of ideas that many reckoned were the best he had ever dreamed up. *The (S)Tory of Oz*, for example, was an attack against the inhumanity of Thatcherism, with Stanley playing Dorothy, The Tin Man, The Scarecrow, The Lion and the Wizard – who turns out to be Ronald Regan.

'Jeffrey Archer had become the Tory propaganda chief at the time. But taking on politics like that had me worried.'

The show had more conventional laugh winners, such as Sir

James Anyone, a crotchety retired Army Major, a geriatric Rambo with a machine gun who, for a punch line, breaks into George Formby singing the 'Chinese Laundry Blues'.

He also created the brilliant *A Raj Too Far,* a satirical swipe at Granada's epic of the British Raj, *The Jewel in the Crown*, with shades of Combined Services and the world he left behind long ago.

Director John Bishop and Stanley worked well together. But at the end of filming scenes, when Stanley looked to the director for approval, John would say, deadpan, 'Well, that was rotten, wasn't it?'

'It was just his way. But I needed praise. I know it sounds wimpish but that's that way performers are. John certainly wasn't a natural spirit-lifter, like Tyrone Guthrie.'

When *Stanley Baxter's Christmas Hamper* went out to 14 million people on December 27 even the hypercritical Kenneth Williams said, 'There's no one to touch you in this kind of show.'

In the New Year of 1986, Stanley had more reasons to be cheerful. Edinburgh loved his Twankey and as soon as he took his last curtain call, Stanley took off to Hong Kong to film a series of commercials for a pager company, taking Marcus along as a freebie. (But not sitting together, just in case).

Back at home, the next task was to come up with six half hours for the BBC. But now the ideas bank was empty. Once again, Stanley refused to use hired guns. Instead, it was deemed the next – and as it turns out his final – production would be another 50-minute special.

The Stanley Baxter Picture Annual featured 37 different characters, including Noel Coward as a wild west gunslinger and a *Gone with the Wind (Wind from the West)* pastiche in which Stanley played Vivien Leigh's Scarlett O'Hara, Clark Gable's Rhett Butler, Black Mama plus a very convincing Mae West as cousin Lulabelle who constantly argues with the father also played by Stanley.

He is speaking to Lulabelle as she sashays out of the drawing room door:

> 'So you want to wind up an old maid?'
> 'Why, you got any old maids that need winding up?'

'Pure Ken Hoare,' says Stanley, in heartfelt thanks for such lines.

The show also contained a risqué gag about a lesbian horse-riding lady and he appeared again as the Duchess of Brendagh in *The State Opening of Television*, where Brendagh (rather presciently) vents her spleen about the drop in programme quality and future cuts. To no one's surprise, *The Stanley Baxter Picture Annual*, transmitted in December 1986, received the same level of praise as his previous BBC effort.

But Stanley could no more wallow in the accolades than he could take Marcus to the showbiz ball. He certainly wasn't relaxed back in Glasgow with *Aladdin* in November. He told the *Glasgow Herald*, 'the fear of failure is lurking in the darkness waiting to pounce'. He also spoke of his worry about memorising lines. Was he being a drama queen? Probably. It's only in very recent times that Stanley has shown any real difficulty with short-term memory.

Yet, while each passing year revealed a diminished confidence, the ego, the need to be in control wouldn't allow for an easier option, such as using a writing team or sharing the spotlight. He could have taken the weight of the workload and expectation off his own shoulders but he wouldn't. As a result, Stanley felt as bowed as Atlas.

But he wouldn't have to take a time-out from television, to reflect on when he would be fit to offer up his next series or perhaps an hour-long special. When Stanley read the December media reports of John Birt leaving LWT and switching to the BBC he felt a deep shudder. And he knew instinctively it was time to hang up his false breasts and support tights.

35
The Languid Moon Vanishes

NOT ONLY DID Stanley see the writing on the wall of his television career, he recognised his panto career too was all but over. The star who'd packed the King's Theatre in Glasgow was told he'd have to wear cheap, tatty hand-me-downs. At least, that's how he saw it.

King's Theatre boss Tom Malarkey had complained about Stanley having ordered £20,000 worth of custom-made, sequin-encrusted frocks for the last Glasgow-Edinburgh double. And so Malarkey came up with the idea Stanley should recycle his costumes.

Stanley Baxter wearing cast-offs? (Even if they were his own). Bessie Baxter would have been horrified to hear of such a thing. And so he decided to walk away rather than compromise. Was this professional integrity or sheer madness? At the time he didn't connect the dots; television had recently been telling him his shows were too expensive and now panto was doing the same.

However, the panto news was just the beginning of his woes. In the New Year of 1987 Stanley's P45, as expected, arrived from the BBC. Stanley had again been sacked by John Birt who was now Deputy Director-General of the BBC – and above Michael Grade.

'Jim Moir wrote me a lovely letter saying he was terribly sorry and they would drop me for one season. But I felt as long as that bastard Birt was there I'd never get back. I'd made my last spectacular.

'I'll never be sure if Birt's motives for getting rid of me were financial or personal – given that he'd gotten rid of me at LWT.

'And what added to the upset was that the decision to stop making television was taken away from me. Yet, at the same time I seemed to have pastiched every movie ever made so when the end came, I reckoned maybe it was all meant to be.'

At 61, Stanley needed a game plan should the work offers dry up completely. His accountant gave him the figure he needed to earn to make retirement comfortable, but where to get it? David Bell suggested sitcom. Mmm. Return to variety theatre? Not a chance. It was dying. What about a West End run? No, the nerves couldn't stand that.

Think. Think money.

Meantime, Stanley had other concerns. David Bell was looking far less like a matinee idol these days. And there was increasing worry over Kenneth Williams' mental state. Stanley says he was by now seeing less of his friend; Williams' bitchiness, huffiness and paranoia made their regular dinner arrangement almost too much to bear. But that didn't dent the loyalty Stanley felt for him. And he offered regular reassurance. Williams recalls in his *Diaries*:

> Stanley telephoned and said, 'You were very good on *Wogan*; less of the camp now you're developing into an elder statesman sort of comedy… very grand and urbane…' He has forgotten that he's told me this before and it doesn't matter. It is a friend saying, 'You're very good at something' and it is enormously comforting.

It was a pity Williams' generosity of spirit all too often appeared only on the diary page. Stanley would have appreciated the thanks. And he too needed his ego massaged. Often. But at least the next time the pair met at Osteria, Stanley had great news to share. A magical job offer had arrived. And it was the answer to his pension prayers.

Mr Majeika was a children's series, based around the adventures of a banished wizard sent to teach in a small country school because he has failed his sorcery exams for the 17th time. To keep the kids in order, Majeika applies a little magic now and then. Filmed in Kent, it seemed a great role for Stanley, a pre-Harry Potter-ish part calling for a large character who could appeal to kids. There were certainly no long speeches to learn – Stanley had already checked that out.

'The scripts were pretty naff, which was frustrating, and I tried to make an input, suggesting structures and so on, but they elbowed me. All the producer allowed was my idea of *Majeika* having a moving hair tuft.

'But that and the filming boredom apart, I had a great time making the series in the summer of '87. I was put up in a very nice hotel where I could spend my spare time thinking about how *Majeika* was conjuring up a very nice pension for me. I can't recall what I was paid in total but I do remember that for the last series (there were three) I was paid £84,000 and I thought, "This is fantasy money! And I don't even have to think up a line. I don't have to go through all those costume changes."'

Filming over in September, Stanley put his hair tuft back in its box and took a break in Greece. On his return, he called to check up on Kenneth Williams – and wisely so. Williams' depression was getting worse.

'Stanley phoned,' Williams wrote in his *Diaries*:

> He said he'd not liked the Ionian Islands – 'mosquitos and all that scratching'. When he asked about the ulcer, I told him, 'Oh, I wish I was dead.' And he said, 'Oh no! Not you!'
>
> He said he's going to do panto next year. 'It does keep one fit doing twice nightly.'

Stanley was considering panto outside of Scotland, in which he could wear new frocks. But when the English offers came in, they lacked the production values he'd been so used to – hand-me-downs or not.

Yet, while Stanley was contemplating future curtain calls, Williams' *Diaries* now showed clear signs of a man pulling down the curtain on his own life. And in early October he was counting his 'poison capsules in preparation'.

Stanley was of course oblivious to any real intent on the part of Williams and the pair even worked together when, on 14 October 1987, they did a voice-over for Vauxhall Senator cars. But over the next six months Stanley checked up regularly on his friend; he knew his mind was especially fragile. And if the reception were favourable, the Scot would suggest dinner.

The rest of the time, before filming *Majeika 2*, was spent relaxing, enjoying lunches with Moira and spending time with Marcus. Stanley certainly enjoyed reading about John Reid's progress. The former shirt salesman from Paisley was now said to be worth £12 million.

By March 1988 however, Kenneth Williams was becoming progressively more impossible to contend with, due in part to pain from ulcers and intestinal problems. 'Why do I linger? Not from a love of life. I've always found it awful... no, it's rather from a sense of curiosity... not wanting to miss the Third Act.'

Williams was hospitalised and Stanley worried more and more about him. The hospital stay revealed he wasn't exaggerating his pain. Yet, Stanley believed his friend would never really take his own life. Williams was a drama queen. He lived on a diet of hyperbole.

But while driving down Regent's Street on 15 April 1988, Stanley heard a news flash on the radio which almost caused him to crash his car. Kenneth Williams was dead. His friend had taken an overdose the night before.

'I don't know how I didn't run into a wall,' Stanley recalls, the horror of the day still in his voice.

'I thought, "Christ, he's done it! He's been threatening it for years and now he's done it."'

The constant threat of suicide had somehow made it seem all the less likely. Williams' complaining was always more about attention seeking than deep suffering or pain. Yes, the pair had talked about not wishing to live to an age where the body and mind fell to pieces, but that was small talk. Not stated intent.

Stanley was in shock. The pals had done their real growing up together during their stint in Singapore. Williams had befriended him when he needed a support system. Williams had shown him a confidence on stage he'd seen in few others. He was never the greatest friend in the sense he was selfless, prepared to put others before his own needs but there was a spark between the pair of intellects that could take conversation off into undiscovered worlds. And they had shared so much over the years; the angst of missed opportunities, the delights of glorious movies, the friends in common, the gossip, the backstage bitching, the tattle tales. And they were both men who found themselves marginalised; both had few friends with whom they could connect with. And they were both gay men who didn't want to be.

The death of Kenneth Williams was a massive blow. Sure, he hadn't been a solid, dependable chum like Bruce, but he had displayed moments of remarkable kindness. Stanley's feelings are understandably confused when it comes to summing up his friendship. In early interviews for this biography he indicated he 'hadn't really seen Kenny for years before his death' (which Williams' *Diaries* reveal wasn't true at all). Stanley had claimed, 'he was just so difficult to know', adding: 'I didn't feel a sense of loss. That would be hypocritical because I was avoiding him for so many years.'

That would also be nonsense. Stanley *had* avoided his chum – at times – but only when Williams became particularly difficult. The truth was Stanley never gave up on him at all. But why say he had? They were brothers of sorts. They mirrored each other. They had similar traits, more similarities than either of them would have wished to acknowledge. Perhaps they held a mirror up to each other? Perhaps Stanley's revisionism was a way of denying that. Perhaps he was upset to the point of anger at his friend for leaving him?

'Perhaps you're right,' Stanley says now, in soft voice. 'And he had so many good points. He was very fond of Gordon Jackson and Rona and the children. In fact, in another life he would have had a family. He was just not so good with adults. There were very, very few of us that he cared about.'

That was true.

'There was no rhyme nor reason to his dislikes. For example, he loved Olivier, whom he knew personally, and he'd smoke the Olivier brand cigarettes. But he hated Sir John Gielgud and we'd argue lots about that. I'd say, "I don't know why you go on and on about Gielgud, he's a great actor." And he'd come back at me with [adopts Williams' loud whine]: "No, dear. He's a great queen. Comes through in everything he does." But Kenny's criticism was probably an example of self-hatred.

'I accept he was a man who was never happy with his lot. He should have had a different birth. And he should have been an academic and gone to Oxford or Cambridge where he would have inspired young people. They'd have found him funny and learned that he was a great teacher. And his sexual inhibitions would have prevented him from getting him into trouble with any of them.'

Stanley reckons part of the reason for Williams' continued melancholy was being stuck with the *Carry On* comic fool, and overly reliant on his old gags and mannerisms. He was 'running around in ever-decreasing circles'.

'Since his death however he has become an industry. He would have loved to have seen the impact his demise has created.'

Williams would also have loved to have seen his own funeral, where a sky-full of stars turned out to pay their respects.

'Maggie Smith was there [who, incidentally, had once been an item with Stanley's old friend Ian Bannen] and she provided a great showbiz moment. No sooner had the coffin been lowered than Maggie declared 'Come on, darlings, it's showtime!' and swept off to the theatre she was starring in at the time.'

Soon after the funeral, Stanley swept off to work on *Majeika* and during filming received another great pension-building work offer. He agreed to play Hook in a vast production of *Peter Pan* alongside Glasgow legend, Lulu and the show was set for the West End the following year and then a national tour.

To get to know his co-star, Stanley went to dinner with Lulu at the Hampstead home she shared with then husband John Frieda. And he thought the singer 'delightful, and very intelligent'. Lulu says the two Scots got on like a house on fire.

'I was in awe of Stanley,' she says. 'Over dinner he came across as the funniest man. He truly is an icon.'

A bonus was the icon knew the *Peter Pan* book backwards, from the original records by Mary Martin, who played Peter. It all made sense. The co-stars got on famously, the show had top production values.

But then Stanley turned it down. Even though the press had announced it was a go-er.

'My agent David White had acted without my final go-ahead,' he explains.

But why dump such a lucrative job?

'I just lost my nerve. There were too many lines. And I didn't think I could cope with the touring schedule. I was just so insecure and I took stage fright.

'But I was disappointed from the point of view I really like Lulu.'

That year, the actor also turned down Bristol, and he was asked to replace an ill Les Dawson and appear with Canon and Ball at the Palladium.

Stanley says he would rather have been shot from a canon than appear with the pair, whose talent he reckoned never quite matched their on-stage enthusiasm. Yes, the money would have topped up the pension plan nicely, but again he found excuses not to work, such as the production values of southern pantos.

'I loathe it when it's done badly.'

And there was also the factor of sharing a spotlight.

But while he was turning down big panto money, Stanley allowed himself a smile on 12 December when he saw *The Sun* splash headline 'SORRY ELTON'. After the paper ran a false expose on Elton's alleged rent boy story, sales dropped by as much as 200,000.

'John Reid told me he stood over the printing presses making sure the apology headline was as large as possible. And he took great delight in seeing the *Sun* pay Elton £1 million.'

Hitting out at the Queen Mum of Pop had angered *Sun* readers. Was this an indicator that the public had become fed up with newspapers' slaughtering of gay celebrities?

Perhaps.

But it didn't stop *The Sun*'s flow of invective. Soon after, the dying Russell Harty, a close friend of David Bell, was labelled 'another self-confessed homosexual'. The onslaught of irrational prejudice, as Stanley would soon discover, simply wouldn't stop.

36
Ugly Flowers

THE *MAJEIKA* SERIES which aired in the New Year of 1989 attracted rather undeserved favourable reviews.

'I didn't enjoy watching it at all,' says Stanley, wincing. 'And neither did a lot of fans of my own show who wrote saying, "What are you thinking of?"'

At the time, the actor had far more to contend with than duff dialogue. David Bell, who'd looked ill for some time, now seemed emaciated.

'He was directing Barry Humphries in a straight play and during the run he called me up in a panic and said, "I was on the floor with a view finder and I just fell over, dear! And a tooth fell out! It just fell out!"'

John Reid recalls the moment he heard the shocking truth of David's illness.

'Right after Russell Harty's funeral we met in a restaurant and David announced, "Right, dear, I'm HIV positive, and I've got two years to live!" It was announced with the same stoicism he had shown throughout his life. It was as if to say, "Well, I'm dying, but meantime let's get on with it, dear." I was so stunned I couldn't speak.'

David had contracted the disease, Stanley reveals, during his last American holiday with Bruce. Totally out of character for David he had picked up a rent boy in Los Angeles.

'This was his one and only excursion into that world. And he paid for it with a death sentence.

'We were all so desperately sad. For a little while he was in St Mary's Hospital, trying to direct the goings-on. Then he discharged himself from hospital for fear of cross infections. And as the illness developed John Reid hired a team of nurses who kept him alive.'

John, Stanley recalls, was heartbroken to watch his former partner descend into this living hell. But he too struggled to cope with the loss of his best friend. He had had to deal with the loss of Bruce, then Kenneth and now here was David counting down his own final moments.

To add to the growing awareness of mortality, in January Stanley learned of the death of Freddie Carpenter, at the age of 81. The pair hadn't seen much of each other over the years – the director's waspishness had worked against him – but Stanley still missed this outrageous creature and knew the theatre had lost one of its most enigmatic characters. It was all the actor could do to film another series of *Majeika* in the summer. At least the money was great.

By autumn, much of Stanley's time was spent looking in on David, marvelling at the bravery of the man who showed an awesome spirit in the darkest of time. Then it was back to Glasgow to front *The Hogmanay Show*. Stanley performed his *Parliamo Glasgow* sketch which STV said would 'heighten cultural awareness' for Glasgow's upcoming 1990 City of Culture celebrations.

'Culture? A comedy sketch which lampoons Glaswegians who distort English? It's hard to see how phrases such as "Apunaburrafurramurra" (A pound of butter for my mother, please) could prove to be invaluable for anyone but those who love to laugh at those who torture polite speech.'

But it was acutely funny. It was in fact, says Billy Connolly, 'fucking genius': 'Scotland is the only nation, as far as I know, that makes fun of its own language. But there's a line you can't cross because audiences don't really want to be identified as working-class, as people who use the vernacular. You have to be very, very clever to get a Glasgow audience to laugh at themselves – and Stanley is the master.'

The Hogmanay show went well but the beginning of the year arrived with very depressing news. Gordon Jackson died on 15 January 1990 of bone cancer. Stanley had never been *that* close to Gordon, in spite of the background they shared (and Bessie had cast Gordon as a rival), but he liked Gordon's wife Rona very much and he deeply regretted Gordon's passing.

For the next few months, Stanley's focus was on the third series of *Majeika*, which at least proved a little more of a performing challenge. He took on two roles, as Majeika and his evil twin, Majolica. The *Majeika* money still wasn't enough to retire on, however. Stanley needed another big pay day. Thankfully, fate intervened and he was presented with two.

King's Theatre panto boss Tom Malarkey (he of the old dress demands) had quit and new manager Billy Differ reckoned Edinburgh and Glasgow could afford Stanley after all. Or more likely, they couldn't afford *not* to bring him back. Both cities missed their greatest-ever Dame. Stanley's currency was now as high as the flies and he was offered £7,000 a week to star in the productions for the winter of '90 and '91.

'I said I had retired after *Aladdin*. But I came back so's I could retire.'

The two pantos were to be revivals, of *Cinderella,* the same show Stanley had starred in ten years before. The new outfits cost 'thousands'.

'It suited me to do the revivals because I wasn't prepared to dream up all new ideas.'

Of course, now that he was financially secure and didn't need to work again, offers arrived like buses. One which Stanley chose to board was, astonishingly, a sitcom. Why this volte-face? Back in 1959, old Citizens' pal Jimmy Gilbert had given Stanley his London lifeline and his first real job in television. Thirty-six years later it was Jimmy's son, Colin, on the phone, offering Stanley a stint in an episode of cult sitcom *Rab C. Nesbitt*, in which he would play an ex-footballer. Stanley explains why he kicked his old sitcom misgivings into the long grass.

'Ian Pattison is such a brilliant writer,' he says. 'That was one reason. There was the money, which wasn't bad at all. And the episode, filmed in June 1990, involved the Nesbitt team going off to support Scotland in the World Cup in Italy. I'd never been filming abroad before, and I liked the idea of going to Genoa.'

Stanley enjoyed playing Matt, the old striker who gets the chance to go to the World Cup. Yet, the enthusiasm for the part wasn't unbridled. He wouldn't be the star of the show. Gregor Fisher was.

'That felt odd, I must admit. The best lines went to Rab. And having a wee room above Gregor's suite compounded the feeling. No, I didn't like being so far down the cast list at all. Having said that, the cast were all very nice.'

Gregor Fisher recalls working with Stanley was 'a dream'.

'At drama schools across the nation there should be classes in Baxter,' he says. 'He's that good.'

The football scenes were filmed before the Scotland vs Costa Rica match but instead of waiting for the kick-off, Stanley took a taxi back to the hotel.

'I think people were amazed I didn't want to stay but I can't be bothered with football. Later when I learned Scotland had lost (Scotland 0, Costa Rica 1) I knew I had missed only heartbreak.'

Not real heartbreak, however. That was to come about within days. The Genoa trip coincided with the death of David Bell on 9 June 1990, aged just 53. And although he was grief-stricken, Stanley knew death had brought with it some merciful relief for his friend.

'It had gotten to the point where he was in nappies. That's when the morphine dose should have been upped to finish him off. There's no question David should have been helped on his way. No one should have to suffer to that level.'

Stanley didn't return from Italy for David's funeral.

'The BBC offered to fly me back but I declined. I said, "I was there when David needed me. He doesn't need me now."'

Watching his closest friend in the world being laid to rest would have been too much to bear. Although Stanley would have marvelled at this epic production.

'I was at his bedside when he was organising it, when he was still lucid of course, and he would call out orders such as, "At the crematorium, there are always ugly flowers placed before the coffin, dear. You know, just before we see it for the last time. Is there any way we can get rid of them? And I'd like to have a little orchestra in the chapel, or perhaps the gravel fore court..."

'It was explained to David that the flowers actually covered up the machinery that slides the coffin out of sight. And when he heard that he said, "Oh, so it's a *production* device, dear. Well, they'll have to stay."'

David's bravery was matched only by his sense of great theatre.

'He staged the whole thing. He was an incredible man…'

Stanley voice trails off and tears form in his eyes. 'He was a great, great chum.'

Back in London after the *Nesbitt* sojourn, Stanley had time to reflect on the sitcom experience. His verdict? Never again. 'I realised that could be my future, playing old farts in other people's shows.'

In October, *The Stanley Baxter Moving Picture Show* was repeated as a tribute to David Bell, a fitting honour. Yet, while television was honouring the talented producer, newspapers were behaving in a far less dignified fashion. The *Sunday Mirror* revealed in a story thick with suggestion:

> Scots comedian Stanley Baxter was left £32,000 in the will of a TV boss. David Bell was just a 21-year-old cameraman when he linked up with the star. Mr Bell died from a 'lingering illness' in his Edinburgh home four months ago.

What it didn't mention was that Stanley was one of six pals who received the same amount.

'David's legacy was shared with pals such as John. Of course, the inference was that we had been an item, which was never the case. As a result of the story, the *News of the World* chased me along the road asking me if I had AIDS. I turned around to this reporter and said, "Do I *look* as if I've got AIDS?" which was a stupid thing to say, considering in early stages you don't see the symptoms.'

David Bell was dead. But homophobia in the media was very much alive.

'Homophobia over AIDS even finished *La Cage Aux Folles* at the Palladium,' Stanley recalls.

In November, David Bell was again honoured, this time at the British Comedy Awards at the London Palladium. The gala evening was recorded for ITV. But Stanley was deeply angered at newspaper comment the next day.

'One critic attacked David, saying, "Why glorify this promiscuous homosexual?" Would he ever have made that attack if David had been a heterosexual producer? You can see the hypocrisy of it all.'

Stanley was interviewed by the *Daily Mirror* about the tribute show and explained why he wouldn't appear.

'When David was alive, he knew it was no good asking me to appear on things like *Live at the Palladium*. I am a production comedian and an actor, not a Jimmy Tarbuck.' (Stanley did feature in a pre-recorded film tribute which was featured.)

At the end of November, back in Edinburgh for the first of his two pension plan *Cinderellas*, Stanley still missed his friend deeply. And now 64, the thought of two performances and 20 costume changes a day lay on his shoulders as heavy as the Wicked Stepmother's outrageous head gear.

37
David Niven's Blow Job

MARCUS TRAVELLED TO Scotland to see Stanley perform in his penultimate panto – but still he could never been introduced to those but the closest confidants. The gay landscape if anything, offered an even less attractive view. In January 1991, not only were Britain's gay celebrities haunted by the fear of being outed by the press, there was so much in-fighting many feared being outed by other gays.

The gay divide was underlined by Sir Ian McKellen's knighthood. It could have been a cause for unconditional celebration however film director Derek Jarman attacked the actor for accepting his knighthood from 'the same government that introduced Clause 28' – which stated that no local authority could 'intentionally promote homosexuality'.[26] Should gay men work within the system and hope for gradual change – or throw bricks at the windows?

What Stanley did was stay schtum and put on his Dame make-up each night and a brave face to his old *Herald* pal Andy Young. The journalist asked Stanley how he kept so young-looking at 64.

'Swimming,' he said. 'I thought: if I suddenly go from doing this to 18 changes of clothes twice daily, it's called heart attack. And then I'll be found in my sleeping bag on the floor of the King's Theatre, Glasgow. Someone will be saying, "You're awful cold, Mr Baxter. Did you not hear the quarter?" And then the *Herald* would be saying, "He died as he would have wished." Wrong! The feet up in the Canaries would be much more how I would wish to go. Not deid in a dressing room in mid-winter.'

As always, Stanley loved to offer a dramatic line.

Moira didn't travel up to Edinburgh, content to stay at home, but in the following months she saw Stanley on a daily basis as he relaxed around Highgate.

Just before his 65th birthday, the Grim Reaper appeared again, this time to announce the death of actress and great seducer of gay men, Coral Browne.

For the rest of the year, Stanley did little more than enjoy another holiday, this time in Cyprus in preparation for the final *Cinderella* in Glasgow. He knew this last panto would be his most difficult ever.

'I was longing to retire, and I was finding rehearsals very hard going. I was fit for my age but 65 after all, and still doing exactly what I had done at the age of 24 by way of quick changes, cod ballets, grand *jetés*.'

At the end of the first night performance, Stanley didn't go up to the bar with the rest of the cast and theatre staff to enjoy a celebration drink. In the bar, Stanley was informed, was Rikki Fulton – his old nemesis – so Stanley slipped out the stage door and off quietly into the night with Marcus.

The panto was a success, but it could have done better business, no doubt affected by a *Daily Record* crit of January 1992 which claimed *Cinders* was 'blue' in parts. The star was aghast. He was now being compared to the likes of Jack Radcliffe, someone who was a threat to the moral welfare of minors.

'Thank God I was on a huge guarantee because the business was not what I had played to in the past. The King's people actually kept the adverse publicity from me 'till half way through the run, knowing how it would affect me. And then some taxi driver spilled the beans.'

Not selling out, in his last season, was a disappointing note to end on. However, on the last night the theatre boasted a full house and the King's General Manager Billy Differ was determined to make Stanley's very last panto curtain call one to remember. He would announce to the audience that they had witnessed an extraordinary, historical theatre moment, the end of an era – and so whip them up into showing their appreciation for the departing Grand Dame of Dames.

Oh no he wouldn't.

Stanley was having none of it.

'I said, "Oh, please don't! Don't! If they want to show any added appreciation, they will."'

And at the end of that final night, Stanley walked off stage as usual, came back on, took his bow – and then the storm started.

The walls of the theatre shook as the thunderclaps echoed around the auditorium. Every pair of hands in the place banged together until they ached. Every pair of feet stamped until they hurt. Every voice cheered until it was hoarse.

In a moment worthy of any Hollywood film ending, the entire theatre stood up to honour the man who had been their panto idol for 50 years. And they refused to sit down. The clapping rang louder and louder. It simply wouldn't subside. The audience seemed to believe that if they applauded long enough Stanley would never go away.

Not surprisingly, the greatest-ever star of Scottish panto stood transfixed, the tears pouring down his cheeks as he took the final, final bow. Walking off into the wings he was hugged by Billy Differ who admitted, 'Stanley, you guessed it right.'

And the star turned and said with a glint in his eye, 'If I can't judge an audience after all these years, I've been wasting my time.'

Stanley had judged the last bow right – but not the emotion he felt on realising he had now come to the end of his career, as far as live stage work and TV spectaculars were concerned. The final night and the wonderful appreciation left his head spinning with incredibly mixed feelings. Stanley was so very moved at the real love he felt, however he was walking away from the very force that had kept him motivated since those first church hall appearances. Yet, at the same time there was a sense of relief he wouldn't have to go through all of that hard work again. Ever. And he knew his exit timing was perfect.

'I think it's very sad when actors and comedians appear when they are way, way past their best. Even Sinatra kept on going just too long. You think, "Why did you do that?" We should be left with the memory of the greats. And British journalists are lethal when you use idiot boards (cue cards). I didn't want that. I wanted to go out when I was flying high, not being shot down in flames by some 12-year-old writer who reckons I should be put out of my misery.'

Stanley walked off into the quiet of the Glasgow night with

Marcus, and from that point onwards the actor's nights were always quiet. Back home in Highgate he would venture out to dinner four or five times a week and take in the odd theatre show. And for the most part he was happy to have surrendered the spotlight.

Television work was gone too. The disappointing Mr Majeika had waved his wand for the last time. But at least the money was in the bank, even more money than he had been aiming to make. And with the windfall, his accountant informed he could afford to buy a holiday home.

Having spent so much time with Moira in Cyprus, the pair had fallen in love with southern town Paphos, the birthplace of Aphrodite, and decided to buy a villa there which they would visit twice a year – June and September – from that point on.

'It cost £100,000 and it all made sense. Moira loved it, thanks to a really nice garden.'

Back home, Stanley may have been retired but he still needed order in his life, he still needed to be in control and this came from structure. He'd get up at 10.00am, have coffee at 11.00am, lunch at 1.00pm and G&Ts at 5.00pm. Then dinner. Daytimes, he would meet Moira for lunch and three times a week he would keep up his fitness regime at the prestigious RAC Club at Pall Mall. During the week he'd eat out with a couple of pals – he hates to eat alone – and see Marcus over the weekend, taking in a Saturday movie matinee.

The odd weekends would be spent visiting the European cities he never had chance to see, sometimes with Marcus, sometimes with friends such as Les Dryden or David Holt. And he would enjoy holidays such as the trip to John Reid's place in St Tropez, meeting up with the likes of Joan Collins, John Standing and his wife Sarah Forbes, who was of course John Reid's ex.

The following year, 1993, ran delightfully enough. But the autumn calm was suddenly shattered by an awesome storm – Hurricane Kenneth.

Williams' *Diaries* were published by HarperCollins. And Stanley was deeply worried about what would be revealed; either the truth or, perhaps worse, Kenneth's embroidered version of the truth. Williams had often asked Stanley for gossip, for details about his pal's indiscretions. Stanley of course had no idea, at first, that

Williams was recording – in his perfect copperplate handwriting – the detail of his life.

'Kenny, I guess, was the auditory equivalent of a voyeur. He wanted to hear about other people's sex lives because he didn't have one himself.

'He was living entirely vicariously. And he'd pick up tales and then he'd tell these stories at his little dinner parties.

'I remember him at one party telling a story about someone being given a blow job at a stairheid, and the punchline came when he revealed "the man being given the blow job was – David Niven!"

'In the car on the way home I took him to task and said, "Kenny, it wasn't David Niven. I *know* this story. It was the man up the stairs from you who was at it." But he just grinned at me and said, "Mmm, yes, I know. But nobody knows *him*, do they!"'

Stanley grins. 'He was a wicked little bastard.'

And worrying. Stanley twigged – eventually – that Williams was writing down the tales told by him. But it was too little too late. Stanley was terrified the *Diaries* – all 28 volumes of them – would reveal all and he grabbed the phone to call his solicitor like a drowning man clinging to a life raft.

'Luckily, I was able to point out to HarperCollins that much of what Kenny wrote was embellished or made up. And that's why the material which appeared was safe.'

The 28 volumes of diaries were condensed into one book and the published material was fairly anodyne, that which didn't threaten or harm lives or careers. But would the day come when the publishers would feel braver, when someone at HarperCollins would decide to publish and be damned?

Stanley may have laid to rest his performance anxieties but the fear of being outed was now very real indeed. This was the one area of the actor's life he was unable to control completely.

38
Shadows Becoming Darker

NEWS OF JOHN BIRT brought a smile, a wicked, self-satisfied smile to Stanley's face in 1994. His former terminator had been forced to surrender his LWT shares when he became a BBC employee. And now that Granada had bought out LWT those shares would have been worth 'millions'.

'Served the bastard right.'

Stanley meantime was enjoying life, luxuriating in the joyous state of mind that comes with having zero commitments to the world of work. And Moira was happy too, gardening, drawing and reading. Interestingly, as Stanley's relationship with Marcus progressed to a deeper level, so did that of Moira and Marcus.

'They were as thick as thieves.'

Stanley however never contemplated living with Marcus; as well as fearing the publicity, he was too protective of his privacy, his little routines and not prepared to surrender space to anyone. Marcus wasn't put out. He hadn't come out to his own family and would have struggled to explain why he was living with an actor.

On the rare occasion Stanley attended a function – a book launch or whatever – he didn't – or couldn't – take Marcus along. Yes, he thought it might be nice, but then some adverse gay story would hit the news. In March 1995, it featured Nigel Hawthorne, who was outed just before the Oscar Awards ceremony. *The Daily Express* ran the headline 'THE MADNESS OF QUEEN NIGEL', while the *Mail* announced 'YES, MINISTER, I'M GAY'.

'With stories like that appearing, how could anyone ever think about coming out?'

And so he and Marcus would keep a very private life, their most public jaunts being weekly trips to the movies such as the most iconoclastic film of the decade, *Trainspotting*.

'Choose life, choose a job. Choose a career. Choose a fucking big television,' declared writer Irvine Welsh in the film's nihilistic monologue, via Ewan McGregor.

'I chose to believe the movie was awful. I hated it. Life is violent enough without seeing it transferred into fiction. A Busby Berkeley musical. It certainly wasn't.'

Indeed. But by December, the actor, now 69, had become a little bored with movie watching. He realised he missed the adrenaline he had enjoyed from performance. He missed the applause.

Thanks to Michael Grade, there was little chance of the Baxter profile slipping too far. Now Head of Channel 4, Grade asked Stanley to choose his favourite bits from '30 glorious years of television' for a Greatest Hits show to be screened in the New Year. Stanley of course didn't need his arm pulled up his back to work with Michael Grade again. But he wouldn't do interviews to publicise the show, thanks to a Sunday broadsheet story in which the journalist claimed to be on an 'extensive hunt for Baxter, the missing comedian'. He revealed he had been 'pursuing Stanley for months, tracking him via vague spoors left in theatrical agents' offices, scouting around TV companies, trawling the North London streets,' and so on, in the way David Attenborough might pursue a rare creature in the wild. It was like a pastiche Stanley could have produced on television. Except it wasn't very funny. The writer wasn't trying to find Stanley; he was trying to find out if he was gay. The reporter eventually doorstepped Stanley – who declined to talk to him – and then made a call to other journalists who knew the Scot well – like Andy Young of *The Glasgow Herald*.

'Andy, who was very gentle, was asked in confidence if I were gay, and he said, 'Well, well, *I think* he is.' And the writer wrote that.

'Andy was horrified when he read the account. And so contrite. He wrote me a letter explaining.

'This writer had really been determined to find out if I were gay, even going to the Voter's Register to find out if I were shacked up with someone.'

Other reporters followed the scent. But Stanley remained resolute. He wouldn't talk.

'I can't remember the writer's name. But I hope he has since disappeared down into the bowels of Hell.'

In February 1996, Stanley was relaxed enough to attend a showbiz party, helping Peter Nichols celebrate his 70th birthday party at his North London home.

'He was up to his arse in celebrities and authors. Glenda Jackson and John Cleese were there. And so too was Beryl Bainbridge.'

The following day however, Stanley's after-party glow dissolved when he heard that Boo Laye had died, at the age of 95 in a nursing home. Although she'd had problems remembering her lines in *Phil the Fluter* at the age of 69, the remarkable lady had carried on working, in review, until the age of 92.

In May, Stanley celebrated his own 70th birthday, in a non-celebratory style of course, although John Reid turned up with champagne and chocolates and turned the day into an occasion.

And in June and September he and Moira again kept up the holiday routine with a return to the villa in Paphos. During these trips Stanley began to become concerned about his wife. She wasn't quite as she should be.

'I realised she was now falling over a little and dropping off to sleep at the oddest times.'

This was a listed side effect of Haloperidol, a treatment used on psychotics.

'I guessed it was the drugs and I spoke to Moira about it and suggested she see her doctor. Perhaps it would be okay to cut down on her drugs dosage?

'Otherwise she was fine. She hadn't had the mental problems for several years. And when we got back, Moira said she was given the green light to come off the often debilitating drug and take a substitute.'

All seemed well. Moira stopped falling asleep at the oddest moments and their old pattern of life returned.

All was well too with Stanley's professional profile in December 1996 when Channel 4 screened *Stanley Baxter in Reel Terms*, another 60-minute Greatest Hits special.

It seemed television didn't want to forget Stanley Baxter and nor did his fans, one of whom was Billy Connolly. The pair had never met, however Billy had, in interviews, professed a long-term admiration for Stanley, while often bemoaning the fact his hero never seemed to be around anymore. Stanley wrote Billy a letter saying he was always around – and would love to meet up. So Billy's people got in touch with Stanley's people etc, etc, and eventually the pair came together at The Ivy. It was a moment in entertainment history terms: two Scottish comedy legends meet, representing different generations and linked both by the immense popularity they enjoyed in Scotland but also in the world beyond. As you would expect, the comic geniuses bonded immediately, sharing an appreciation of the absurd, a healthy cynicism and an acute understanding of the effects of baring the comic soul.

Or rather they would have if perhaps Billy's opener had been different?

'Billy opened up the discussion with a comment about saying some of his best friends are gay!' recalls Stanley in dramatic voice to illustrate his discomfort.

And that was enough to see the Baxter drawbridge being pulled up faster than you could say Dangerous Ground.

'I just didn't know where to go after that. It seemed a bit clumsy. I didn't wish to acknowledge my sexuality with someone I had just met! I really was on the back foot. What really frustrated me though was that I think he truly is brilliant, and there was lots we could have talked about, growing up in Glasgow, favourite Scots comedians, all of that.'

Billy was unaware that he had upset Stanley with those first few words. He was simply trying to say they had a friend in common. And that he had heard some stories about Stanley's past life.

'We spoke about Kenneth Williams,' says Billy of his attempt to quickly find common ground. 'The very first series of *Parkinson* had everyone and his uncle Willie on it, and I was there as well. And so was Kenneth. And later he regaled me with the stories of him and Stanley and what went on in the Far East days, with the CSE boys, the leaping in and out of bed and all of that.'

Billy had also listened as Kenneth Williams impersonated Stanley. So brilliantly, according to Billy, that he lost control of his own body and fell out of a chair laughing. (Williams of course had never offered up this impersonation when he was in Stanley's company, for the same reasons Stanley never sent up his friend.)

'I think Kenneth presumed, rightly, that I was au fait with the whole gay thing. And I guess I was trying to get this across to Stanley.

'I talked about how I had spoken with Kenneth, about how he had said he didn't mind being homosexual but the idea of physical contact appalled him and all of that.

'But if Stanley was unsure about talking about the gay thing I can understand. It's so hard to imagine what it was like for gay men in those days.'

Billy adds, 'Stanley is a private person – he has always had that wonderfully elusive quality about him – and there's something about privacy I like. There are private things people should keep to themselves if they choose.'

What Stanley and Billy did manage to discuss, albeit for a short time, was a film offer. Billy had signed to appear in a new movie, *Mrs Brown*, which explored the relationship between Queen Victoria and her Scottish ghillie. Billy asked Stanley if he would be interested in playing the small role of Dr Jenner, a part which later went to Richard Pascoe.

Stanley's reaction to the offer was predictable.

'Playing a doctor in a film starring Billy Connolly? No, I don't think so.'

Billy was disappointed.

'I wanted him to be in it,' he says. 'But his reply was "Probably not. I'm fed up being nervous. I don't want to be nervous anymore."'

Overall, Billy thought the lunch was 'lovely'.

'I guess I never thought he was nervous because I was such in awe of the man. I don't know what Stanley expected to happen but I got a lot out of it, although I suppose I was tip-toeing around him. And I felt when I was with Stanley that my gas was at a peep, I wasn't firing on all cylinders. I guess that was because I wanted to listen, to absorb all he had to say. The man is a legend. Yet, he probably doesn't realise he's a legend.'

Stanley's take on Billy?

'I think he is a lot more vulnerable than people would imagine.

But then he is a great performer. It comes with the territory. But the lunch itself because of the uncomfortable opener, was, sadly, a bit odd.'

What was also odd was Moira's behaviour at the time. She told Stanley the television was talking to her.

'I panicked at the news and suggested we get her back on the stronger drug. And so she went back to the doctors to arrange it.'

Or so he thought.

In June 1997, Stanley and Moira returned to Cyprus. However, a few days into the holiday Stanley found himself hospitalised after a particularly bad bout of diarrhoea.

Moira was alone in the villa, but she didn't call to see how he was. For someone so devoted to Stanley this was the strangest behaviour. Sadly, she was once again becoming lost in her own world.

'Back home, she deteriorated further. All she would eat was lettuce and tomato and drink water. During her time in remission she'd go round to Marcus's house and chat over tea and digestives. But now when he suggested their usual tea break she'd just take a glass of water.'

Stanley was bewildered by his wife's behaviour. Was the diet restriction some form of self-punishment? Moira swore she was taking the new drug the doctor had prescribed. Was it the new drug which was making her feel worse?

'She seemed so spaced out, so difficult to make connection with.'

While in August the world was rocked by the news Princess Diana had been killed in a Parisian tunnel, Moira was back floating around in her own darkness. Stanley's skin began to tighten with panic. How would she behave this time around? What extremes was she now capable of? He feared for her. And he feared for his own state of mind; he was having panic attacks again. This was far too much responsibility to cope with. Again.

Yet, he had to go about the business of his own life. Part of that business in September meant going back to Cyprus for his second visit of the year. The villa needed tending, the garden sorted out. But this time he didn't want to Moira to come. He argues she was too bewildered, way too divorced from reality. So he determined that instead of taking off for the usual month's break, he would go for a week and deal with the upkeep.

'About a week before I travelled, she called on me and said, "You've got my passport."

'"Yes, I have."

'"Well, I would like it please."

'And I knew what this meant. She had turned up on me before in Edinburgh, with disastrous consequences. And I just knew she'd fly to Cyprus and appear at the villa out of the blue.

'I'm sorry, Moira. Until you are better, you can't come to Cyprus.'

'Then I'll say I've lost it and get a new one.'

'I'll say you're lying.'

'It was then she physically attacked me. She punched me and my glasses flew off. It was the one and only time she had ever reacted in this way. But immediately afterwards she was so sorry and all the love she felt came back.

'Anyway, I went off to Cyprus, and phoned her every day. Each day I would try and sound encouraging, saying little things like, "As far as the garden's concerned, you'll love it! I've got it looking great. Yes, you'll be back next year and you'll see, it looks terrific... and are you taking the new drug the psychiatrist recommended?"

'But I wasn't convinced this new drug was working. Each day she sounded more and more spaced out.'

During this week, Marcus popped in to check things were okay. One day he rang Stanley with some alarming news. A pigeon had been run over in the street and he had found Moira in her living room trying to nurse it in front of the fire.

'One wounded bird helping to look after another.'

That night, Stanley called from Cyprus, just to reassure Moira he would be back home the following day and they could meet for lunch. There was no reply. But that wasn't entirely unusual. Still, he would see her the moment he arrived and make sure she had been taking her new medication, or perhaps insist she go back to the doctors and have it altered.

He called Moira from the airport on his return. Again, no reply. Now he began to worry. He felt this was yet another of her rather dramatic calls for help, but at the same time he began to panic.

What if she had done something stupid? His mind raced with attempts at solutions. She couldn't go on like this, dropping in and out of reality. Something *had* to be done to help her. He would go with her to the doctor and demand improved treatment. Whatever it took. Whatever the cost.

In the taxi over to Cherry Tree Road, his heart thumped, partly with fear and partly with the sheer bloody frustration of it all, knowing this lovely woman was being trapped in the prison of her own mind. At the front door he saw the Chubb lock was opened. His heart beat even louder. Stanley pushed the door open and called out. Nothing. He ran upstairs and there he found Moira lying perfectly still on her bed.

Marion Irving Robertson had at last found peace.

'That was the denouement of that marriage,' he says, his voice filled with sad resignation.

At the autopsy, doctors noticed the scars on the wrist and Stanley confirmed they were the result of the two previous suicide attempts. The doctors then revealed Moira had taken 27 aspirins. What they also discovered was that she hadn't taken a single one of her psychiatric pills; there was no trace of anti-psychotics in her system. She had been pretending to be back on the medication. Why? Possibly because she didn't wish to continue to wander around in a drugged condition. More likely, she didn't want Stanley to see her floating around this half-life of dulled semi-awareness in which she could scarcely contribute. She didn't want to disappoint the love of her life. However, Stanley learned it's common for schizophrenics to refuse to take drugs that will help them.

'Apparently, there is something about the drug that they hate, that causes them to react against it.'

Could the suicide have been a call for help? Did she know Stanley was on the way back from Cyprus and reckoned he would arrive just in time? She hadn't cut her wrists this time, instead, she had swallowed a bottle of aspirins. Not an instantaneous death. Stanley asks himself that question more times than outsiders would understand. And as he speaks tears form in his eyes revealing an overwhelming sadness – coupled with incredible regret.

'Did she carry some hope that I would get off the plane, rush round and save her again? Should I have taken her to Cyprus? Would it have happened anyway? We'll never know.'

The death left him devastated. Life seemed likely to have a premature end for a woman who flitted in and out of reality. Nevertheless, her final act, when it came, broke the dam of all the years of pent-up guilt – and he was rocked by its force.

He had always felt guilty for marrying in March 1952. He felt guilty when he began relations with new partners, when he took off to Australia and North American. He felt guilty when he stopped living with her, unable to share a home with her. And now he felt incredibly guilty because it was he who suggested perhaps she could do without the Haloperidol – even though the medication had turned her into a chemical-dependent zombie. And then at the very end he wasn't there – to do what? Say sorry? Say goodbye? Or even just give her the only thing she had ever asked for in their life together – to be with him.

In the coming days, Stanley gained comfort from the knowing Moira was at least freed from the demons within. But his mind then filled with questions which still exist to this day. Did he ruin Moira's life by giving her false hope when they first got engaged? Should he have walked away when she offered him the chance? Or would her condition have led her down the same path, no matter whom she shared her life with?

'I've often wondered how her life would have turned out had she married a devoted heterosexual husband.'

Did she at least have a happy life in part knowing she was married to someone she worshipped? The adoring letters she wrote to him, which Stanley still keeps, suggest Moira was eternally besotted and a 'devoted heterosexual husband' would never have fitted the bill.

On 24 September 1990, for example, she wrote from 13 Cherry Tree Road:

> Darling Stanley,
>
> I want to thank you for such a wonderful holiday. It will stay in my memory as one of the happiest we have ever spent together and gives me much to think about when you're away in Edinburgh.

Thank you dearest Stanley so much.
All my love,
Moira.

'I will never know why she loved me so much. But I have to say in the end I was glad to see her go. She was being tortured.'

His voice struggles to emerge as he says, 'All seemed to be going so well until the shadows became darker.'

39
The Wasp Sting

IN NOVEMBER 1997, Stanley received one of the greatest accolades bestowed on any entertainer, The British Comedy Awards' Lifetime Achievement Award. And he was overjoyed, despite the fact it meant returning to the LWT building for the first time since he had been sacked. Stanley dedicated the award to Moira.

The rest of the year was broken up with return trips to the villa in Paphos – it was all very strange without Moira around – and to whichever European city Stanley fancied seeing. In between times, he enjoyed lazy days and relaxed dinners, chatting with friends about the news of the day, whether it was John Reid's final split from Elton as his manager or George Michael being arrested for indecency in a Los Angeles toilet.

'That was a disgusting set-up,' he says, his voice revealing an anger not unconnected to his experience with *le scandale*. 'The police were every bit as guilty as he was.'

At Christmas time, the Baxter star again appeared across Britain with the transmission of *Stanley Baxter in Person*, a Channel 4 documentary produced by Karen Steyn. Now 72, Stanley was far less shy about appearing as himself on camera, or rather the version of himself he chose to appear as on the day. And it was not an overly analytical piece of film. Stanley, always in control of the production, agreed to the documentary on the condition he had full content approval.

'I got a list of the questions, scored out the ones I thought would be unproductive, and then worked on some answers for the rest.'

The finished film however did reveal some personal insight.

'When I go to sleep and dream it's always about getting into costume. I'm always waiting in the wings.'

Dream – or nightmare? Probably both. And the line indicates he was always ready to become someone else. Being Stanley Baxter was tough.

It was certainly true that Stanley never studied people in order to impersonate them. Somehow, they arrived in his mind on their own. One night in his house some years later, during interview sessions, Anne Robinson appeared on television briefly with a trailer for *The Weakest Link*. Ten minutes later Stanley asked, 'An hour to go before dinner. Fancy a G&T?' – but it was Anne Robinson's voice that emerged. Not a perfect impersonation. It was better than that, a perfect reproduction, just slightly exaggerated and very funny.

Later during dinner when I asked how long he had been working on Robinson he claimed he had never done her.

'But you did her tonight. The G&T conversation.'

'Did I? I never realised.'

And he hadn't. He'd simply absorbed the voice and character, just as his six-year-old self had when he became Reverend Wadilaw.

Yet, while Stanley's talent for impressions had never subsided, there was no way he'd perform them on television. He did however agree to provide all the voices for ITV kids' 13-part cartoon series, *Meeow*.

'I thought I could have fun with a little pussy,' he says, grinning.

And he did. It was easy money, and life was more relaxed, if still punctuated by reminders of mortality when Ian Bannen and Jimmy Logan exited stage left for the last time.

A few weeks later however, the overall calm was again wrecked. The *Daily Record*'s headline 'CARRY ON CAMPING' carried the sub-head 'Astonishing Insight Into Stanley Baxter's Private Life Is Revealed In Letters To Old Pal Kenneth Williams'. All the positive energy Stanley had built up since retirement poured from his body. And to compound the pain, readers were pulled in by the photographs – a huge pic of Stanley in *Gone with the Wind* Scarlett dress, ringlets and bonnet, a smaller photo of Williams grinning mischievously and a very small insert photo of Stanley as himself.

It transpired that when Kenneth Williams died, he left his money to businessman Michael Whittaker, but the contents of his flat went to Paul Richardson, who lived upstairs, and an unknown godson. Unfortunately, the contents included his diaries. And this wasn't the rather anodyne collection published in 1993, but thousands of pages of Williams' additional writings and his vast collection of letters. Several interested parties, including Stanley and Michael Whittaker, attempted to lay claim to Williams' writings for obvious reasons, but when the case came to court it was deemed the writings should be treated as 'contents'. The letters written by Stanley were sold at Christie's, and their content leaked to the *Daily Record*. And quite damning content it was too. One of Stanley's letters talks about male partners such as Roy and Bill and offers detail of holidays in Tangier.

To the watching world, his secret was out. Having battled to protect the truth about his sexuality for nearly 60 years, it turned out that one of his best friends had offered up the key to the locked door.

Stanley was angered beyond belief. The newspaper copy used every device to present Stanley as a sly, furtive homosexual.

'Stanley and Moira were never pictured in public,' the story said, which was total fabrication. Their wedding pics were in every national newspaper. And Moira was photographed at his side by every publication during *le scandale*.

But although he now feared being hounded, Stanley didn't run off to Cyprus and hide. Nor did he simply hope it would all go away. Instead, the Bessie Baxter-inherited determination kicked in and he went on the attack, calling his lawyers immediately and demanding a retraction. How? By pointing out that he had copyright over the letters he had written to Williams. The *Daily Record* was therefore in breach of this and the Privacy Act by printing any extract. He could also argue that Williams was a fantasist, and that he would take the paper to court to argue some of what he wrote was contrived. And if he could prove *some* of Williams' writings were fantastical, where would judges draw the line?

'The letters were a send-up,' Stanley was quoted as saying at the end of the *Daily Record* story. 'Anything I said to Kenneth about being gay was to send him up, knowing his predilections.'

It wasn't true of course, but this wasn't about honesty, this was about defying intrusion from a newspaper looking to trash a man's character. The *Record* would have to be very sure of all they had printed or he would sue them silly. In the event, the newspaper's lawyers weren't sure at all, and not only did they back down and apologise, their story was wiped from their electronic system. It never existed.

'This had protected me since,' he says, sighing with relief.

'I had to write letters again to HarperCollins, pointing out that in many ways Kenny was a fantasist and often reattributed stories (such as the David Niven blow job), so if anything defamatory appeared I would certainly go to law. But it seems we can't protect what they may choose to reveal.

'I think the legal term is we are in "jeopardy". The letters are another story. As long as I'm alive, I own the copyright.

'The man who copied them down and sent the details to the *Daily Record* sent his fee back to us, the £500. So the letters are not a problem.

'It's the diaries.'

Stanley had hoped that in his 70s the media would allow an older man some quiet. But that wasn't the case. And the episode only served to cast a darker shadow on his feelings on Kenneth Williams. Williams was once described as 'a wasp with adenoids'. Now, Kenny had stung his pal from beyond the grave.

There was more bad news to follow in the months ahead. In June, Joan Sims passed away but he couldn't manage to the *Carry On* star's funeral because that same week, Stanley's favourite cousin Alma died.

In the summer of 2001, BBC Scotland made a documentary to record Stanley's 75th. As expected, the actor had full control over the edit. Stephen Fry was one of the contributors on the film and Stanley wrote him a letter thanking him. Stephen wrote back and suggested a drink or lunch, but Stanley declined.

'It would be too cerebral a lunch, I reckoned. I chickened out.'

Stanley also turned down an offer of lunch with the programme's narrator, Denis Lawson. And Denis lived just along the road.

'I'd like to have met his nephew though,' he says with a wicked grin, referring to film star Ewan McGregor. 'He seems to have huge charisma. And every time I see him on television or film he seems to be getting it out.'

The reality is Stanley would have turned down a lunch invite with the heartthrob nephew as well. Incredible as it sounds, he would have worried that *he* disappointed. And he was worried the issue of his sexuality would come up. Would there ever come a time when the sword didn't hang over him?

40
Cancelling the Newspapers

MOVING INTO THE NOUGHTIES, signs emerged to suggest Britain was travelling in the direction of tolerance of sexuality.

'Yes, Coronation Street has gays now,' says Stanley, a fan of the show. 'Yet, the central homosexual character Sean, the sewing machinist role [played by Anthony Cotton] *is* rather nelly. And that is unfortunate. You know, Morris the newsagent should have been the gay man in the Street. He really did have the character traits, the fussiness, the nosiness. But the move towards gay acceptance hasn't convinced me I wouldn't still get grief.' He adds, in defiant voice, 'It's all very well for younger men such as John Reid [now a theatre producer – he had a huge West End hit in 2000 with *The Graduate* and was back in the West End in 2016 with *Mrs Henderson Presents*] to come out, but the papers would still label me an old queen.'

March 2003 offered a happy moment when Stanley was awarded an Honorary Arts Degree (MA) from the University of Glasgow. And he wished Fred Baxter had been around to see his son collect his certificate.

A few months later, more searing reminders of time rushing forward emerged when John Schlesinger died in Los Angeles from a heart attack.

'Another of my CSE chums gone,' Stanley reflects, his eyes almost teary.

At least he was fit and well, he had had a heart stent fitted thanks to a routine angiogram. And in the Noughties, Stanley felt the need to return to work. Why? If it's said 'a dark theatre eats its head off', so too does a talented actor who has lived for the love of an audience.

F Scott Fitzgerald once wrote, 'There are no second acts in American lives', suggesting that stars had but one chance at fame before returning to the seats in the audience. But Fitzgerald's theory never applied to talents such as Stanley, who returned to acting, starring in *Stanley Baxter and Friends*, a series of comedy plays for Radio 4.

The light was switched on again; a softer, more gentle, controllable light. But a light nonetheless. And it grew brighter as Stanley agreed to appear on television interviews for documentaries on the likes of the Citizens' Theatre in Glasgow.

The actor enjoyed the radio work, realising he didn't have to learn a single line nor come up with an idea. And he loved the great reviews the series attracted. But some of the media attention left him burned, and reinforced his argument that coming out would let the detractors in. To promote his Radio 4 broadcasts, Stanley had agreed to be interviewed by *The Scotsman*.

The feature began jolly enough: 'A dapper man in contrasting winter shades, beige scarf at a jaunty angle, he marches across the nosherie floor to greet me.'

But then came the stinger: 'That fine head of hair is now silver and he appears to be wearing a light coating of theatrical panstick.'

Panstick? Make-up? In public? Oh dear. This was Barri Chatt land the writer was describing. Or David Jacobs. (The facial colouring was down to the many sunshine holidays Stanley had enjoyed that year.)

The writer went on to underline the actor's perceived femininity.

'Baxter can't throw away the trusty make-up box which has accompanied him round the theatres of the land.'

Baxter was enraged.

'I've never worn make up in the street in my life. I don't even like it when other men wear it. In fact, I have a horror of it.'

The journalist then informed the world that Stanley was 'off on holiday next week to Egypt with a "chum",' the inverted commas clearly a device to indicate there was more to the relationship than mateyness. He was wrong. Stanley's travelling partner was his old friend Les Mackenzie, who lived around the corner.

And of course, the tricky question was saved for last.

'And what about your sex life, Stanley?'

'On that issue the drawbridge comes up."

'You won't talk about it?'

'No, I certainly won't.'

And then the copy said: 'Stanley refused to talk about his sex life, of which there have been many rumours over the years.'

'Really, the interviewer was trying to establish "poofie" from the word go.'

Still, the radio experience had reminded the actor he was still valued. And Stanley began to consider more offers of work. But he wouldn't accept the many television or film offers to play 'old farts' – even a *Harry Potter* – despite assurances his character would be heavily disguised under prosthetics.

'I'm not like Joan Crawford, who insisted on being photographed in the nude in her 60s.'

Indeed.

Stanley believed life to be too short to subject himself to unnecessary. That message was brought home in February 2004 when Rikki Fulton passed away, having suffered from Alzheimer's.

'I wouldn't wish that on anybody.'

Life was now about strolling in comfortable semi-obscurity, enjoying the half-light that radio offered – and remaining in complete control.

From time to time, Stanley felt relaxed enough to talk about the possibility of releasing his biography during his lifetime. But then another media flurry around the world of homosexual intrigue saw him recoil. The publication of Piers Paul Read's Alec Guinness authorised biography resulted in the *Daily Express* in October 2005 running a story that Gordon Jackson was 'a closet queen'.

Every now and then Stanley would accept the world was becoming more gay tolerant, a world in which rugby players could come out, young good-looking high divers would reveal their sexuality – with the news barely making a splash. But he still feared being judged. He still feared the media would reveal him to be a 'nelly'.

In 2016, aged 90, Stanley celebrated his birthday with dinner with John Reid. But earlier in the day he had been making a new series of *Stanley Baxter and Friends*. It was a remarkable achievement.

'I could never have imagined when I did my first radio at 14 with Auntie Kathleen, I'd still be working for Auntie at 90.'

In early 2017, Stanley's health deteriorated rapidly. Back pain joined knee stiffness (two knee replacements hadn't really helped the pain) and saw him confined to quarters. Initially, he could have strolled outdoors using a walking stick, a Zimmer perhaps, but he wouldn't.

'I didn't want to be seen as someone who once was Stanley Baxter,' he admits.

At the end of January, Stanley took to his bed. Permanently. But it wasn't just worsening joint ache or vanity that prompted his decision. A few months before, Marcus had contracted terminal lung cancer (he never smoked in his life but grew up with older sisters who did).

His sisters took Marcus back to Cyprus to attempt a last-ditch treatment, of combined chemo and radio therapy, which isn't given in Britain. Stanley didn't say as much but in his heart he knew he was saying goodbye to his partner for the last time. The loss was too much to bear. Stanley no longer saw a reason to embrace the new day.

Thankfully, friends didn't allow him to surrender completely to the night. Actor pal David Holt visited regularly, facilitating the practical needs in Stanley's life, fixing up a TV in his downstairs main bedroom etc. John Reid kept more than an eye on his old pal, paying for him to have round-the-clock care, making sure his garden looked great.

But Stanley's chums faced an uphill challenge to life their friend's spirits. One afternoon, John took round a *La La Land* DVD for the pair to watch.

'I hated the opening five minutes,' Stanley told John, then refused to watch anymore. 'It was total nonsense.'

It wasn't *that* bad a movie. But with Marcus gone, Stanley had lost not only the willingness to surrender disbelief but some of the joy of shared experience. A phone conversation with him revealed so much.

'How are you passing the day, Stanley? Are you watching television?'

'Don't see the point. I feel too ill?'

'What hurts?'

'Nothing, really. But everything.'

'Are you reading? You love a good showbiz biography?'

'Not interested.'

'You're at least keeping up with the news?'

'I've cancelled the newspapers.'

Oh, God. This was so revealing. Stanley was a three papers-a-day man.

'What? You love to know the world around you?'

'I'm tired, darling. I don't care anymore.'

But at that point he realised the sadness in his own voice, and another Stanley emerged. It was the bolder Stanley, the one who loves to work, to entertain, to receive the acknowledgement his talent deserves. It was the Stanley who captured Glasgow's hearts with *The Tintock Cup*, who won over a British audience with *On the Bright Side*, who made cinema audiences laugh at *The Fast Lady*, who became a television icon with *The Stanley Baxter Picture Shows* and who out-Damed any Dame before and since.

'I hear *42nd Street* is wonderful,' he said of the West End revival, reaching for a positive.

We met a couple of weeks later. He lay in bed, speaking in short sentences. He was tired, he said. And he was. Reluctant to say much, yet not wishing to be alone either.

But then after an hour and a Bloody Mary he came alive and rewound on parts of his life. He travelled back in time, to 5 Wilton Mansions, the days when he dreamed of becoming a star. And his memories suddenly burst out of his mouth, singing 'Everything's Coming Up Roses.

Now that he's looking back, does he have regrets in life?

'None,' he says, dismissively.

'Are you sure, Stanley?'

'Well, perhaps. I should have worked in America. And I turned down too many parts.' He added, laughing: 'Almost as often as a chambermaid turns down bed-sheets.'

Sometimes it was ego, he admits. He was too good for them. Often, he felt not good enough.

We speak of paradoxes; the continual pleasure he sought during his performance years didn't come about until he stopped doing what he did best. The more the actor bathed in the spotlight, the darker he felt inside. The greater the applause he achieved the more anxious he became that he couldn't sustain the performance.

'That's so true,' he says, softly. 'However, I would never convey to an audience anything but total enthusiasm. Those who saw a show would often say, "I could tell you loved every minute of it!", but I was probably having diarrhoea and feeling ill. They would never know.'

Let's lift the mood a little. What were life's irritants?

'Football, eating alone, war films, bad manners, intolerance and vacuous television such as reality shows,' he reels off, then adds, grinning 'Who wants to see desperate fame-seekers eat maggots and try to shag each other?'

Stanley was not keen on public transport – Hell really is other people, in a subway – and he hates the perpetual association with drag.

'I was in the *Audience with Dame Edna* and met Barry Humphries afterwards with a group of people,' he recalls. 'But Barry insisted on meeting us as Edna. That struck me as very odd. I hated wearing women's clothing and I'd get out of it as soon as a show was over.'

He defends his assumed eagerness to don a dress.

'I know I impersonated a lot of women but it was because they are easier. Try taking off Don Ameche or John Payne. You can't.'

On the subject of his content, Stanley regrets relying upon too much pastiche of old films, of not continuing to have sharper material, such as *Parliamo Glasgow*, which poked fun with wit and style and paid Glaswegians, and tangentially all working-class Scots, the compliment of treating us as adults, capable of amused self-awareness.

But what he perhaps regrets most is his need to be in control – which meant he wouldn't subcontract work to anyone else.

'My mother instilled I always had to get it right. I was too afraid to take the chance on others.' He adds, wistfully, 'Perhaps it was ego too.'

Does he feel happy to know he has made so many happy?

'Yes, and it's awfully nice when people say to you, "I can't tell you the pleasure you've given me over the years, the laughs..." Yet, while it's lovely to hear compliments like that, it's not the reason you perform. The truth is no artist, no comedian, singer, whatever, goes into the business to give the public joy. I mean it. You don't do it to bring pleasure to millions. You do it to fulfil this egotism, the desire to show off in the areas you think you are strongest in. It's about the need for love and attention.'

He adds, grinning, 'Now, you may argue that Mother Theresa was a woman without ego. Wr-ong! What she did was wonderful – but she was getting her kicks. She wouldn't have done it otherwise. Jesus was just the same, all these men worshipping him and hanging on his every word. If he'd been around now, he'd have been up there on stage with Saint Bob (Geldof) of Africa.'

There are more regrets. He regrets he didn't have the confidence to meet up with people he admired, such as Stephen Fry. He regrets he wasn't closer to his dad. He deeply regrets that he never managed to get approval from his mother, the person from whom he wanted it most. A great regret was in marrying Moira, for her sake.

'She guessed wrongly what being with a gay man entailed. Although to be fair, no woman could have known what to expect.' He breaks into a smile. 'Except Coral Browne. She married two. But I have to say I never treated Moira with anything other than kindness.'

At times, Stanley regrets not having had children, and says it would be 'quite nice' to be a grandfather right now. But then a more pessimistic overview prevails.

'I'm neurotic, Moira was psychotic. At the time I didn't want to bring any child into the world who suffered what I suffered, at least some of the time. A wean would surely have grown up with problems and taken drugs.'

What saddens him most however is growing up in an era in which being gay meant you could go to prison, an era in which homophobia followed him around like a contagion – and resulted in his horrendous courtroom experience. Actor pal John Fraser one wrote: 'What use is talent, or even genius, for God's sake, if you have to live a lie and deny love?' Stanley regrets he and Marcus had never really been partners in the outside world.

But there's little doubt that Stanley's greatest regret is his sexual predilection. He has never wanted to play the role of Gay Man.

'Anybody would be insane to choose to live such a very difficult life,' he says, in solemn voice.

Stanley believes his sexuality offered him a special insight, an overview of life, of mores and behaviours, and it helped him capture female characters in particular. Yet, it also stunted his career. Had he not been gay he could have reached bigger audiences. He could have appeared on chat shows and wowed audiences as Kenneth Williams had. But he feared the more the public knew of him, the more he would be found out. And no longer loved.

'There are many gay people these days who are fairly comfortable with their sexuality, fairly happy with who they are. I'm not. I never wanted to be gay. I still don't.'

He adds, his voice dark, 'The truth is, I don't really want to be me.'

Stanley was certainly poised to absorb new accents and voices from the earliest times; his has always been a temporary identity, with his body keen to play host to new visitors. And they were given easy access, given his willingness to allow entry.

'I take on the character of whoever I'm doing,' he says. 'And as soon as I'm into the character I lose the self, whom I have never really cared for.'

Aware of his dark tones, his mind switches back to Ethel Merman mode and he spoke of his best work. And as he lies in bed unable to walk, never mind dance across the living room the way he had just a few years before, he remembers the fun he had creating so many outrageous characters.

'I can't believe I got away with the likes of Faith Douche,' he says, smiling.

What we witnessed was so many different versions of the man, prismed via his take on film or television, beamed out in the hope the world would laugh at him, and perhaps adore him. Before Stanley took to the stage, he would always feel the warmth of a radiator as he left his dressing room, a great metaphor for his emotional need. But even now, his self-belief isn't strong enough for him to acknowledge his place in film, TV and theatre history.

He never felt, truly, that he had arrived.

'I never did,' he says. 'Even when I was making films and starring in the West End at the same time. I still don't. You're only as good as your last show.

'But then again, I never wanted to be a high-profile entertainer. All I ever wanted was to be awfy good.'

And to be loved, of course. And he was. And he is.

'I hope so,' he says, grinning. 'I'd hate to think all that effort and angst had been for nothing.

With that, the Bloody Mary glass is clinked back onto his bed tray, and he lays back down on his bed. Within seconds his body yields to the demands of the day and his eyelids flicker, signalling the curtain is set to come down, perhaps for the very last time, on our chats.

'I need to have a wee sleep now, darling. I hope I've told you enough over the past ten years.'

'Twenty, Stanley.'

'Has it been that long? Well, after all that blethering you should have enough material anyway.'

The eyes close fully as his last sentence emerges.

'It's been fun chatting. Perhaps I'll see you again soon. Now, it's time to dream.'

A last question. 'Do you remember you once told me the dream you dreamed most often is where you're standing in the wings, waiting to go on. Terrified. And yet so excited?'

'Absolutely,' he says, smiling. 'Life's a bastard.'

Endnotes

1 Tall, gangly Tommy Morgan was born in 1898 in Glasgow. He left the chocolate factory where he worked from the age of 14 to become a clown comedian, starring at the city's Pavilion Theatre for 14 consecutive years.

2 Tommy Lorne, born in 1890 as Hugh Corcoran, was a Kirkintilloch-born former steel company draughtsman who first found fame at the Royal Princess's Theatre in Glasgow's Gorbals and the Palace Music Hall next door. His stage costume saw him wear white make-up, oversized boots and a jacket that was too small. The comedian graduated to become a panto star who toured the north of England. Lorne died from pneumonia aged 45.

3 Dave Willis was born David Williams in Glasgow in 1895. The comedian's hugely successful, bemused style saw him become a music hall and panto star. He also appeared in two films. Willis holds the record for his 32-week stint Half Past Eight shows at the city's Theatre Royal in 1943 and had a wartime hit record with 'My Wee Gas Mask'.

4 Sir Harry Lauder, born in 1870, was a Scots music hall singer who exported tartanalia around the globe, at one point becoming the highest paid performer in the world.

5 Howard & Wyndham were Scots producers and impresarios, who staged revue shows and pantos. H&W became Britain's largest owner of quality theatre companies.

6 Band of Hope was a temperance organisation for working-class children.

7 Brian Aherne starred as the decent French family man who is called to act as a juror and takes pity on the accused, played by Rita Hayworth. In fact, he takes pity on her so much he takes her home, much to the consternation of his wife.

8 Roddy McMillan became famous in Scotland for his role as a tug boat skipper in BBC comedy *The Vital Spark* and starred as a down-at-heel private detective in the BBC's *The View From Daniel Pyke*. During his career he played the role of tough, aggressive Scots in a vast range of film, TV and theatre roles such as the '70s drama, *Hazell*. He died in 1979.

9 Born John Brown Chatt, the 40-year-old singer, actor and drag artist from County Durham had, in his own words, 'signed on for sun and fun'. He

was one of many civilian performers 'recruited' by the army to aid troop morale.

10 Guthrie, a former radio broadcaster and producer, had an incredible CV which included setting up the Shakespeare Repertory Company and directing the Metropolitan Opera in New York. Ironically, he had also set up the Young Vic Theatre School.

11 *Scotch and Wry* was a Scottish television comedy sketch show produced by BBC Scotland, starring Rikki Fulton and a revolving ensemble cast which over the years include Gregor Fisher, Tony Roper, Claire Nielson, Juliet Cadzow and John Bett. Initially running for two series from 1978 to 1979, the show went on to become a top-rating annual Hogmanay special for over a decade.

12 Scottish theatres were categorised – the biggest and most prestigious were Number Ones. The less artistically credible were Number Twos. The likes of the Citz were outside the categories and seen as arts theatres.

13 Alec Finlay was a Glasgow-born seaside comic and variety performer who could dance and play the bagpipes at the same time.

14 Kenneth McKellar was an opera-trained tenor who had moved into variety and panto and would later represent Britain in the Eurovision Song Contest.

15 Dickie Henderson was the son of music hall star Dick Henderson. Young Dickie appeared in the film of Noel Coward's *Cavalcade* at the age of ten in 1953 and went on to enjoy success as a languid comedian and sitcom star, with *The Dickie Henderson Show* in the early '60s. He died in 1985 aged 62.

16 Once the epicentre of the American film industry, the first film studio in Culver City in Los Angeles County was built in 1918. A year on, silent film producer Hal Roach built his studios there and MGM followed a few years later.

17 Lonnie Donegan was a Glasgow-born musician who would become the 'King of Skiffle' and have 31 hit singles in the UK Top 30.

18 *Juke Box Jury*, presented by radio DJ David Jacobs, was a music panel show which ran on the BBC from 1959 to 1967. At its peak it attracted 12 million viewers.

19 *Dee Time* was the chat show vehicle for presenter Simon Dee, a flash, E-Type Jag driving former DJ who achieved spectacular fame and an 18

million strong audience in 1967. (Stanley would later pastiche the show as 'Bee Time'.) Dee's career slid downhill after he left the BBC and would find himself impoverished and subsequently jailed twice.

20 Welsh theatre manager producer Hugh 'Binkie' Beaumont was famed for his lavish productions, starry casts and the knack of knowing what a West End audience expected from a show. He had great success with the likes of *My Fair Lady* and *West Side Story*. Described as the 'éminence grise' of the West End, Beaumont preferred to stay in the shadows rather than court publicity.

21 Peter Barkworth was a BAFTA-winning actor, most famous for his roles in ITV's 1970 Second World War drama *Manhunt* and the 1979 BBC series *Telford's Change*, in which Scots actress Hannah Gordon played his wife.

22 Patricia Michael was a ballet school-trained performer and a talented singer who could play a vast range of roles from comedy such as Elvira in Noel Coward's *Blythe Spirit*, to Shakespeare, playing Bianca in *Othello*. She was also a variety theatre and a panto regular – very often playing Principal Boy – and worked with Stanley on four productions. Michael moved to the US where she became a panto director.

23 Maurice Chevalier was a French actor and crooner who became the highest paid star in in Hollywood in the 1930s, appearing in hits such as *The Merry Widow*. He is best remembered for his 1957 hit *Thank Heaven For Little Girls* – an appropriate title given his fondness for young chorus girls.

24 Bruce Gowers certainly had great talent and imagination. At the end of 1975 he had directed the Queen video to promote their (soon to be) UK Number One hit 'Bohemian Rhapsody'. Gowers later complained to the *Daily Mail* he'd been paid just £500 for his work, despite the pop video being regarded as one of the best ever.

25 John Birt was a producer with Granada Television before moving to LWT in 1972. Ten years later he would become the station's Director of Programmes. He then moved to the BBC, becoming Director-General in 1992, and imposed a policy of radical change to deliver efficiency savings.

26 Derek Jarman was a controversial, outspoken film director responsible for art house classic such as *Sebastiane* (1976) and *Caravaggio* (1986), both of which had homosexuality as a central theme. Jarman died in 1992 aged 52 of an AIDS-related illness.

TIMELINE

Personal Life

1926 Stanley Livingstone Baxter is born in Glasgow, 12 days after the General Strike.

1933 At the height of the Depression, while five-year-old Shirley Temple is signing with Hollywood, Stanley appears in a series of local talent competitions, competing against adults.

1939 As the Second World War approaches, Stanley makes his radio debut, playing the role of 'daft, excited boy' with the BBC's *Children's Hour*.

1943 As the UK wallows in the sentimental delight of *Lassie Comes Home* and the songs of Frank Sinatra, Stanley falls in love.

1944 The slim, sensitive young Scot becomes a skin-chaffed Bevan Boy, working at the mines as part of his National Service.

1946 Stanley, now in the army and based in Singapore, teams up with Kenneth Williams in the Forces' concert party outfit Combined Services Entertainment.

1948 In the hopeful year of the creation of the NHS, Israel and the UN's Declaration on Human Rights, the excited young actor joins the Citizens' Theatre as an Assistant Stage Manager.

1949 George Orwell's dystopian novel *Nineteen Eighty-Four* shakes the world, but Glasgow is being lit up by Stanley's co-writing and production of *The Tintock Cup*, a pseudo panto so successful the theatre brings the curtain down, in case the Corporation grant is cancelled.

1952 Elizabeth II becomes Queen of England, never realising she will one day become a Baxter parody, The Duchess of Brendagh. In the same year, Stanley marries Moira Robertson, an actress with the Citizens' company.

1952 Stanley's dad, Fred Baxter dies, aged 63, after suffering a heart attack as Stanley is set to join variety theatre giants, Howard & Wyndham.

1956 While Elvis is entering the charts with 'Heartbreak Hotel' and *The Ten Commandments* is breaking film records, the comedy star joins tartan troupe The White Heather Club on tour in North America.

1959 Fidel Castro is now in power in Cuba and Barbie has emerged in the US. But Stanley is now living in London, ready to storm the world of television and theatre.

1962 The world is rocked by the Cuban Missile Crisis but Stanley's world is crashing as he is finds himself facing career-ending charges.

1965 Stanley's chum Julie Christie is starring in the fabulous *Dr Zhivago*, but the Scot's career is in free-fall and he flees to Australia.

1966 Stanley is delighted to see Harold Wilson's Labour Government in power, but not as happy as he is to meet up with new best friend, TV director David Bell.

1967 The Summer of Love and the immense energy of the Beatles' *Sgt. Pepper's Lonely Hearts Club Band* album contrast with the tragic loss of new friend, Joe Orton.

1968 Bessie Baxter, star-creator, mother, performer, piano player, mahjong expert, home entertainer, and housewife, dies.

1973 The UK may have been darkened by the blight of the three-day week but real, big love re-enters Stanley's life

1983 Thatcher's Britain is heaping monetarism on the nation's shoulders as Stanley is being sacked by LWT, his programmes deemed to be too costly.

1988 Pubs can now remain open all day long, but the doors close forever on Kenneth Williams, ending a remarkable love/hate relationship.

1990 Stanley is enjoying the Spanish sun while filming in Spain yet it doesn't soothe the tragic loss of his closest chum, David Bell.

1992 The world is captured by sad, confessional television from the likes of Jerry Springer and Oprah Winfrey while Stanley's is walking out of theatre for ever.

1997 Princess Diana's death is followed by the death of Stanley's wife, Moira. Two months later Stanley is awarded the British Comedy Awards' Lifetime Achievement Award.

2003 Stanley is now enjoying the (honorary) Arts Degree from the University of Glasgow his dad Fred Baxter had hoped he would achieve.

2016 The 90-year-old Stanley is celebrating his birthday, having dinner with close pal John Reid. But earlier in the day he had been with the BBC, making a new series of *Stanley Baxter and Friends*.

2017 Stanley is saddened by the inauguration of President Donald Trump. Soon after, with the death of his partner and love of his life, he takes to his bed.

TIMELINE

Stanley Baxter on... Radio, TV and Film

1940	*Children's Hour*, BBC Radio Scotland, playing 'an excited idiot'.
1952	*Shop Window* BBC London-based talent showcase,
1955	*Geordie*, film, playing the role of village postie.
1957	*This Is Scotland,* heralding in the new television station STV.
1959	*On The Bright Side*, BBC satirical TV revue show.
1961	*Lunch In The Park*, BBC comedy by Galton and Simpson.
1961	*Very Important Person*, film lead, alongside James Robertson Justice.
1962	*Crooks Anonymous*, film lead, alongside Leslie Phillips.
1962	*The Fast Lady*, film lead, with Julie Christie.
1963	*The Stanley Baxter Show*, BBC.
1964	*Espionage* drama, BBC.
1964	*Baxter On...*, BBC.
1965	*Joey Boy*, film lead alongside Harry H Corbett.
1965	*The Confidence Course*, part of the BBC's Wednesday Play series.
1967	*The Stanley Baxter Show*, BBC2.
1968	*The Stanley Baxter Show*, BBC1.
1971	*The Goodies*, BBC1.
1972	*Time For Baxter*, BBC1.
1972	*The Stanley Baxter Picture Show*, ITV.
1973	*The Stanley Baxter Big Picture Show*, ITV.
1974	*The Stanley Baxter Moving Picture Show*, ITV.
1975	*The Stanley Baxter Big Picture Show*, ITV.
1976	*Stanley Baxter's Christmas Box*, ITV.

1977	*Stanley Baxter's Greatest Hits*, ITV.
1977	*Bing Crosbie's Merrie Olde Christmas*, ITV.
1979	*Stanley Baxter on Television*, ITV.
1982	*The Stanley Baxter Hour*, ITV.
1985	*The Stanley Baxter Christmas Hamper*, BBC1.
1986	*Stanley Baxter's Picture Annual*, BBC1.
1988	*Mr Majeika*, ITV.
1989	*Mr Majeika*, series 2, ITV.
1989	*The New Year Show*, ITV.
1990	*Mr Majeika*, series 3, ITV.
1990	*The British Academy Awards.*
1991	*Rab C. Nesbitt*, BBC2.
1995	*Stanley Baxter is Back*, Channel 4.
1995	*Arabian Knight*, film animation.
1996	*Stanley Baxter in Reel Terms*, Channel 4.
1996	*Stanley Baxter is Back*, Channel 4.
1997	*British Academy Awards*, Lifetime Achievement.
1998	*Stanley Baxter – His Best Bits*, Channel 4.
1998	*Stanley Baxter in Person*, ITV.
2000	*Meeow*, part one of three, cartoon series, ITV.
2001	*This is Stanley Baxter*, BBC1.
2001	*The Unforgettable Kenneth Williams*, ITV.
2006–16	*Stanley Baxter Comedy Playhouse*, BBC Radio 4.
2008	*Stanley Baxter Now and Then*, ITV.
2010	*Artwork Scotland When Alan Cumming met Stanley Baxter*, BBC2.
2013	*The Many Faces of Stanley Baxter*, BBC2.
2019	*Comedy National Treasures*, Channel 5.

Acknowledgements

To those who dabbed a tissue to the often tear-stained face of frustration during the writing of this book I will be forever grateful.

They include John Reid, Ed Crozier, Mark Smith, Ford Kiernan, Richard Ross, Ian Pattison, Robert C Kelly, Garry Scott and Russell Kyle.

And Jonathan Hayden, super-agent, has been ever-ready with a man-size box of Kleenex.

Picture Credits

All pictures are from Stanley Baxter's private collection apart from the following:

Photo by Popperfoto via Getty Images/Getty Images: Stanley Baxter (front cover)

David Holt: Stanley Baxter (dust jacket)

Courtesy of The Herald and Times: Brian Beacom (dust jacket)

Kirsty Anderson, *The Herald*: Brian Beacom as Buttons (dust jacket)

Courtesy of the King's Theatre: Stanley Baxter and Angus Lennie star in *Cinderella*.

Courtesy of SMN Archive: Stanley and Ronnie Corbett play the Ugly Sisters in *Cinderella* at the King's Theatre.

Courtesy of BBC: The cast of radio hit *It's All Yours*, with Jimmy Logan (centre).

Luath Press Limited

committed to publishing well written books worth reading

LUATH PRESS takes its name from Robert Burns, whose little collie Luath (*Gael.*, swift or nimble) tripped up Jean Armour at a wedding and gave him the chance to speak to the woman who was to be his wife and the abiding love of his life. Burns called one of the 'Twa Dogs' Luath after Cuchullin's hunting dog in Ossian's *Fingal*.
Luath Press was established in 1981 in the heart of Burns country, and is now based a few steps up the road from Burns' first lodgings on Edinburgh's Royal Mile. Luath offers you distinctive writing with a hint of unexpected pleasures.
Most bookshops in the UK, the US, Canada, Australia, New Zealand and parts of Europe, either carry our books in stock or can order them for you. To order direct from us, please send a £sterling cheque, postal order, international money order or your credit card details (number, address of cardholder and expiry date) to us at the address below. Please add post and packing as follows: UK – £1.00 per delivery address; overseas surface mail – £2.50 per delivery address; overseas airmail – £3.50 for the first book to each delivery address, plus £1.00 for each additional book by airmail to the same address. If your order is a gift, we will happily enclose your card or message at no extra charge.

Luath Press Limited
543/2 Castlehill
The Royal Mile
Edinburgh EH1 2ND
Scotland
Telephone: +44 (0)131 225 4326 (24 hours)
email: sales@luath. co.uk
Website: www. luath.co.uk